*DESIGNING PARTS WITH*

# **Solid**Works®

## *Roy Wysack*

Designing Parts with
**Solid**Works ®

**Roy Wysack**

Published by:

CAD/CAM Publishing
1010 Turquoise Street, Suite 320
San Diego, California 92109 USA
Web site: http://www.cadcamnet.com

Copyright © 1997 Roy Wysack
Copyright © 1998 Roy Wysack

Second Edition, 1998

10 9 8 7 6 5 4 3 2 1

Printed in the United States of America

ISBN 0-934869-22-7

## Trademarks

## Warning and Disclaimer

## About the Author

Roy Wysack began his career 30 years ago as a draftsman. Since then he has risen through the ranks as designer, drafting supervisor, CAD manager, and chief draftsman. He has worked in the automotive, aerospace, and heavy construction industries. His many years of experience in design layout, and design and drawing management gives Wysack an edge when it comes to understanding the problems the industry faces learning CAD and making CAD pay. This practical experience and knowledge has shaped his writing style into one aimed at designers and design managers, not computer scientists. His *Smart Managers' Guide to Effective CAD Management* has become a best-selling reference volume. He is also a developer of innovative CAD management and CAD training programs, and has conducted workshops in both areas. Wysack has served the research staff of the *CAD Report* since it was founded in 1981, and he is now an independent consultant in CAD.

## Acknowledgments

The author would like to acknowledge the staffs of SolidWorks Corporation and CAD/CAM Publishing for their support and technical advice. A special thanks to Mr. Jon Hirschtick, CEO of SolidWorks Corporation, whose SolidWorks software turned out to be as amazing to me as his magic tricks. I would also like to thank Scott Harris of

SolidWorks Corporation for his patience, support, and technical guidance throughout this project. Also, I am very grateful to Jon Hirschtick, Mike Payne, Scott Harris, and Bob Zuffante for hiring me to review the prereleased versions of SolidWorks. This opportunity to work with the SolidWorks founders gave me the knowledge and inspiration to write this book. Finally, a big thanks to the editors of CAD/CAM Publishing. First, thanks to Steve Wolfe, who helped me to maintain the balance required to incorporate details without losing sight of the big picture. And secondly to Steve, Geoff Smith-Moritz, and Nancy E. Rouse for their technical support and editing skills.

# Forward by L. Stephen Wolfe – Publisher CAD/CAM Publishing

## WHY SOLID MODELING?

The biggest cost saving from solid modeling comes from avoiding mistakes. CAD vendors don't like to say this because salespeople never like to bring up unpleasant subjects, and mistakes are invariably unpleasant. So the CAD marketing types yammer about "competitiveness" and "time-to-market," and make up cute phrases such as "electronic product definition" to describe what their products do. Yet the real reason solid-modeling systems help companies bring products to market faster is that they enable engineers to understand more thoroughly how their designs will look and perform before committing themselves to the costly processes of preparing manufacturing documents and making production tools.

All but the simplest products are hard to visualize solely from 2-D drawings. So designers supplement drawings with physical prototypes, such as clay, wood, or plastic models. Working prototypes, handmade from materials similar to those that will be used in the production product generally follows these models. In the case of custom products, the product *is* the prototype. Mistakes are reworked as the machine or device takes shape.

Solid computer models permit designers to better understand how their products will look and function before physical models are made. Solid-modeling systems automatically remove hidden lines, allow mating conditions between parts to be clearly defined, and permit interference to be detected both visually and analytically. If designers did no more than assure that parts fit together properly and looked right, solids-based CAD systems would justify their costs. Physical models are expensive and can't be changed easily.

But solid models can be even more useful. The geometry from solid models can be used in a variety of analytical systems including finite-element analysis, boundary-element analysis, computational fluid dynamics, and kinematic and dynamic analysis. These analytical tools let engineers estimate working stresses, temperatures, and deflections in models to assure that they don't fail in service, that they're sufficiently stiff, and that they don't have annoying or destructive vibrations.

In many cases, computer models aren't sufficient to assure that a product looks right or works right or feels right in the hand. So users of solid models can convert them to physical models using a variety of technologies such as stereolithography, fused deposition, or laminated object modeling. Each month the *Rapid Prototyping Report* newsletter describes examples of firms that have used rapid prototypes to validate designs. In nearly every case, these users discovered small flaws in their designs that would have been costly and time-consuming to fix in production.

Once a design is released for production, the cost of making changes grows exponentially. For each part of a product, dozens, or even hundreds of manufacturing documents are produced. The documents include purchase specifications, assembly instructions, tool and fixture design drawings, and users' manuals. Tools, such as molds, dies, jigs, and fixtures, costing tens or hundreds of thousands of dollars may be made. A change to a single part in production affects many of these tools and documents. Late changes increase costs and extend production schedules. Sometimes overtime wages – a 50 percent premium – must be paid for rework to keep products on schedule.

Even more costly are defective products that reach customers. Such products must be fixed under warranty, may engender liability suits, and often cause the customer to buy someone else's product instead of yours the next time he or she needs one.

Accountants and managers don't like to hear about mistakes when they're reading cost justifications for CAD systems. But until companies understand how and why errors creep into their designs, they can't begin to improve their processes. Making a mistake is regrettable, but all people make some. Making the same mistake again and again because of error-prone procedures is inexcusable.

## Other Savings

When parts are described as solid models, it is no longer necessary to create fully dimensioned drawings for manufacturing. Instead, CAD models can be given directly to tool makers and manufacturing departments accompanied by a simplified drawing showing tolerances and material requirements. In some cases, CAD models can be used to drive numerically controlled tools to cut parts or tool cavities. They can also be used for "soft gauging" with coordinate-measuring machines.

Drawings are not only expensive to make, but they take time to produce. Eliminating the production of fully detailed drawings enables design data to be released for production of tools and parts sooner.

Solid models can also simplify document production in manufacturing. Assembly instructions with exploded views, technical manuals, and change-order requests can be made much more quickly with complete, three-dimensional models.

Design reuse can be a third type of savings afforded by solid-modeling systems. It's often faster to take an existing solid model and modify it than it is to start afresh with a blank screen. Often new designs are simply larger or smaller versions of an existing product. In other cases, they may be improved versions.

**When Solids Don't Pay**

Deriving maximum benefits from solid models isn't easy. Firms that don't realize most of the benefits outlined above have trouble justifying system costs or complain that productivity has not met expectations. Why do these problems occur?

The most common reason is that solid-modeling programs still won't create certain types of geometry. In other cases, it is so hard to create a particular shape that most workers give up before they're done.

A second reason productivity lags expectations is that users of solid-modeling programs are not properly trained. This book is intended to help designers learn to create solid models the right way. In writing this book, the author has employed a highly graphical approach, which we hope you will find easier than traditional books and manuals. We would appreciate any suggestions from readers about ways that we can make future editions of our SolidWorks book series more helpful to you.

I dedicate this book to my wife Val. Thanks for your love and support.


Love, Roy

# Table of Contents

## Table of Figures

*Chapter*

**1**

# Chapter 1 – INTRODUCTION TO SolidWorks

## What is SolidWorks?

SolidWorks is a computer-aided design (CAD) software package that you can use to create parts, assemblies, and drawings. Parts, assemblies, and drawings are associated with each other so that a change to any part is automatically reflected in both the assembly models that use it and the drawings of it. SolidWorks runs under Microsoft's Windows 95, Windows 98, or Windows NT operating systems on computers based on Intel's Pentium or Digital Equipment's Alpha microprocessors.

## Why it's hot

SolidWorks combines a unique blend of capabilities, user friendliness, and competitive price in a productive solid-modeling product that is fun to use and easy to learn. The software is based on state-of-the-art, feature-based parametric modeling technology that allows users to quickly create and change solid model parts and assemblies. If you are a mechanical engineer or designer, SolidWorks makes you more productive by helping you to visualize complex designs by displaying them as 3-Dimensional, color-coded, shaded images and by also letting you reuse combinations of previously designed parts to create new designs. You can calculate mass properties of part models and assemblies, check fit of parts in assemblies, and create rapid prototypes of your designs. You can generate 2-Dimensional drawing views of solid parts and assemblies automatically and annotate drawing sheets with notes and dimensions.

SolidWorks is designed specifically to be used in a multitasking Windows environment. Because it conforms to Microsoft's Windows' user interface guidelines, engineers who are familiar with other Windows programs, such as word processors or spreadsheets, can perform a number of routine SolidWorks functions without additional training. You can open, close, and save files; drag and drop features from one part to another, and cut and paste images from one window to another using standardized techniques. Third-party software is available that provides optional capabilities for SolidWorks, including photo-realistic renderings, stress analysis, and manufacturing automation.

## Who should use it?

SolidWorks can be used productively by any company that designs mechanical parts and assemblies for manufacture.

## How it works

SolidWorks employs solid features to create part shapes. To create most features, first sketch a 2-Dimensional profile. Then move this profile through space to create a volume. You can create additional features to add or remove material from this first feature. Features can also be related to each other to preserve design intent, so that a change in one feature will automatically update related features. These constraints can be applied by dimensions, geometric relations (such as tangent to), or by equations of mathematical formulas (such as base to equal one-half of height).

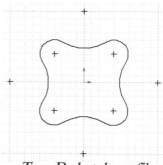

*Two-D sketch profile*

SolidWorks keeps track of what is inside and outside your part. Hence, the parts appear on the computer display to be "solid" and can be used for functions such as interference checking and volumetric calculations.

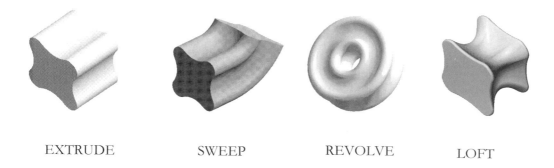

EXTRUDE          SWEEP          REVOLVE          LOFT

Figure 1.1 – Sample Solids Created from a Single Sketch Profile

**Using different operations, all of these solid models were created from the single two-dimensional sketch profile shown above. Geometry can be sketched on construction planes or on planar surfaces of parts.**

You can use a sketch profile to cut material from a part or to add material to a part in a number of ways.

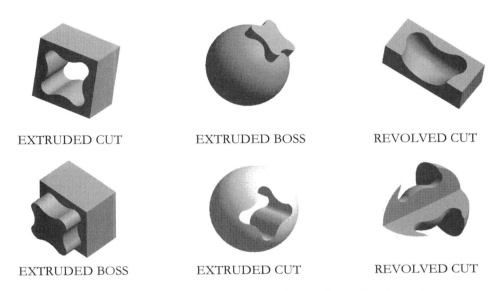

EXTRUDED CUT   EXTRUDED BOSS   REVOLVED CUT

EXTRUDED BOSS   EXTRUDED CUT   REVOLVED CUT

Figure 1.0 – Variations to Parts Created from a Single Sketch Profile

In addition to the samples shown above, you can "sweep" a sketch profile along a trajectory to form a tube or to cut a channel in a part. You also can form a shape by "lofting" between multiple sketches.

SolidWorks features are dimension driven. When you change a feature dimension, the geometry of the entire part will be updated to suit the change.

SolidWorks offers a modern approach to constructing drawings. Once you create a model, the software can automatically produce geometry for orthographic and auxiliary views, thus liberating you from this otherwise tedious chore. Drawings can then be embellished with additional sketch geometry, dimensions, notes, and other annotations as required. Because SolidWorks takes advantage of the Microsoft Windows graphical user interface, multiple windows of parts, assemblies and drawings may be displayed simultaneously, and because of the associativity between these files, changes to one file will be reflected in the associated file.

Figure 1.3 – Typical Solid Parts

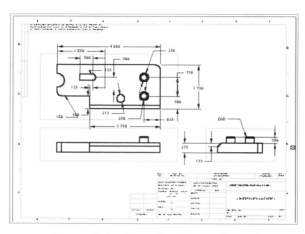

Figure 1.4 – Drawing Views Created
Automatically from Solid Parts

**Because SolidWorks has a multiple-document interface, you can display multiple views and windows of one or more models at the same time. Changes in one window appear in all associated windows. This capability makes it easier to visualize your work and simplifies the design iteration process.**

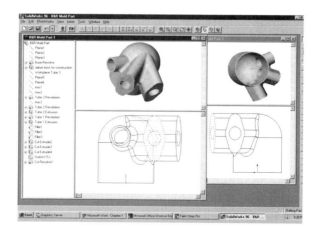

Figure 1.5 – Typical Multiple Window Display

One way to be productive with CAD is to reuse work already done. Employing "copy and paste" and "drag-and-drop" techniques makes it easy to reuse existing work. You can copy sketches to and paste them from the clipboard, and you can move or copy part features with the mouse. These translations can be carried out within a part model, or from one part to another part, assembly, or drawing.

*The sketch used for this cut can be reused in other parts as shown below*

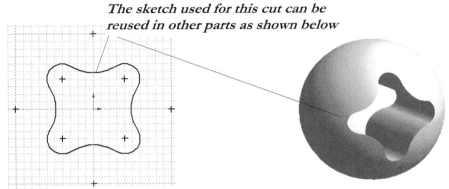

Figure 1.6 – Sketch Used for a Cut Feature

Below, the sketch from **Part A** was copied into the clipboard and pasted into **Part B** to make the cut through Part B.

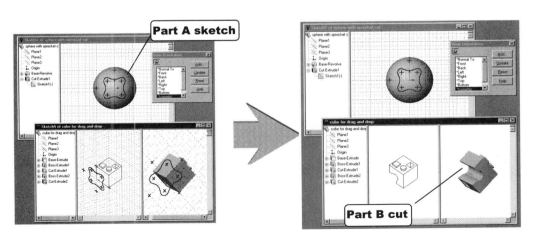

Figure 1.7 – Copying and Pasting Sketches to Part Surfaces

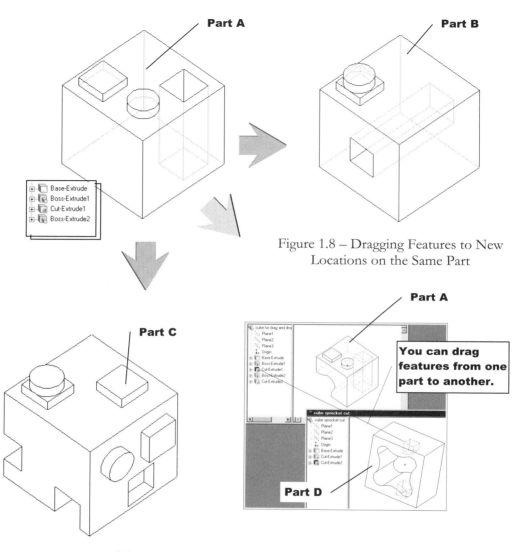

Figure 1.8 – Dragging Features to New Locations on the Same Part

Figure 1.9 – Copying Features to New Locations Using Drag and Drop

The examples shown above demonstrate some drag-and-drop techniques. **Part B** was made by dragging features in **Part A** to new locations. **Part C** was made from Part A by (CTRL) dragging to copy features to new locations. **Part D** was revised by dragging and copying the rectangular cut from Part A to Part D.

SolidWorks allows you to share data between different Microsoft OLE-compliant (Object Linking and Embedding) software applications. For example, with OLE, you can insert SolidWorks documents into word documents or insert Excel spreadsheets into SolidWorks documents. In the example below, an Excel spreadsheet used to calculate pump and tank data for the water gun assembly shown, was inserted into a SolidWorks assembly document as an icon. Double-clicking the icon opens Excel and activates the spreadsheet. A designer can keep both programs open and switch between them as required. Spreadsheets can also be used to generate bills of material, and if set up as a "design table," can drive geometry to generate families of parts simply by editing the values in the design table.

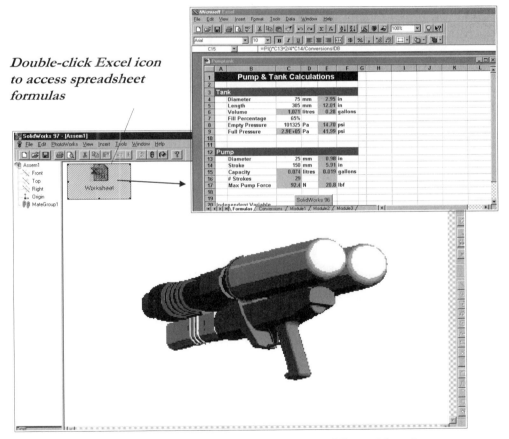

*Double-click Excel icon to access spreadsheet formulas*

Figure 1.10 – OLE Application Linking an Excel Spreadsheet into a SolidWorks Assembly Document

A Word document can be used for interdepartmental communication and a SolidWorks model can be inserted into it. The model can then be accessed from within the Word document by double-clicking the model. Double-clicking on the part from within Word will load the SolidWorks program window shown at the right. From here, you can work on the SolidWorks model with any SolidWorks tool.

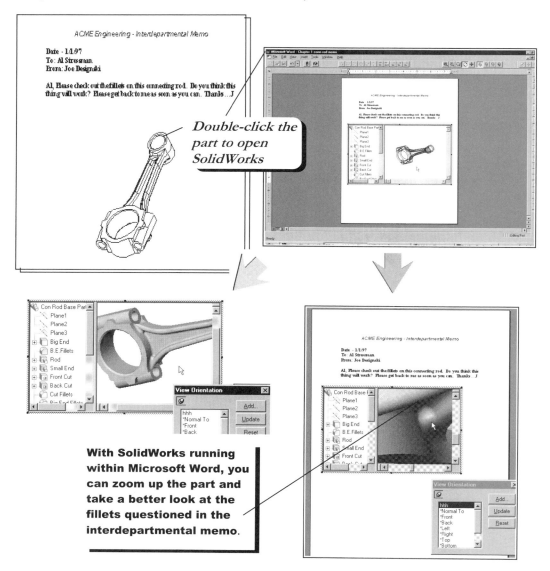

Figure 1.11 – OLE Application of SolidWorks Part Embedded in Word Document

Creating assembly files of SolidWorks parts is also easy to do. You can insert components into an assembly and add mating relations to other parts, or you can construct parts right in the assembly.

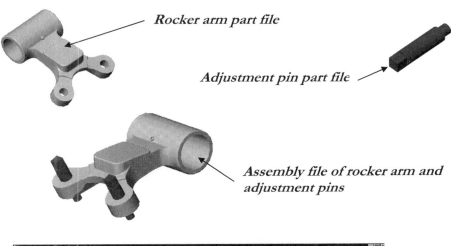

*Rocker arm part file*

*Adjustment pin part file*

*Assembly file of rocker arm and adjustment pins*

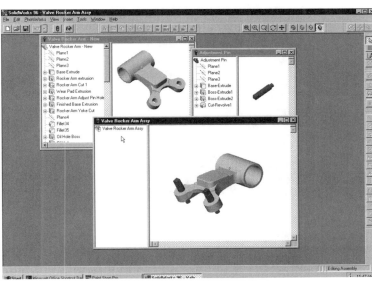

Figure 1.12 – Using Existing Parts to Make an Assembly

**You can create or modify the oil filter shown below right in the engine assembly.**

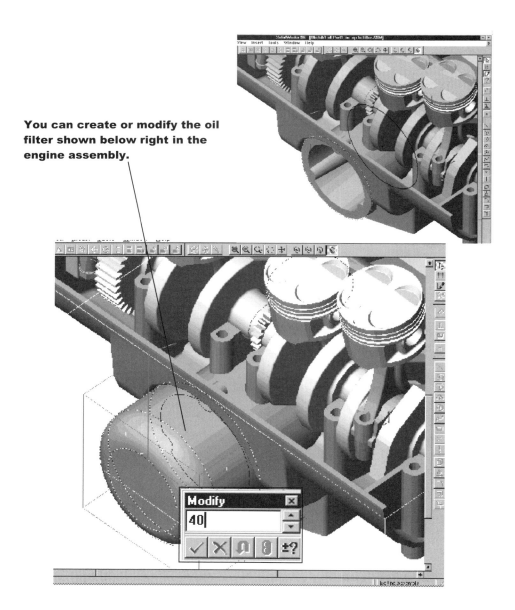

Figure 1.13 – Creating and Revising Parts While in Assembly Mode

## Examples of images completed with SolidWorks

The following illustrations show some samples of tasks that you can accomplish with SolidWorks.

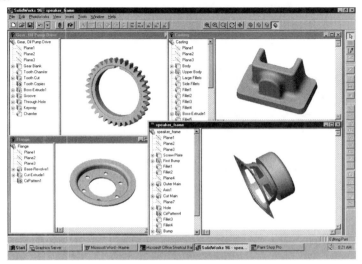

Figure 1.14 – Various Types of Parts Created as Solids

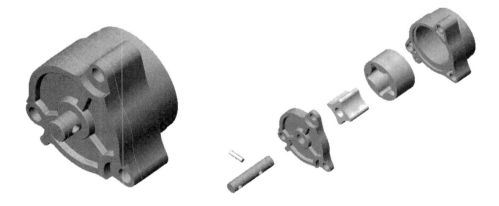

Figure 1.15 – Assemblies and Exploded Views of Assemblies

Figure 1.16 – Patterns and Multiple Instances in Parts or Assemblies

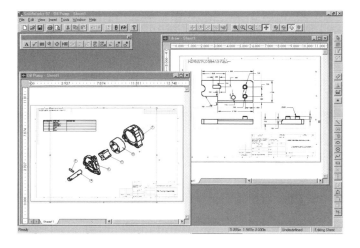

Figure 1.17 – Isometric and Orthographic Drawings

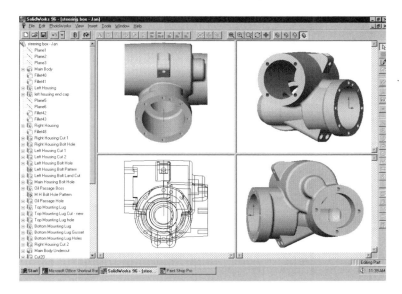

Figure 1.18 – Castings with Draft, Complex Fillets, and Rounds

Figure 1.19 – Section Cuts that Allow Designers to Visualize Complex Parts

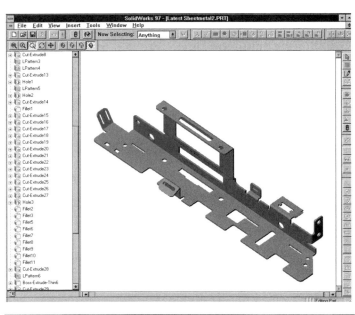

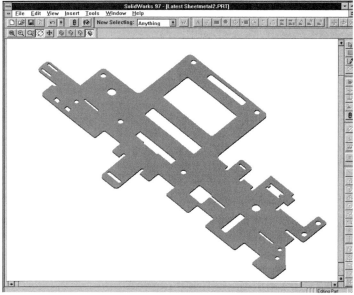

Figure 1.20 – Sheet Metal Including Flat Patterns

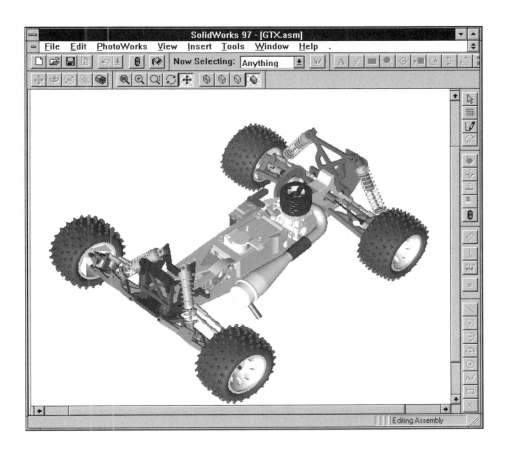

Figure 1.21 – Complex Assemblies

### chapter contents

**Building a simple part**
**Modifying parts**

## Chapter 2 – GETTING STARTED WITH SolidWorks

### Building a simple part

#### Lesson 2.1.1 - Creating a Base Feature

In SolidWorks, parts are created by building a "base feature," and adding other features such as bosses, cuts, holes, fillets, or shells. The base feature may be an extrusion, revolution, swept profile, or loft. To create a base feature, sketch a 2-dimensional geometric profile and move the profile through space to create a volume. Geometry can be sketched on construction planes or on planar surfaces of parts.

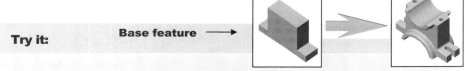

**Try it:**    **Base feature** ⟶

Create a base feature for the Pillow Block shown. Start by sketching the predominant shape found in the front view and extruding the sketch into space. **Sketch on default Plane 1**. Follow the steps numbered 1-14 below.

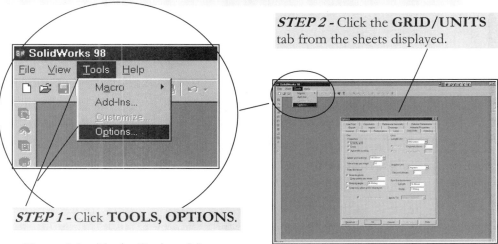

*STEP 2 -* Click the **GRID/UNITS** tab from the sheets displayed.

*STEP 1 -* Click **TOOLS, OPTIONS**.

Figure 2.1 – Tools, Options Menu

**Note: When you see this symbol, be sure to follow the directions very closely to ensure the best success with the lesson.**

*STEP 3 -* Fill in the **GRID/UNITS** tab so it looks like this one, then click **OK**. Be sure to use the proper units and grid spacing.

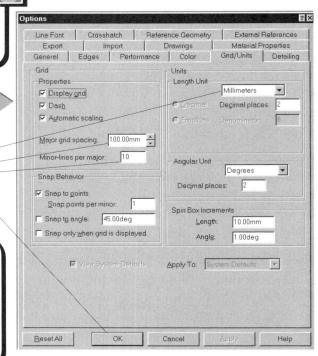

Figure 2.2 – Options Tabs

**Note: Preferences set in TOOLS, OPTIONS from the startup menu (no parts open) affect all modeling sessions. To change OPTIONS for a single part, select TOOLS, OPTIONS, in an active part TOOLS pulldown menu.**

*STEP 4 -* Click the **NEW PART** icon or from the **FILE** menu, click **NEW**. Click **OK** for a new part.

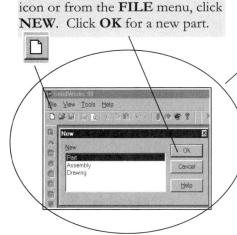

*STEP 5 -* **INSERT SKETCH** by clicking the **SKETCH** tool icon.

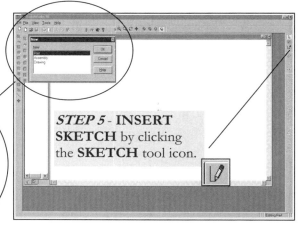

Figure 2.3 – NEW PART Initial Window

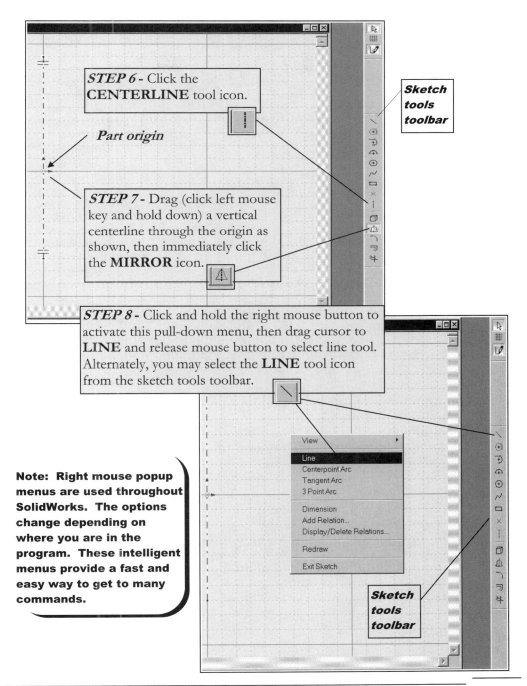

***Sketch tools toolbar***

*STEP 6* - Click the **CENTERLINE** tool icon.

*Part origin*

*STEP 7* - Drag (click left mouse key and hold down) a vertical centerline through the origin as shown, then immediately click the **MIRROR** icon.

*STEP 8* - Click and hold the right mouse button to activate this pull-down menu, then drag cursor to **LINE** and release mouse button to select line tool. Alternately, you may select the **LINE** tool icon from the sketch tools toolbar.

**Note: Right mouse popup menus are used throughout SolidWorks. The options change depending on where you are in the program. These intelligent menus provide a fast and easy way to get to many commands.**

View

Line
Centerpoint Arc
Tangent Arc
3 Point Arc

Dimension
Add Relation...
Display/Delete Relations...

Redraw

Exit Sketch

***Sketch tools toolbar***

**STEP 9 -** Draw this shape by sketching to grid points. Click and drag to sketch each line. With the **MIRROR** tool on, the geometry you sketch will be mirrored about the centerline as shown below. Be sure to construct your sketch **exactly** as shown.

**Note:** To delete lines, return to SELECT mode and select the lines by clicking them with the left mouse button (hold Ctrl and click for multiple line selection), then press the delete key – or click the UNDO icon on the top toolbar after inserting the lines. Selected sketch elements turn green.

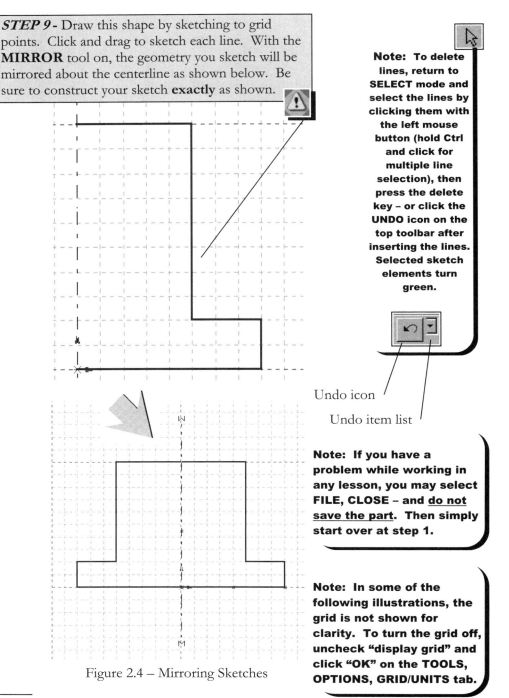

Undo icon

Undo item list

**Note:** If you have a problem while working in any lesson, you may select FILE, CLOSE – and <u>do not save the part</u>. Then simply start over at step 1.

**Note:** In some of the following illustrations, the grid is not shown for clarity. To turn the grid off, uncheck "display grid" and click "OK" on the TOOLS, OPTIONS, GRID/UNITS tab.

Figure 2.4 – Mirroring Sketches

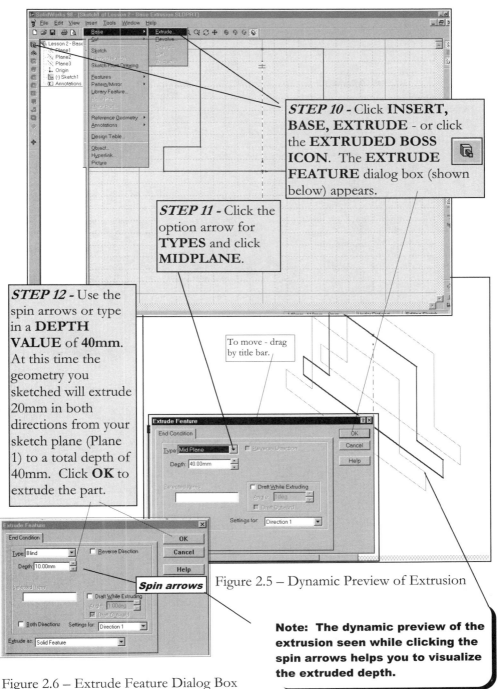

**STEP 10** - Click **INSERT, BASE, EXTRUDE** - or click the **EXTRUDED BOSS ICON**. The **EXTRUDE FEATURE** dialog box (shown below) appears.

**STEP 11** - Click the option arrow for **TYPES** and click **MIDPLANE**.

**STEP 12** - Use the spin arrows or type in a **DEPTH VALUE** of **40mm**. At this time the geometry you sketched will extrude 20mm in both directions from your sketch plane (Plane 1) to a total depth of 40mm. Click **OK** to extrude the part.

To move - drag by title bar.

*Spin arrows*

Figure 2.5 – Dynamic Preview of Extrusion

**Note: The dynamic preview of the extrusion seen while clicking the spin arrows helps you to visualize the extruded depth.**

Figure 2.6 – Extrude Feature Dialog Box

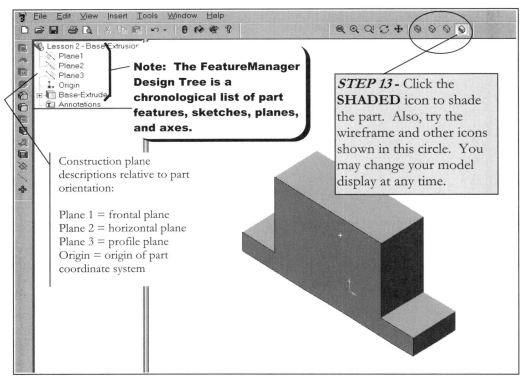

Figure 2.7 – Construction Planes and FeatureManager

You just modeled a base feature that will be used for two different parts. For base features, a sketch must be created on a construction plane. In the part you just made, the sketch was automatically created on Plane 1 (the default and frontal plane of the part, activated by selecting the sketch tool icon). To add additional features to the base feature, sketches may be created on <u>construction planes</u> or on <u>planar surfaces</u> of existing parts. This will be demonstrated next.

*STEP 14* - Save your model as two different files – from the menu toolbar, click **FILE – SAVE AS –** and enter **"Lesson 2 – Base Extrusion,"** then save again as **"Lesson 2 – Adding Bosses."** Now the part is ready to use in the next lesson.

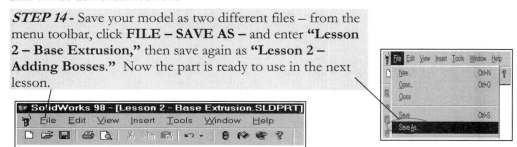

Figure 2.8 – FILE Pull-Down Menu

## Lesson 2.1.2 - Adding Bosses to a Base Extrusion

**Try it:** (*) Lesson 2 – Adding Bosses    **objective**

Extrude two bosses onto the part you just created. Follow the steps numbered 1-12 in the following illustrations. Save your work often.

(*) If necessary, open Lesson 2 – Adding Bosses filed in the last lesson. Use **FILE, OPEN,** or click **OPEN ICON**.

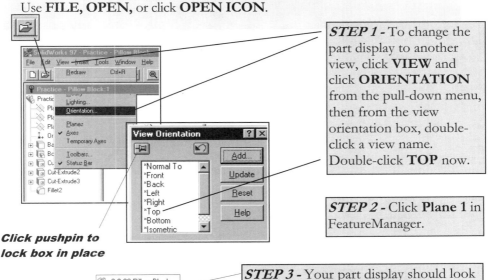

**Click pushpin to lock box in place**

*STEP 1 -* To change the part display to another view, click **VIEW** and click **ORIENTATION** from the pull-down menu, then from the view orientation box, double-click a view name. Double-click **TOP** now.

*STEP 2 -* Click **Plane 1** in FeatureManager.

*STEP 3 -* Your part display should look like this. Notice how your previous extrusion was created symmetrically about Plane 1 because you used the **MIDPLANE Extrude** option.

**Plane 1**

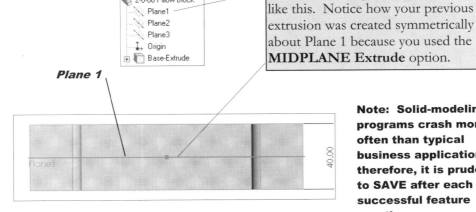

Figure 2.9 – Midplane Extrusion

Note: Solid-modeling programs crash more often than typical business applications, therefore, it is prudent to SAVE after each successful feature creation.

**STEP 4 -** Double-click **FRONT** from the view orientation box to display the front view. Use "Z" or "Ctrl Z" on keyboard to zoom up or down.

**STEP 5 -** See Figure 2.2 for grid settings. Select **Plane 1** and **INSERT SKETCH**. (Click the **SKETCH TOOL** icon.)

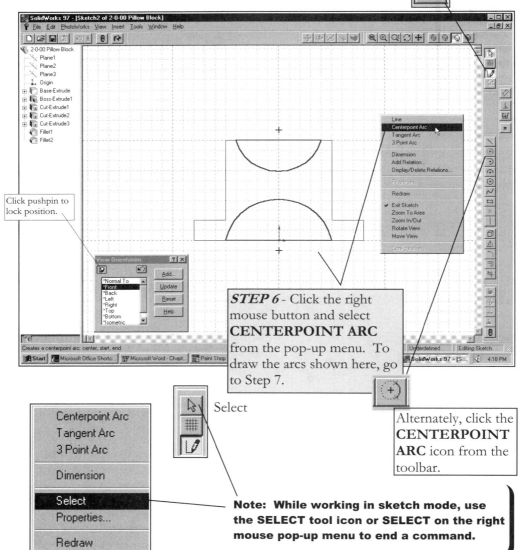

Click pushpin to lock position.

**STEP 6 -** Click the right mouse button and select **CENTERPOINT ARC** from the pop-up menu. To draw the arcs shown here, go to Step 7.

Select

Alternately, click the **CENTERPOINT ARC** icon from the toolbar.

Centerpoint Arc
Tangent Arc
3 Point Arc

Dimension

Select
Properties...

Redraw

**Note: While working in sketch mode, use the SELECT tool icon or SELECT on the right mouse pop-up menu to end a command.**

Figure 2.10 – Right Mouse Pop-Up Menu

**Note:** When sketching, notice the cursor inferencing which shows the active sketch tool and cursor alignment with existing sketch points. Also, see Figure 2.12 for images of some inferencing symbols used in SolidWorks.

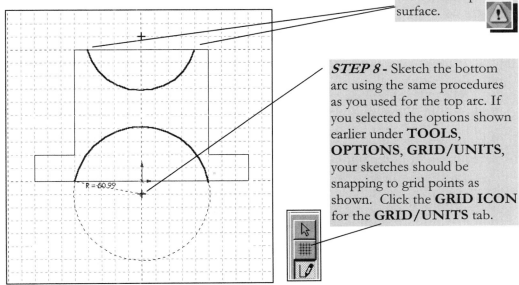

*Pick here first*

A

B

C

R = 41.23

Plane1

*STEP 7 -* To sketch a centerpoint arc, click the centerpoint **A** and drag out the arc to the circumference **B**, then release the mouse button. Next, click at **B** and drag to arc length **C** and release the mouse button. The completed arc should begin and end at the top surface.

Figure 2.11 – Centerpoint Arc

R = 60.99

*STEP 8 -* Sketch the bottom arc using the same procedures as you used for the top arc. If you selected the options shown earlier under **TOOLS**, **OPTIONS**, **GRID/UNITS**, your sketches should be snapping to grid points as shown. Click the **GRID ICON** for the **GRID/UNITS** tab.

*STEP 9 -* Click the right mouse
pop-up menu and select **LINE**.

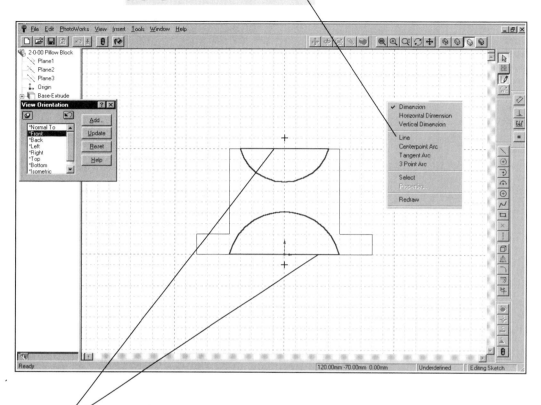

*STEP 10 -* Sketch the two lines shown
connecting the arcs to form closed profiles.
Use the inferencing symbol for **CURVE
ENDPOINT** to ensure that the lines are
coincident with the arc endpoints. See next
page for partial list of inferencing symbols.

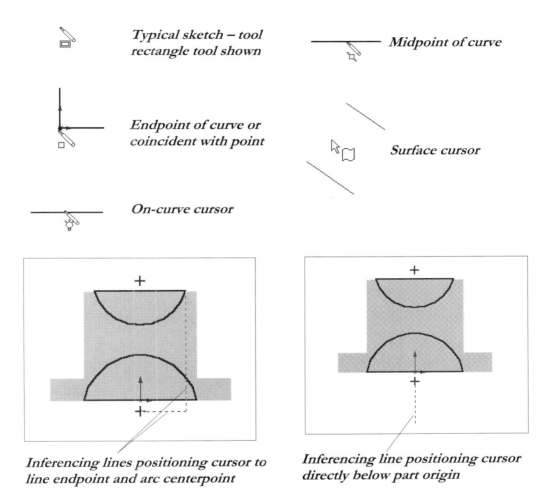

Typical sketch – tool
rectangle tool shown

Midpoint of curve

Endpoint of curve or
coincident with point

Surface cursor

On-curve cursor

Inferencing lines positioning cursor to
line endpoint and arc centerpoint

Inferencing line positioning cursor
directly below part origin

Figure 2.12 – Sketch Inferencing Symbols and Lines

Note: Inferencing symbols and lines aid you in sketching.
They provide information about the current tool in use, the
cursor position, and the geometric relationships to other
sketch elements that are automatically applied while
sketching. For a comprehensive list of inferencing symbols,
refer to the SolidWorks user's manual.

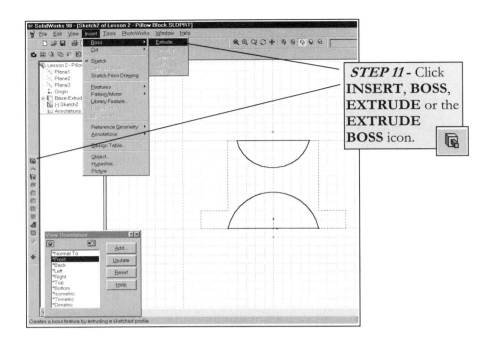

**STEP 11 -** Click **INSERT, BOSS, EXTRUDE** or the **EXTRUDE BOSS** icon.

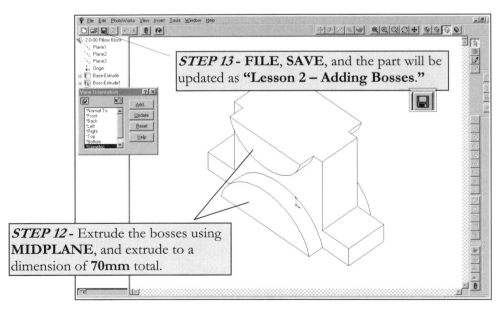

**STEP 13 -** **FILE, SAVE,** and the part will be updated as **"Lesson 2 – Adding Bosses."**

**STEP 12 -** Extrude the bosses using **MIDPLANE,** and extrude to a dimension of **70mm** total.

## Lesson 2.1.3 - Extruding Cuts

The profiles for the base extrusion and extruded bosses were sketched on Plane 1 (the frontal plane of the part). Now for the circular cuts, try sketching on a planar surface of the part.

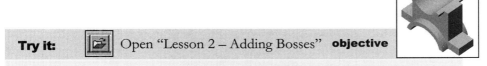

**Try it:** Open "Lesson 2 – Adding Bosses" **objective**

Extrude the circular cuts on the top and bottom of the Pillow Block by sketching on the part surface rather than on a sketch plane.

*Drag top bar to reposition*

*Click pushpin to anchor box in position*

**STEP 1 -** From the view orientation box, double-click isometric.

**STEP 2 -** Click the front face of either boss to establish a sketch plane, then **INSERT SKETCH**.

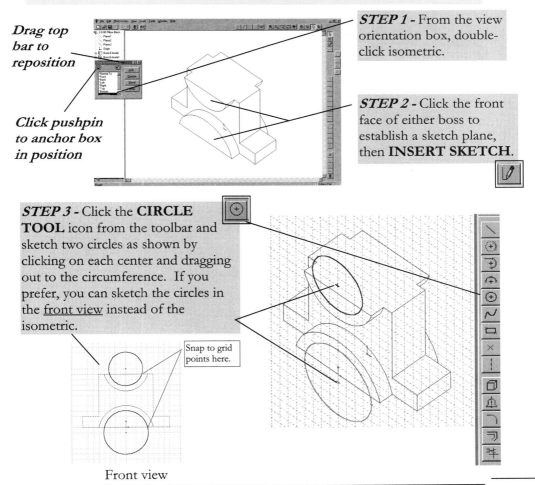

**STEP 3 -** Click the **CIRCLE TOOL** icon from the toolbar and sketch two circles as shown by clicking on each center and dragging out to the circumference. If you prefer, you can sketch the circles in the <u>front view</u> instead of the isometric.

Snap to grid points here.

Front view

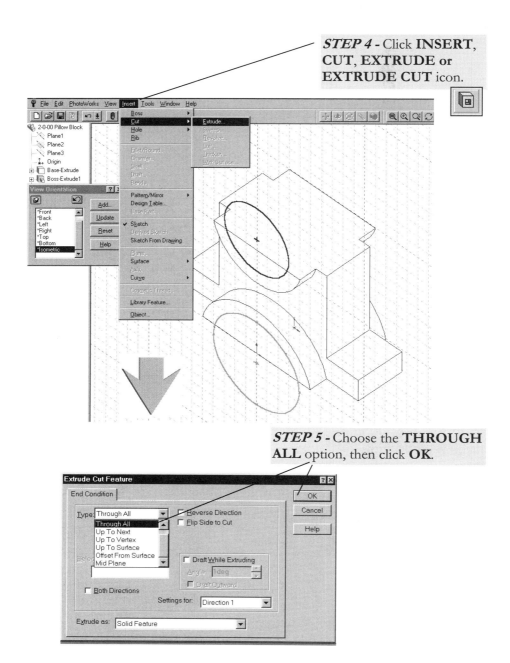

STEP 4 - Click INSERT, CUT, EXTRUDE or EXTRUDE CUT icon.

STEP 5 - Choose the THROUGH ALL option, then click OK.

Figure 2.13 – Extrude Cut Dialog Box

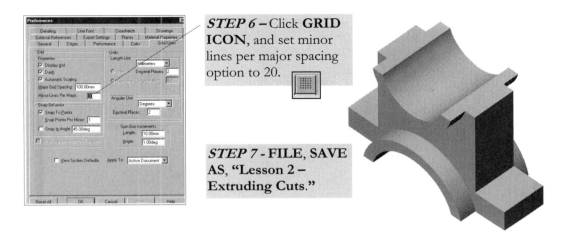

*STEP 6* – Click **GRID ICON**, and set minor lines per major spacing option to 20.

*STEP 7* - FILE, SAVE AS, "Lesson 2 – Extruding Cuts."

### Lesson 2.1.4 - Adding Slots to the Pillow Block Base

When parts have symmetrical features like the slots in the base, simply sketch one of the slots then mirror it.

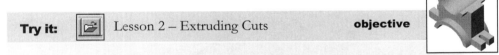

**Try it:** Lesson 2 – Extruding Cuts **objective**

Sketch a centerline and the slot on one side of the base. Then mirror the sketch and extrude the cuts. Note minor grid spacing should be 20.

*STEP 1* - Click **HIDDEN LINE REMOVED** icon, the top surface of the base, then the **SKETCH** tool icon.

*STEP 2* - Draw the centerline as shown through part origin.

*STEP 3* - Begin to sketch the slot using the right mouse menu. Select and sketch a **LINE**, then **TANGENT ARC**, and then **LINE**.

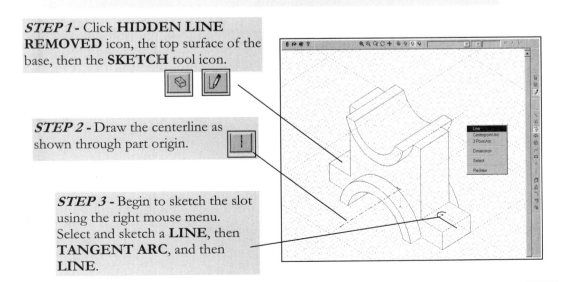

**STEP 4 -** Complete the sketch of the slot as shown, then right mouse on **SELECT** to end command.

Note: Be sure that all sketch elements (including the centerline) are enclosed in the box in order for them to be selected.

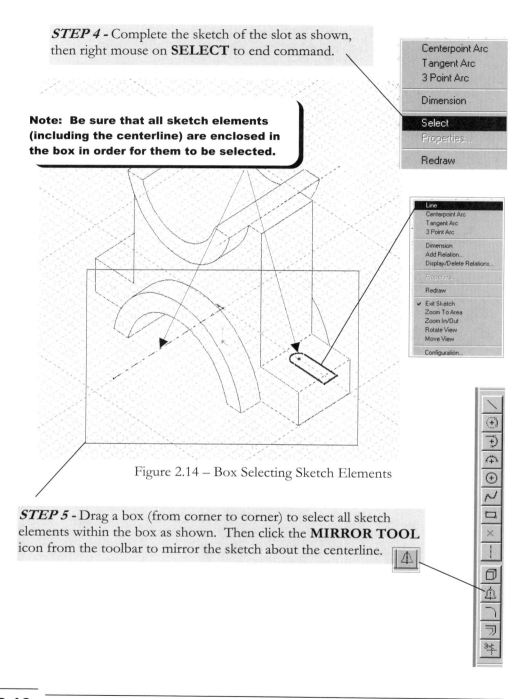

Figure 2.14 – Box Selecting Sketch Elements

**STEP 5 -** Drag a box (from corner to corner) to select all sketch elements within the box as shown. Then click the **MIRROR TOOL** icon from the toolbar to mirror the sketch about the centerline.

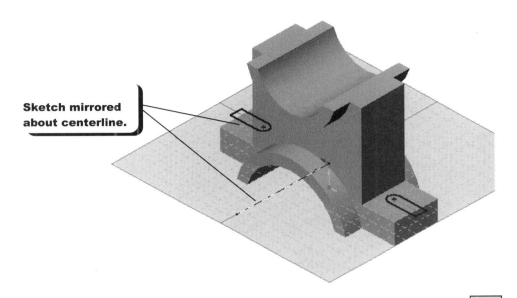

**Sketch mirrored about centerline.**

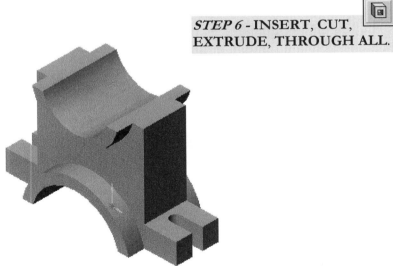

*STEP 6* - INSERT, CUT, EXTRUDE, THROUGH ALL.

*STEP 7* - FILE, SAVE AS – "Lesson 2 – Pillow Block."

### Lesson 2.1.5 - Adding Holes

You can add holes to a part by using **INSERT**, **CUT**, **EXTRUDE** (see previous lesson) or by using the Hole Wizard.

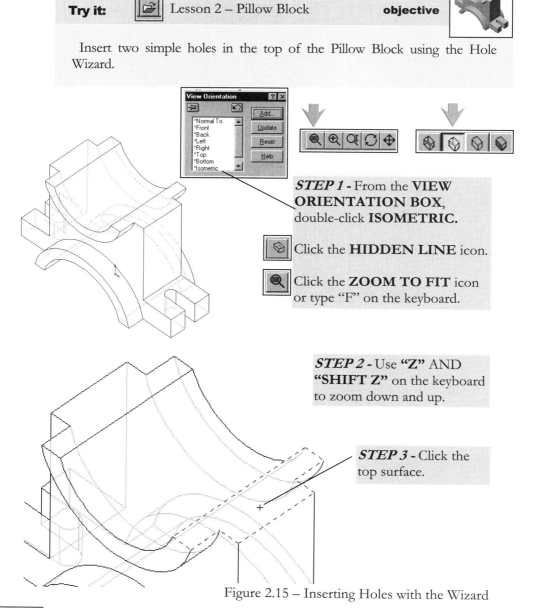

**Try it:**    Lesson 2 – Pillow Block     **objective**

Insert two simple holes in the top of the Pillow Block using the Hole Wizard.

*STEP 1 -* From the **VIEW ORIENTATION BOX**, double-click **ISOMETRIC.**

Click the **HIDDEN LINE** icon.

Click the **ZOOM TO FIT** icon or type "F" on the keyboard.

*STEP 2 -* Use **"Z"** AND **"SHIFT Z"** on the keyboard to zoom down and up.

*STEP 3 -* Click the top surface.

Figure 2.15 – Inserting Holes with the Wizard

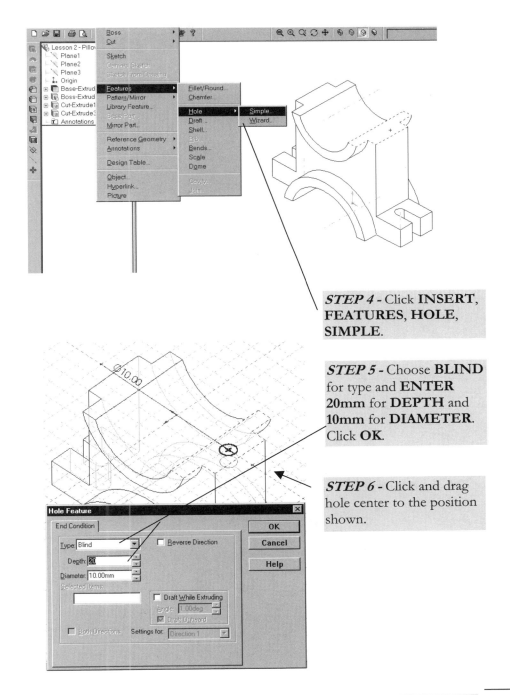

*STEP 4* - Click **INSERT**, **FEATURES**, **HOLE**, **SIMPLE**.

*STEP 5* - Choose **BLIND** for type and **ENTER** **20mm** for **DEPTH** and **10mm** for **DIAMETER**. Click **OK**.

*STEP 6* - Click and drag hole center to the position shown.

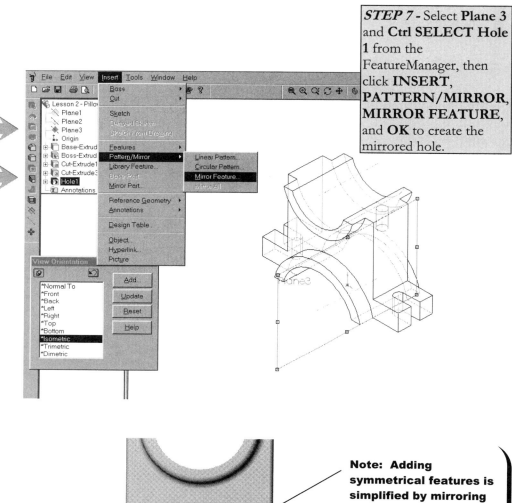

**Note: Adding symmetrical features is simplified by mirroring them about default construction planes such as Plane 3, therefore, it is a good idea to model most parts with the origin centered in the part as shown.**

Figure 2.16 – Mirroring Features

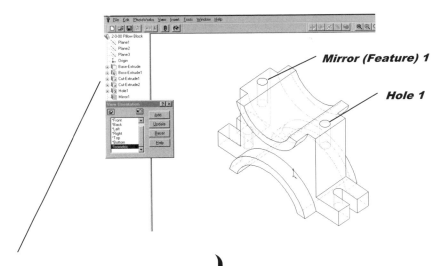

Mirror (Feature) 1

Hole 1

Note: The FeatureManager keeps
track of the features you add to a
part automatically.

**STEP 8** - FILE, SAVE
or click icon.

**STEP 9** - Try some other hole
patterns from the Wizard for fun,
however, do not overwrite the file
just saved. Redo Step 4 but click
**WIZARD** instead of **SIMPLE**
hole.

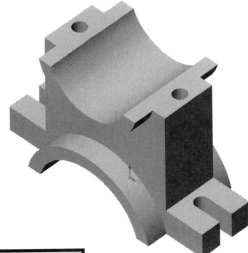

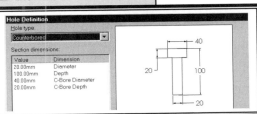

### Lesson 2.1.6 - Adding Fillets

You can add fillets to a part by selecting an edge, face, or loop. A loop is one contiguous edge on a face.

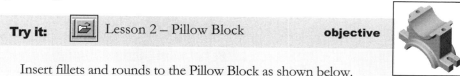

**Try it:**    Lesson 2 – Pillow Block       **objective**

Insert fillets and rounds to the Pillow Block as shown below.

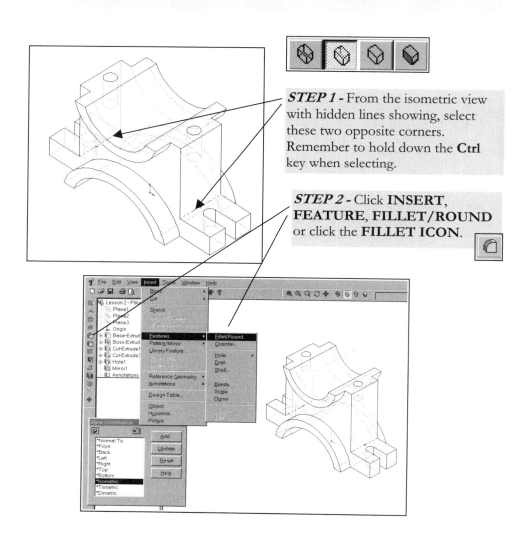

*STEP 1 -* From the isometric view with hidden lines showing, select these two opposite corners. Remember to hold down the **Ctrl** key when selecting.

*STEP 2 -* Click **INSERT, FEATURE, FILLET/ROUND** or click the **FILLET ICON**.

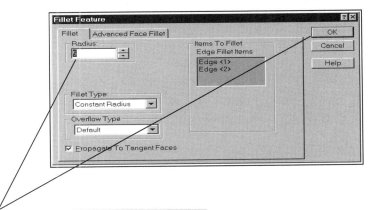

**STEP 3 -** From the **FILLET FEATURE** dialog box, enter 5mm and click **OK**.

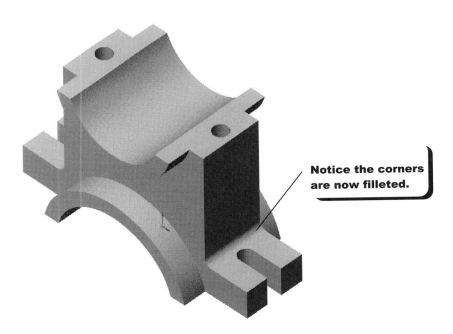

Notice the corners are now filleted.

STEP 4 - **Ctrl SELECT** (hold down the control key while selecting) 8 edges as shown, and **INSERT 4mm FILLETS/ROUNDS**.

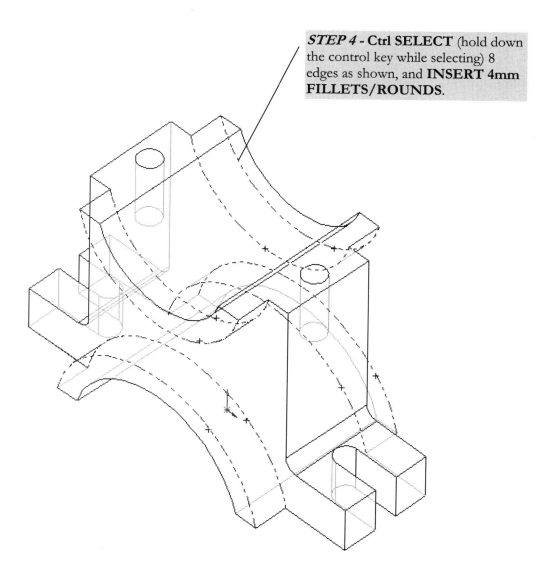

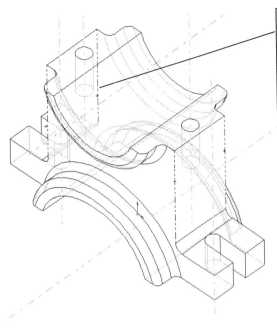

*STEP 5* - **Ctrl SELECT** 4 edges as shown, and **INSERT 3mm FILLETS/ROUNDS**. Make sure that the **Propagate Along Tangent Edges** option is checked in **Fillet Feature** dialog box.

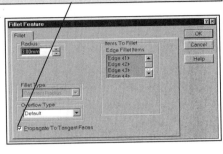

*STEP 6* - Shade the part, then use "Z" and "Shift Z" and the keyboard arrow keys to zoom and rotate the part to look over the fillets and rounds you added. Finally, select the isometric view, zoom to fit, and save.

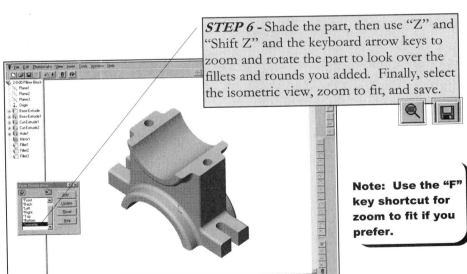

**Note: Use the "F" key shortcut for zoom to fit if you prefer.**

### Lesson 2.1.7 - Displaying Features and Sketches

You can scroll through the sketches used in your part and the features that were generated from them by using the **FeatureManager Design Tree.** You can also display features and sketches by clicking right on part features.

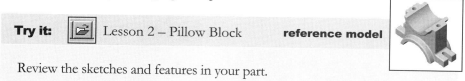

**Try it:** Lesson 2 – Pillow Block    **reference model**

Review the sketches and features in your part.

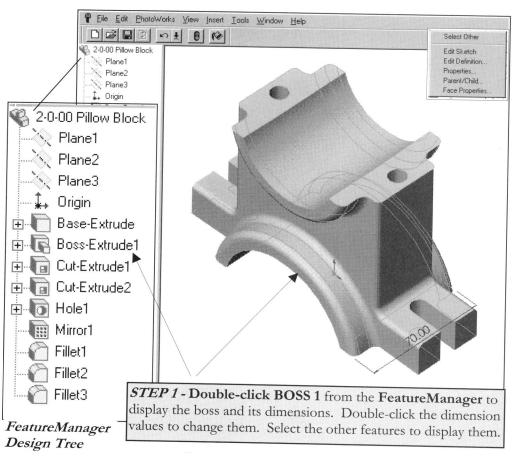

*FeatureManager Design Tree*

*STEP 1* - **Double-click BOSS 1** from the **FeatureManager** to display the boss and its dimensions. Double-click the dimension values to change them. Select the other features to display them.

Figure 2.17 – Displaying and Editing Sketches

*STEP 2* - Click each plus sign to expand the FeatureManager list and the minus sign to collapse it. When the sketches are displayed, click each sketch to see it. Click the **REDRAW** icon to clean up the screen and the **REBUILD** icon to rebuild the part and reset the FeatureManager.

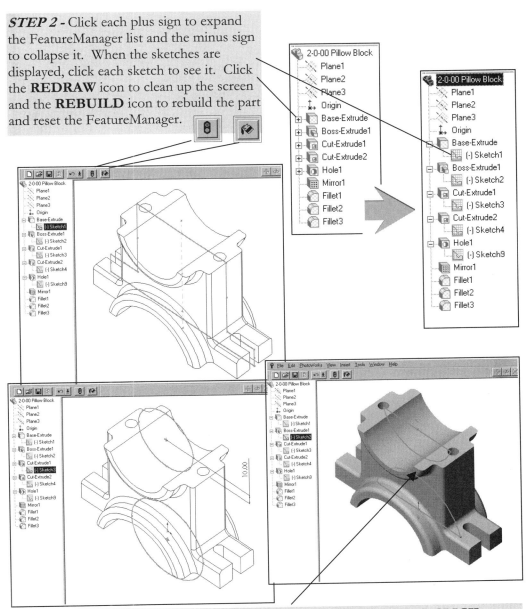

*STEP 3* - You can **CLICK, DOUBLE-CLICK**, or **RIGHT MOUSE CLICK** on features right in the part to activate various options. For example, right mouse click on the boss shown and select **EDIT SKETCH** from the pop-up menu if you want to modify it. Try these options to see what they do, then **REBUILD** before going on.

## Modifying parts

In SolidWorks, you can change anything at any time. You can revise sketch geometry or dimensions, change feature definitions, locations, or dimensional values, or change the sequence in which features are built into a part. You can also change geometric relationships in a sketch or a feature. The following examples represent typical design changes made by modifying the part at the right.

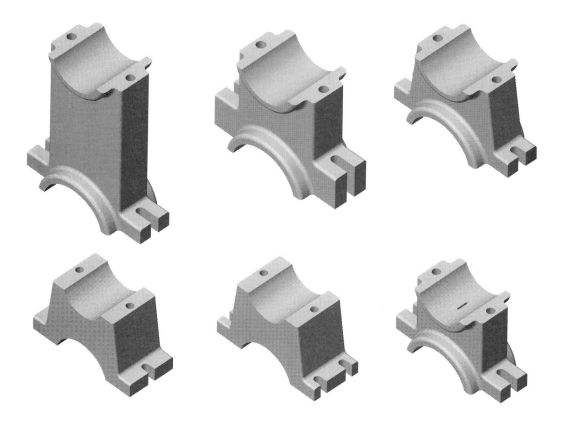

Figure 2.18 – Modified Parts

## Lesson 2.2.1 - Reshape a Sketch by Dragging Sketch Elements

In SolidWorks, you can drag sketch elements or element endpoints to reshape a sketch. Rebuilding the part updates the feature.

**Try it:** Lesson 2 – Pillow Block **objective**

Constrain the top of the upper boss and Cut 1 to the top face of the base extrusion. Then stretch the part higher by dragging the top of the base extrusion sketch. The boss and cut will remain attached to the top face.

**STEP 1 -** Right mouse click on Boss 1 and click **EDIT SKETCH** from the pop-up menu.

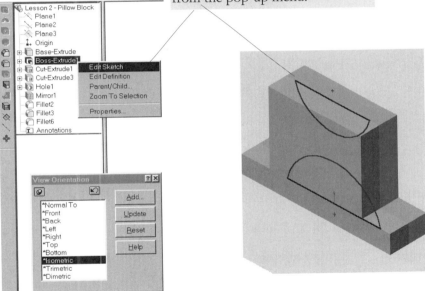

**Note: You will notice different colored lines on your sketches. Black lines are "fully defined," blue lines are "under-defined" until dimensioned or constrained, red lines are "over-defined" with redundant dimensions or constraints. Lines turn green when selected. To see the current list of other line colors, click TOOLS, OPTIONS, COLOR, SKETCH COLORS.**

**STEP 2 - Ctrl SELECT** this line and edge.

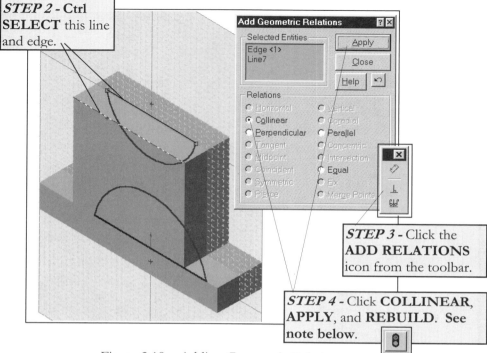

**STEP 3 -** Click the **ADD RELATIONS** icon from the toolbar.

**STEP 4 -** Click **COLLINEAR, APPLY**, and **REBUILD. See note below.**

Figure 2.19 – Adding Geometric Relations

**Note: GEOMETRIC RELATIONS describe relationships among geometric entities in parts in order to preserve design intent. For example, in Step 4 above, the COLLINEAR relationship "constrains" the "CUT 1" sketch to the top surface. Therefore, CUT 1 will move with the surface when the surface is modified.**

**STEP 5 -** You can tie the cut location to the top surface by adding a constraint to the cut sketch. Right mouse **Cut 1** and **EDIT SKETCH** from the FeatureManager or from the part.

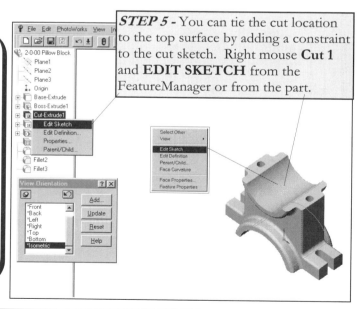

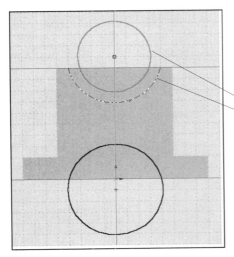

Note: Use your preference of the isometric or front view for this construction.

*STEP 6* - **Ctrl SELECT** the two diameters shown.

*STEP 7* - Click **ADD RELATIONS** icon, choose **CONCENTRIC** and click **APPLY**.

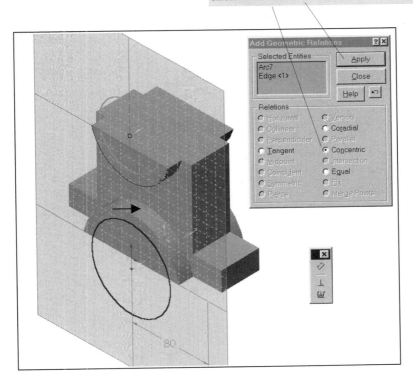

*STEP 8 -* To stretch the height of the part, **EDIT THE SKETCH** of the base feature.

*STEP 9 -* Drag the top line up to the location shown.

*STEP 10 -* Rebuild and **SAVE AS - Lesson 2 - Pillow Block Mod 1.**

**Note: Your sketch should look like this.**

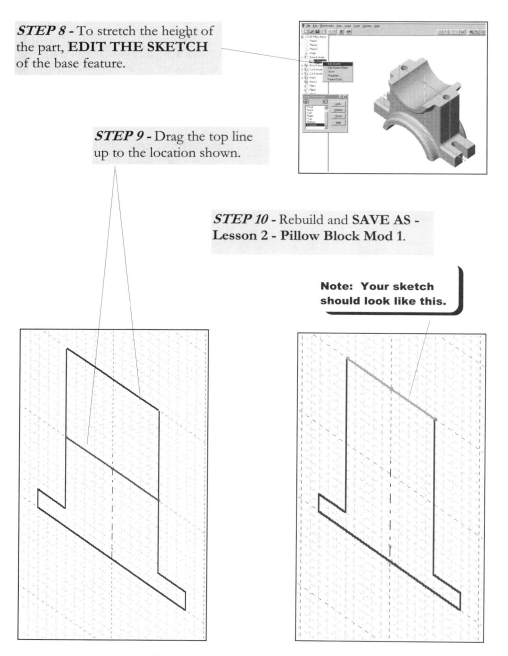

Figure 2.20 – Dragging Sketch Elements

## Lesson 2.2.2 - Reshape a Sketch by Changing Dimensions

SolidWorks is a dimension-driven program; changing dimensions automatically changes geometry. You can add and change these dimensions at any time.

**Try it:** 　　 Lesson 2 – Pillow Block 　　　 **reference model**

Dimension the height of the base-mounting lugs, change the dimension, and rebuild the part. Be sure to start with Lesson 2 – Pillow Block, not Mod 1.

*STEP 1* - Edit the sketch of the base extrusion.

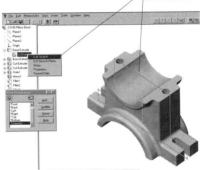

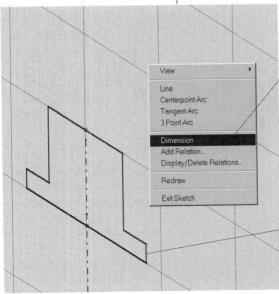

*STEP 2* - Click the dimension icon or select **DIMENSION** from the right mouse pop-up menu.

*STEP 3* - To dimension lug, click this line then a location to place the dimension.

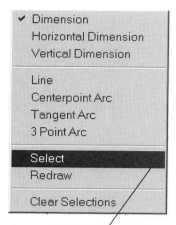

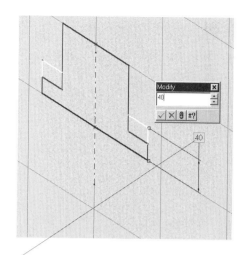

**STEP 4** - From the right mouse menu click **SELECT**.

**STEP 5** - Double-click the dimension.

**STEP 6** - Change the value to 40mm, press enter key, or select checkmark to view the modified sketch. Try the other options in the Modify box to learn what they do.

**STEP 7** - Rebuild and save as **"Lesson 2 - Pillow Block Mod 2."**

Figure 2.21 – Dimension-Driven Sketching

**Note: You can also double-click on any feature to bring up its dimensions. Double-click the dimensions to change them. The changes you make will take affect after you rebuild the part.**

**To delete a dimension, select it and press the delete key.**

**Lesson 2.2.3 - Reshape a Sketch by Dragging a Line Endpoint**

**Try it:**  Lesson 2 – Pillow Block **objective**

Make the following revisions to the base extrusion sketch.

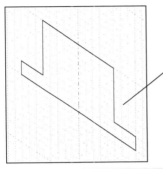

*STEP 1 -* Edit the base extrusion sketch.

*STEP 2 -* Click the original (not mirrored) vertical line and click the **DISPLAY/DELETE RELATIONS** icon.

*STEP 3 -* From the pop-up dialog, click **DELETE** to delete the automatically applied **VERTICAL CONSTRAINT**. Click close to finish.

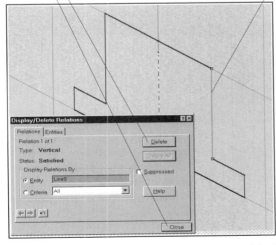

Figure 2.22 – Display/Delete Relations Tool

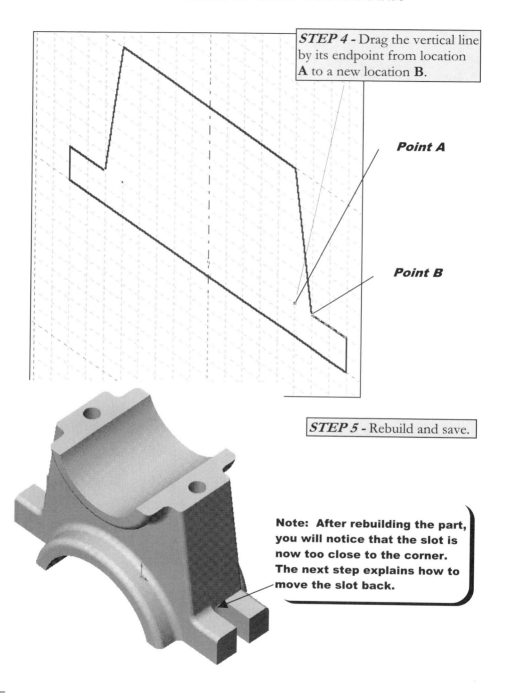

**STEP 4** - Drag the vertical line by its endpoint from location **A** to a new location **B**.

**Point A**

**Point B**

**STEP 5** - Rebuild and save.

Note: After rebuilding the part, you will notice that the slot is now too close to the corner. The next step explains how to move the slot back.

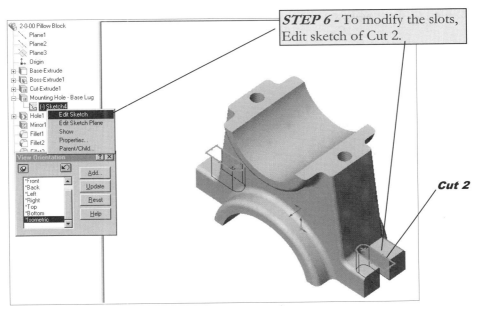

**STEP 6 -** To modify the slots, Edit sketch of Cut 2.

Cut 2

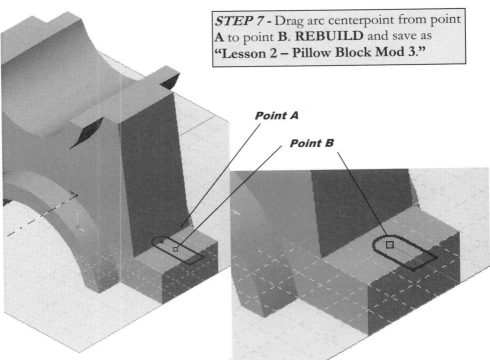

**STEP 7 -** Drag arc centerpoint from point **A** to point **B. REBUILD** and save as **"Lesson 2 – Pillow Block Mod 3."**

Point A

Point B

## Lesson 2.2.4 - Modifying Feature Depth

Modifying a feature's depth can make a dramatic change to a part's appearance. This capability makes it easy to iterate designs, or to use existing parts to make new ones.

**Try it:** Lesson 2 – Pillow Block Mod 3    **objective**

Create this part by modifying the base feature depth.

*STEP 1* - Open the part version Mod 3 and file as **"Lesson 2 – Pillow Block Mod 4."** Then delete Cut 1.

*STEP 2* - Edit the **SKETCH PLANE** for the remaining cut sketch and move it to Plane 1. Select Plane 1 from FeatureManager and click Apply.

*STEP 3* - Delete Boss 1. Notice that dependent features are deleted automatically. *Note: Step 5 will solve the rebuild error warning.*

*STEP 4* - Delete the sketch used for deleted Boss 1.

*STEP 5* - Edit Sketch 3 and delete all relations applied to it. Rebuild part.

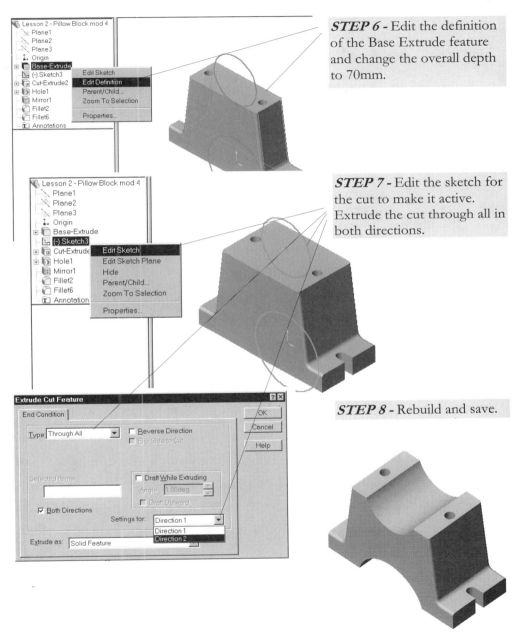

**STEP 6 -** Edit the definition of the Base Extrude feature and change the overall depth to 70mm.

**STEP 7 -** Edit the sketch for the cut to make it active. Extrude the cut through all in both directions.

**STEP 8 -** Rebuild and save.

Figure 2.23 – Modifying Feature Definitions

## Lesson 2.2.5 - Moving and Mirroring Features

You can modify existing features by moving, copying, or mirroring them.

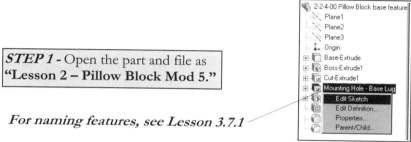

**Try it:**    Lesson 2 – Pillow Block Mod 4    **objective**

Modify the part so that it has four base-lug mounting holes as shown at the right.

**STEP 1 -** Open the part and file as **"Lesson 2 – Pillow Block Mod 5."**

*For naming features, see Lesson 3.7.1*

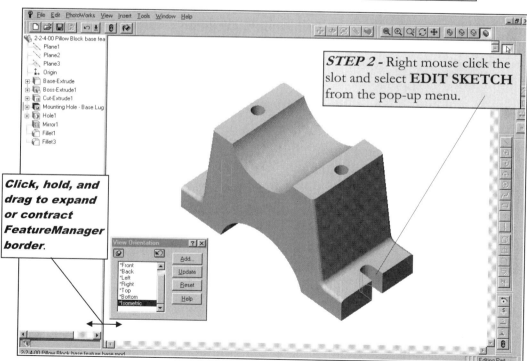

**STEP 2 -** Right mouse click the slot and select **EDIT SKETCH** from the pop-up menu.

*Click, hold, and drag to expand or contract FeatureManager border.*

**STEP 3 -** From right mouse pop-up menu, select **DIMENSION** tool.

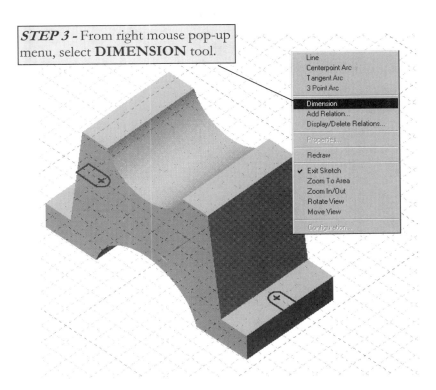

Line
Centerpoint Arc
Tangent Arc
3 Point Arc

Dimension
Add Relation...
Display/Delete Relations...

Properties...

Redraw

✓ Exit Sketch
Zoom To Area
Zoom In/Out
Rotate View
Move View

Configuration...

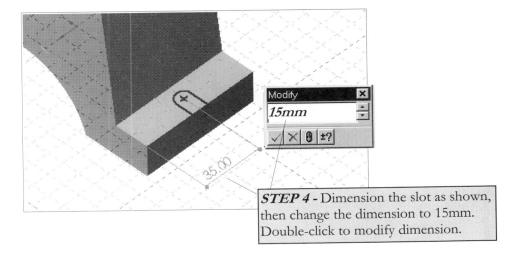

Modify

*15mm*

35.00

**STEP 4 -** Dimension the slot as shown, then change the dimension to 15mm. Double-click to modify dimension.

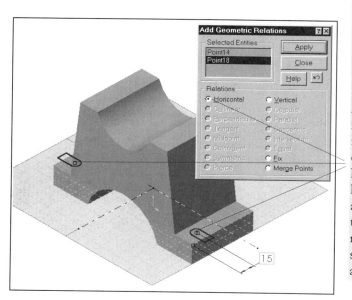

***STEP 5*** - Add a relation between the slots so that they are in line. **Ctrl SELECT** the two slot centerpoints. Click the **ADD RELATION** icon and make the mounting slot centerpoints horizontal. (To be in line, the slots would appear horizontal in the top view, the view normal to the work surface.) Click **APPLY** and **CLOSE**.

**Note: The newly constrained slot lines up to the dimensioned one.**

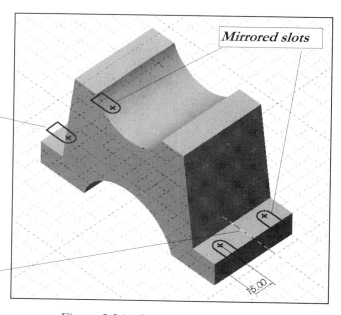

***STEP 6*** - Sketch a centerline as shown, then select all of the elements in both mounting slots and the centerline to mirror the slots about the centerline.

Figure 2.24 – Mirroring Feature Sketches

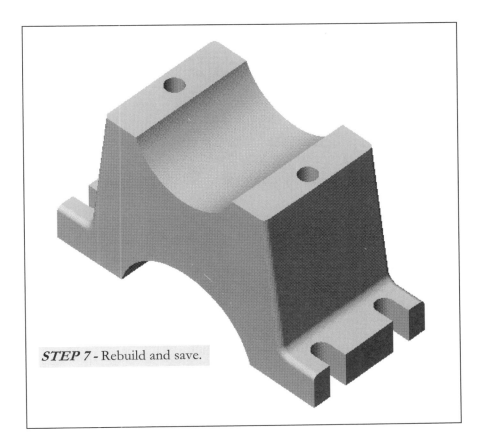

*STEP 7 -* Rebuild and save.

Note: You can delete practice part files from disk from within SolidWorks using this procedure:

1. Select the OPEN part icon or select FILE, OPEN
2. Select the part you want to delete from disk (delete Lesson 2 – Base Extrusion)
3. Press the DELETE key and click YES to confirm the deletion

## Lesson 2.2.6 - Adding New Features

You can add new features to existing parts by sketching on a reference plane or a planar surface of the part and inserting a feature from the sketch.

**Try it:**  Lesson 2 – Pillow Block **objective**

Add an oil passage between the circular cuts as shown.

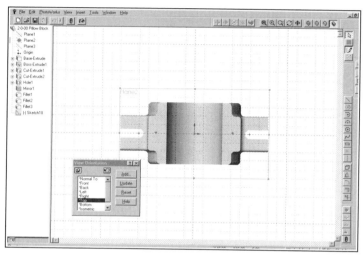

Top view

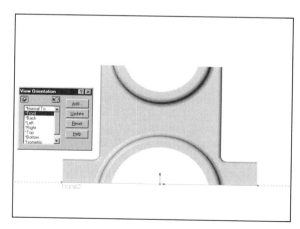

*STEP 1* - Select Plane 2 and go to the top view of the part. Save as **"Lesson 2 – Pillow Block with Oil Hole."**

Front view reference

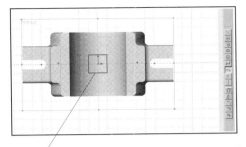

**STEP 2 -** Insert a new sketch, then click the **RECTANGLE** tool and sketch as shown.

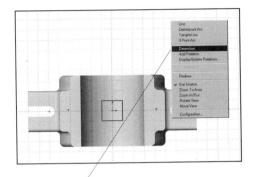

**STEP 3 -** Right mouse click for **DIMENSION** tool and dimension as shown.

**STEP 4 -** Add and revise dimensions as shown in the next three illustrations.

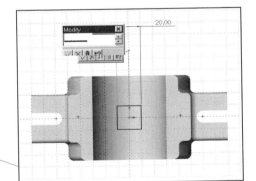

Note:
*Placing a dimension provides a preview of how the dimension will look before clicking its position. Move the cursor around sketch elements to place a horizontal, vertical, or point-to-point dimension. You can reposition dimensions after they are placed.*

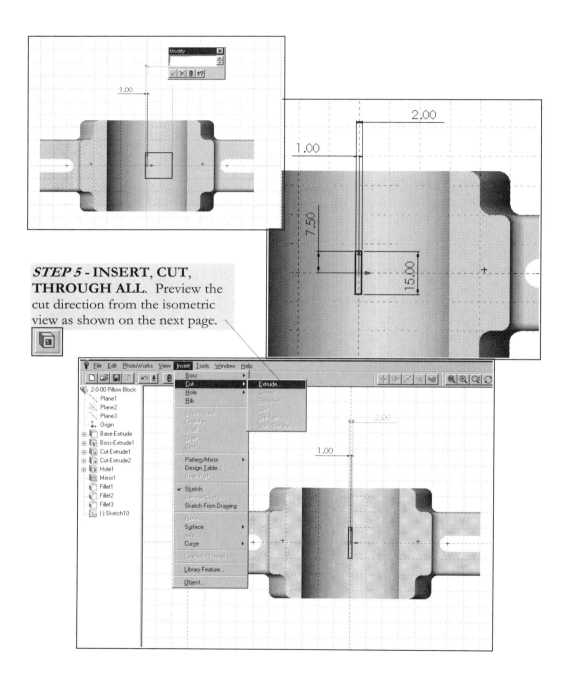

**STEP 5 - INSERT, CUT, THROUGH ALL.** Preview the cut direction from the isometric view as shown on the next page.

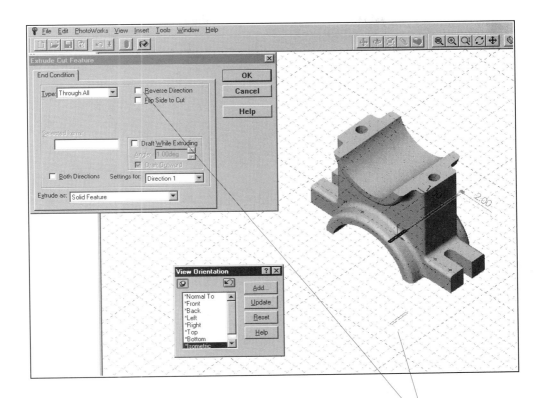

**STEP 6 - REVERSE DIRECTION** if **CUT PREVIEW** appears here. When you are satisfied with the cut results, **Save the part**.

It is recommended that you review all of the pages in this chapter before moving on to the next chapter. Redo any lesson that you are not confident with.

**Proficiency comes with practice.**

*chapter contents*

**Displaying origin, axes, and planes**
**Arranging windows**
**Part color and edge display options**
**Zooming, panning, and rotating**
**View orientation settings**
**Section-cutting parts**
**Naming and suppressing features**

# Chapter 3 – VISUALIZATION TOOLS

## Displaying origin, axes, and planes

**Lesson 3.1.1 - Hiding the Part Origin**

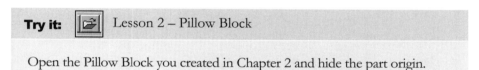

**Try it:** Lesson 2 – Pillow Block

Open the Pillow Block you created in Chapter 2 and hide the part origin.

**STEP 1 -** Right mouse click the **ORIGIN** in the FeatureManager and click **HIDE** from the pop-up dialog.

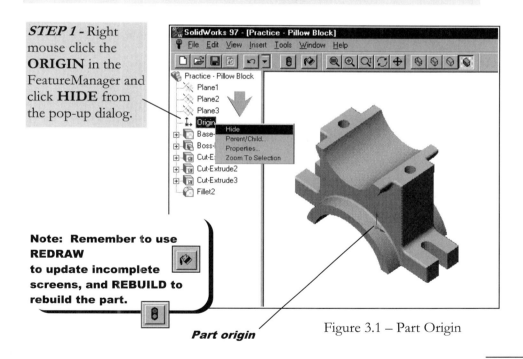

**Note: Remember to use REDRAW to update incomplete screens, and REBUILD to rebuild the part.**

*Part origin*

Figure 3.1 – Part Origin

### Lesson 3.1.2 - Showing, Moving, and Resizing Part Construction Planes

You can show or hide individual or all construction planes. You can resize or move the planes to aid in visualizing your part orientation at any time.

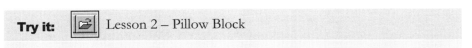

Toggle planes on, show, move and resize the default construction planes.

**STEP 1 -** Click **VIEW**, **PLANES** to toggle the display of planes on. Click **PLANES** again (no checkmark) to toggle off. Be sure **VIEW**, **PLANES** is checked before going on to step 2.

**STEP 2 -** Right mouse click a plane in the **FeatureManager** and click **SHOW** from the pop-up dialog. Repeat and click **HIDE** to hide a plane. **SHOW** all of the planes before going on to step 3.

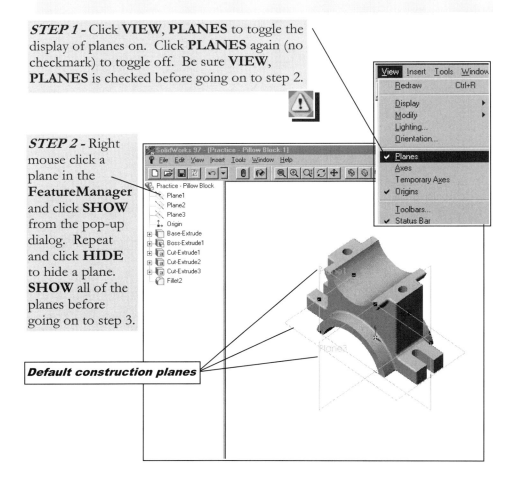

**Default construction planes**

Figure 3.2 – Default Planes 1-3

**STEP 3 -** Using the view orientation box, click some other views and notice all planes are shown.

**STEP 4 -** When you click on a plane to select it, "handles" will show up on the corners and edge midpoints. Click and hold a handle to reshape the plane. Move the cursor over the plane until the cursor "move" symbol appears, then move the plane to a new position that helps you to visualize the part better.

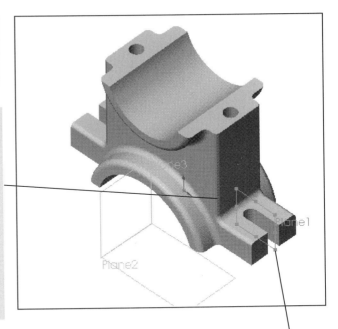

*Plane resizing handles*

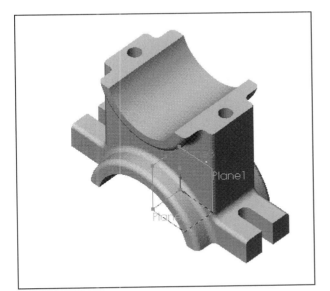

*Planes moved and resized around the part origin*

### Lesson 3.1.3 - Converting Temporary Axes to Reference Axes

All holes and circular features have axes that are automatically created by SolidWorks. These axes are defined as "temporary" until you convert them to a "reference axis." On complex parts, displaying all of the temporary axes on the display would be overwhelming. For this reason, SolidWorks allows you to separate important axes from the others by converting them to reference axes. Reference axes are listed in the FeatureManager along with other axes you create, such as an axis created at the intersection of two planes or planar surfaces. Any axis may be used for locating, constraining, or dimensioning part features. Any axis may also be used as an axis of rotation for circular patterns.

**Try it:**   Lesson 2 – Pillow Block

Show the system-generated "temporary" axes of holes and circular features, and convert a temporary axis to a reference axis.

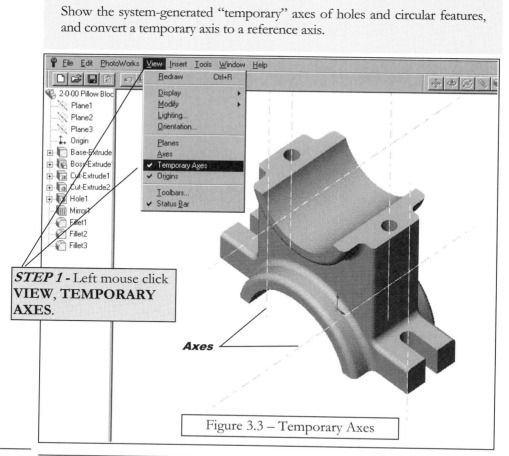

*STEP 1* - Left mouse click **VIEW, TEMPORARY AXES**.

*Axes*

Figure 3.3 – Temporary Axes

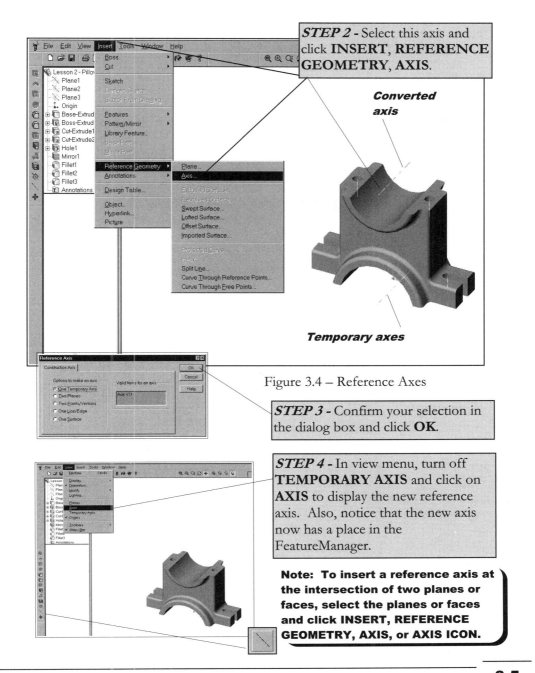

**STEP 2 -** Select this axis and click **INSERT, REFERENCE GEOMETRY, AXIS.**

*Converted axis*

*Temporary axes*

Figure 3.4 – Reference Axes

**STEP 3 -** Confirm your selection in the dialog box and click **OK.**

**STEP 4 -** In view menu, turn off **TEMPORARY AXIS** and click on **AXIS** to display the new reference axis. Also, notice that the new axis now has a place in the FeatureManager.

**Note: To insert a reference axis at the intersection of two planes or faces, select the planes or faces and click INSERT, REFERENCE GEOMETRY, AXIS, or AXIS ICON.**

## Arranging windows

### Lesson 3.2.1 - Opening New Windows of the Same Part

You can display two or more windows of a part at one time and orient the parts in the windows for optimum viewing. Since changes in one view appears in all views, design iterations are easier to visualize. The new windows are simply another view of the same document.

**Try it:** Lesson 2 – Pillow Block

Open a **NEW WINDOW** and display both part windows at once.

*STEP 1* - Click **WINDOW, NEW WINDOW**.

*STEP 2* - Click **WINDOW, TILE VERTICALLY**.

**Note: Click in a window to activate it.**

**Note: In the view orientation box, double-click a view name to change the view display.**

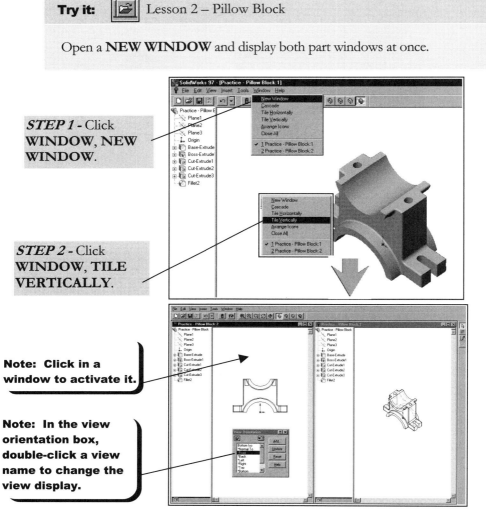

Figure 3.5 – Windows Tiled Vertically

### Lesson 3.2.2 – Split-Screen Windows of the Same Part

You can also split the display screen horizontally and vertically to add up to four panes to the same window.

**Try it:** Lesson 2 – Pillow Block

Create another window by dragging the vertical split-screen display bar, then rotate and move the views in any window.

**STEP 1 -** Drag this bar to create a split screen.

*Drag bar*

**STEP 2 -** Use **ROTATE** and **PAN** tools to arrange parts in windows.

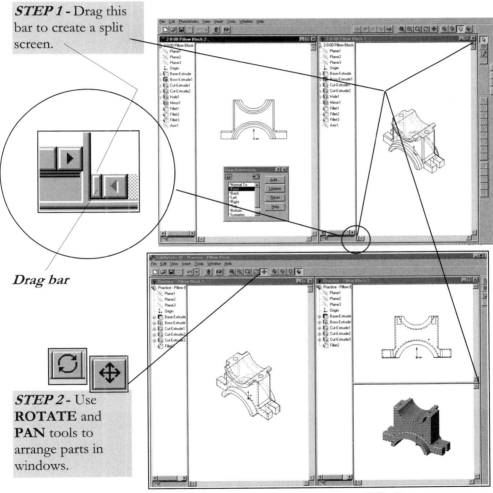

Figure 3.6 – Windows Split Bar

### Lesson 3.2.3 - Tiled Windows of Different Parts

Like other Microsoft Windows applications, you can have multiple SolidWorks documents opened at the same time. This capability is a valuable visualization tool that makes it easier to design parts based on reference models.

**Try it :** 🗗   Lesson 2 – Pillow Block Mod 1 - Mod 4

Open all four parts and display them simultaneously.

*STEP 1* - From **WINDOW** menu, click **TILE HORIZONTALLY**.

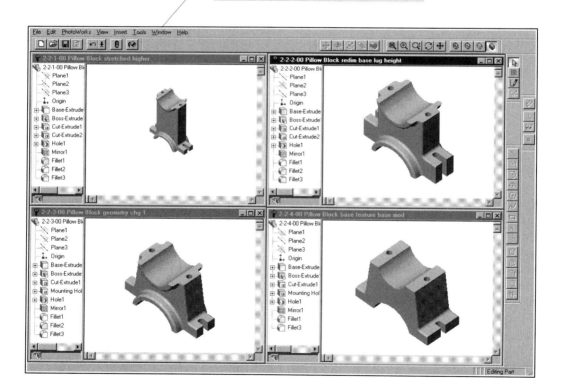

Figure 3.7 – Windows Tiled

*Minimize*

*Maximize*

*Close*

STEP 2 - From Window menu, click **CASCADE**.

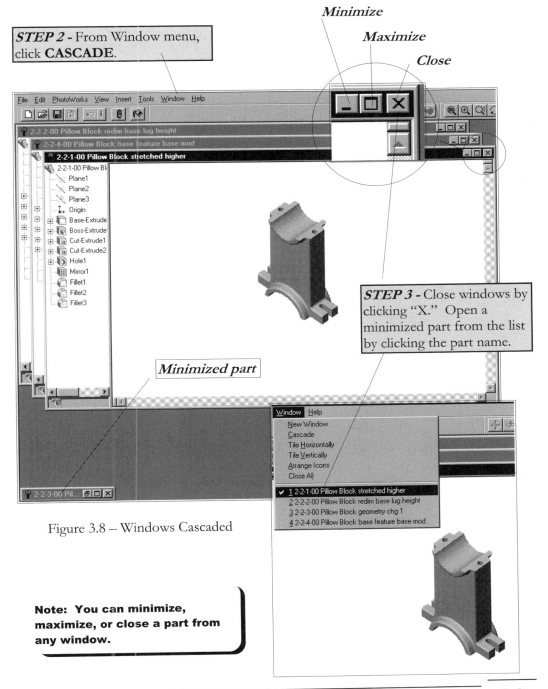

STEP 3 - Close windows by clicking "X." Open a minimized part from the list by clicking the part name.

*Minimized part*

Window  Help

New Window
Cascade
Tile Horizontally
Tile Vertically
Arrange Icons
Close All

✓ 1 2-2-1-00 Pillow Block stretched higher
2 2-2-2-00 Pillow Block redim base lug height
3 2-2-3-00 Pillow Block geometry chg 1
4 2-2-4-00 Pillow Block base feature base mod

Figure 3.8 – Windows Cascaded

**Note:  You can minimize, maximize, or close a part from any window.**

# Part color and edge display options

### Lesson 3.3.1 - Changing Part Color and Edge Display

You can change the part color and edge display in any window.

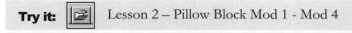

**Try it:** Lesson 2 – Pillow Block Mod 1 - Mod 4

Tile the parts horizontally, then change part colors and edge displays.

*STEP 1 -* Right mouse click a part name and click on **OPTIONS**.

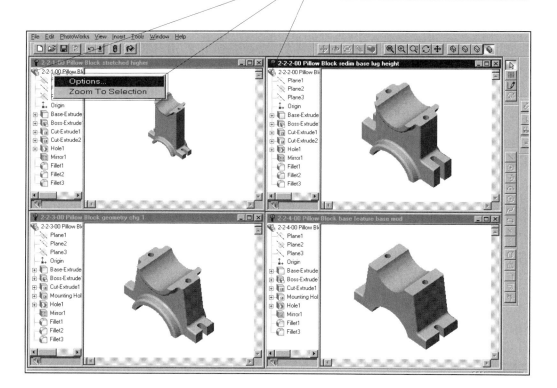

**STEP 2** - Click **COLOR TAB**, **SHADING**, **EDIT**, then choose a color from the palette and click **OK** on each menu.

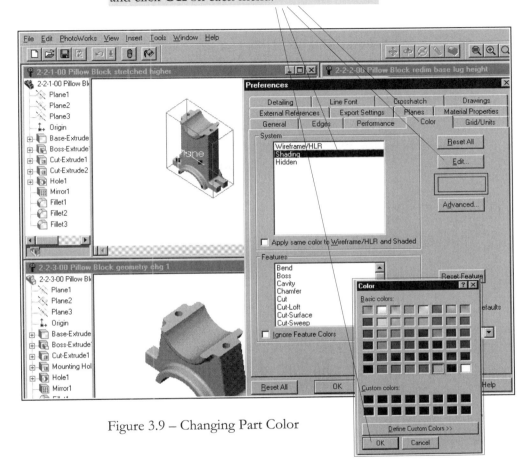

Figure 3.9 – Changing Part Color

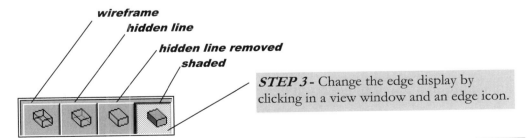

wireframe
hidden line
hidden line removed
shaded

**STEP 3** - Change the edge display by clicking in a view window and an edge icon.

### Lesson 3.3.2 - Changing Part Feature Color

You can change the color of part features to aid visualizing a design. This can be a communication aid for design review meetings or for training.

**Try it:** Lesson 2 – Pillow Block Mod 1 - Mod 4

Using the windows shown in the previous lesson, change the part color, feature color, and face color as shown.

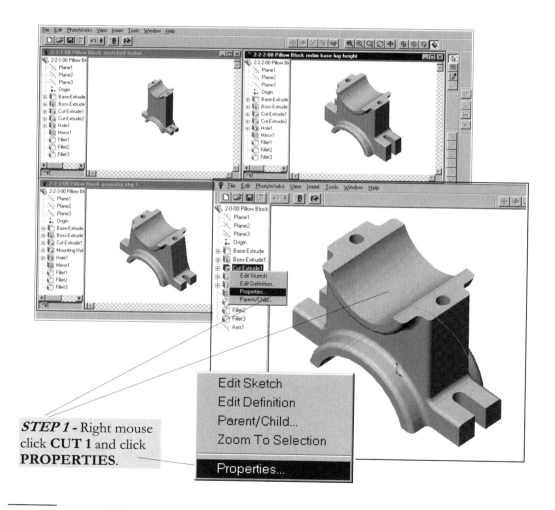

*STEP 1 -* Right mouse click **CUT 1** and click **PROPERTIES**.

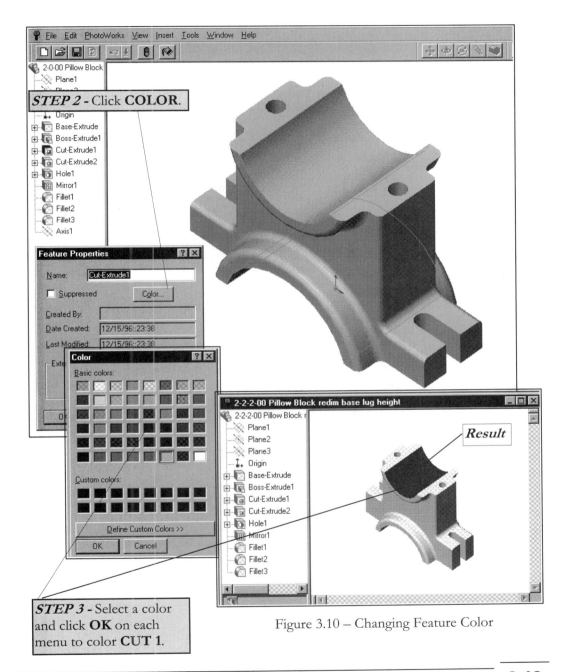

STEP 2 - Click COLOR.

STEP 3 - Select a color and click OK on each menu to color CUT 1.

Figure 3.10 – Changing Feature Color

**STEP 4 -** Click this window, right mouse click the part name, and click **OPTIONS** from the pop-up menu.

**STEP 5 -** On the color tab, click **FILLET** and **EDIT** to color the fillets.

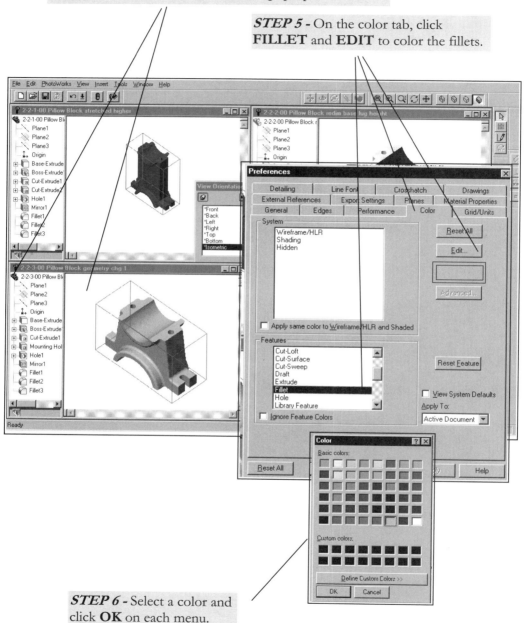

**STEP 6 -** Select a color and click **OK** on each menu.

**STEP 7 -** Right mouse click face and click **FACE PROPERTIES**.

**STEP 8 -** Change the face color.

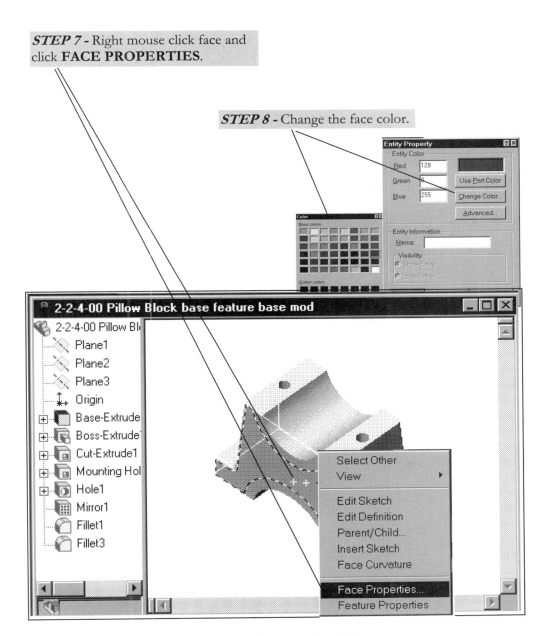

Figure 3.11 – Changing Face Color

*Part colored*

*Cut feature colored*

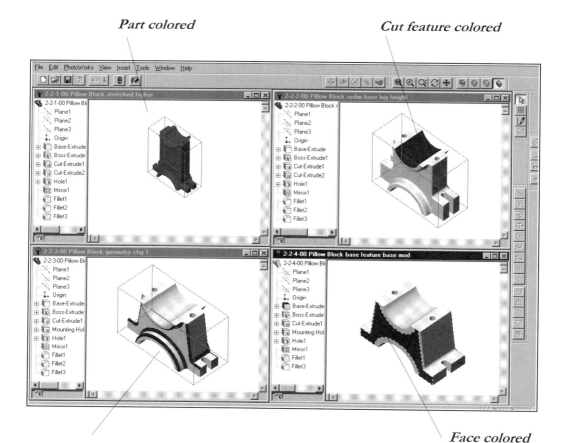

*Fillets and
rounds colored*

*Face colored*

Figure 3.12 – Part, Feature, and Face Color Options

### Lesson 3.3.3 - Displaying Transparent Parts

You can display parts with different levels of transparency to show internal features. When transparent parts are used in assemblies, it becomes easier to see internal assembly components.

**Try it:** Lesson 2 – Pillow Block

Display the Pillow Block as transparent.

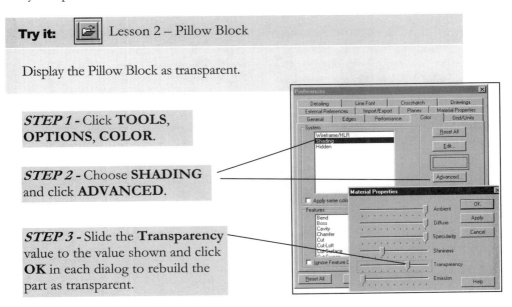

**STEP 1 -** Click **TOOLS, OPTIONS, COLOR.**

**STEP 2 -** Choose **SHADING** and click **ADVANCED.**

**STEP 3 -** Slide the **Transparency** value to the value shown and click **OK** in each dialog to rebuild the part as transparent.

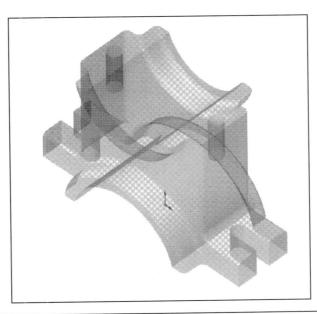

## Zooming, panning, and rotating
### Lesson 3.4.1 - Zooming, Panning, and Rotating Parts

**Try it:**  Lesson 2 – Pillow Block

Use the toolbar buttons described below to change the view size, position, and rotation in each window. To zoom the display for a specific part feature, right mouse the feature from the FeatureManager and choose **ZOOM TO SELECTION** from the pop-up dialog.

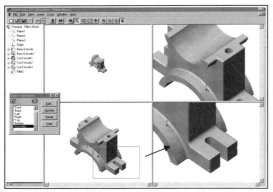

Figure 3.13 – Zooming Parts

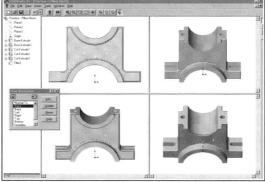

Figure 3.14 – Rotating Parts

🔍⁺ = Zoom area in box (drag out a box) to

🔍 = Zoom part to fit screen automatically

🔍 = Zoom using mouse - Drag mouse up or down in the view window

 = Pan part by dragging it

🔄 = Rotate part by dragging it

*To change part orientation:*
arrow keys = rotate in 15 **(*)** degree increments

Shift+arrow key = rotate 90 degrees with each keystroke

Alt+arrow key = rotate 15 **(*)** degrees about line of sight

*Keyboard alternates* (for toolbar buttons)

| *To change part size:* | *To change part position:* |
|---|---|
| F = zoom to fit | |
| Z = zoom down | Ctrl+arrow keys = move |
| Shift+Z = zoom up | |

**(*)** Rotation angle may be set in **TOOLS**, **OPTIONS**, **GENERAL**, **VIEW ROTATION**.

## View orientation settings
### Lesson 3.5.1 - Changing the Displayed View
You can change a view from the **VIEW ORIENTATION** dialog box.

**Try it:** 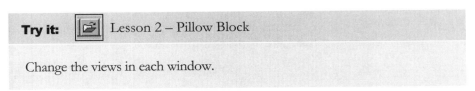 Lesson 2 – Pillow Block

Change the views in each window.

*STEP 1* - Click **VIEW, ORIENTATION**.

**Note: Click and hold the title bar to drag the view orientation box. To keep it always visible, click on the pushpin.**

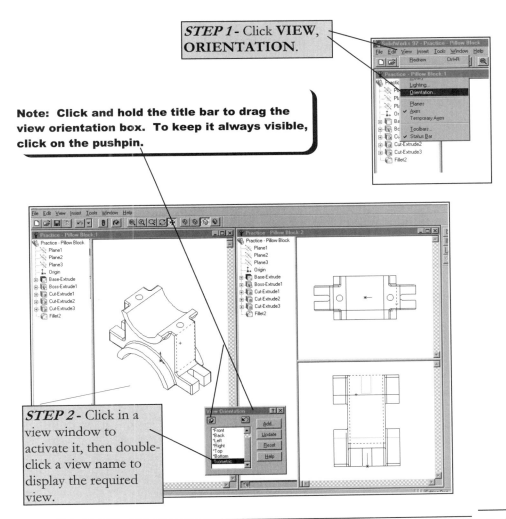

*STEP 2* - Click in a view window to activate it, then double-click a view name to display the required view.

## Lesson 3.5.2 - Setting up Orthographic Views

You can create a very organized work area using split screens and view orientation. The figure below shows a popular way to set up the display when working with split screens because it uses the standard orthographic and isometric view arrangements used in third-angle projection. This arrangement creates a working environment that all designers are familiar with. When changes are made in one view, the resultant change in the other views provides the designer with instant feedback of the change.

**Try it:** Lesson 2 – Pillow Block

Create equally spaced split screens and change each view window as shown below.

**STEP 1 -** After creating the views shown, add a hole to any planar surface in one view and observe the other views update automatically. Use this display orientation in the next lesson.

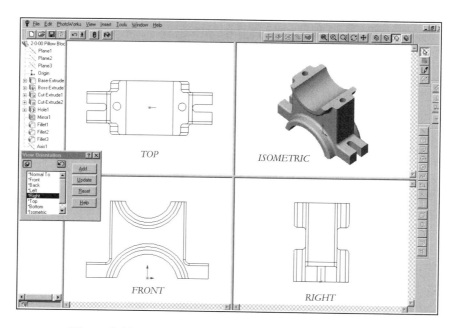

Figure 3.15 – View Orientation – Orthographic Views

## Lesson 3.5.3 - Changing the Default Views

You may change the view orientation in a part so that view assignments become consistent with how other parts are oriented in an assembly. You may also want to change the view orientation in a part to create a better-looking drawing sheet presentation. For example, if a "part" front view is not the best selection for a "drawing sheet" front view, you can change the part's view orientation. The other related orthographic views in a part will automatically update to reflect your new orientation after you make a change to any orthographic view.

**Try it:** Lesson 2 – Pillow Block

Change the orientation of the part so that the old front view is now the right side view.

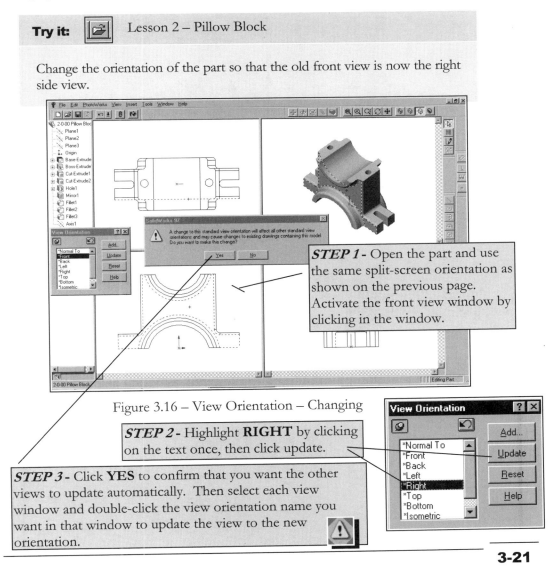

**STEP 1 -** Open the part and use the same split-screen orientation as shown on the previous page. Activate the front view window by clicking in the window.

Figure 3.16 – View Orientation – Changing

**STEP 2 -** Highlight **RIGHT** by clicking on the text once, then click update.

**STEP 3 -** Click **YES** to confirm that you want the other views to update automatically. Then select each view window and double-click the view orientation name you want in that window to update the view to the new orientation.

**Note: All of the views update to the new orientation.**

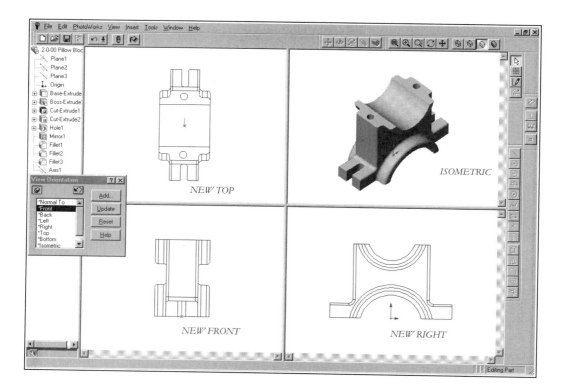

Figure 3.17 – Revised View Orientation

## Lesson 3.5.4 - Creating and Naming a New View

You can save a view of the screen display.

**Try it:** 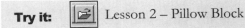 Lesson 2 – Pillow Block

Rotate and size the Pillow Block part as shown below, then save the new view as "Bottom Iso."

*STEP 1* - Display the part as shown, then click **ADD** in the view orientation box.

*STEP 2* - Type in "Bottom Iso" as "view name" and click **OK**.

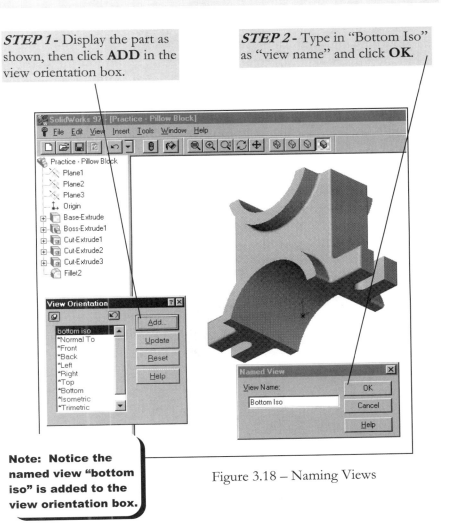

**Note: Notice the named view "bottom iso" is added to the view orientation box.**

Figure 3.18 – Naming Views

### Lesson 3.5.5 - Displaying a Perspective View of a Part

You can display a part in perspective to use in technical publications of SolidWorks documents.

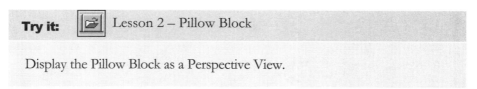

**Try it:** Lesson 2 – Pillow Block

Display the Pillow Block as a Perspective View.

*STEP 1* - Click **VIEW, DISPLAY, PERSPECTIVE**.

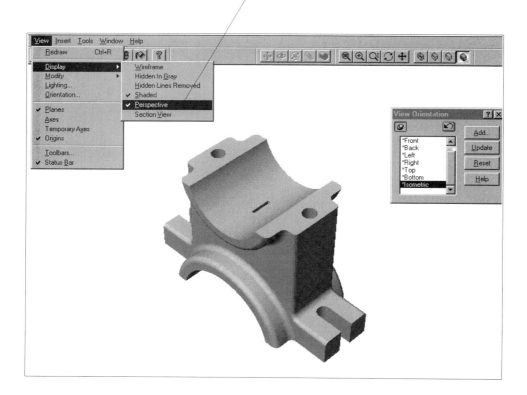

## Lesson 3.6.1 – Section-Cutting Parts

Section cut a part to see internal details.  You can create cross sections of a part by using the **VIEW**, **DISPLAY**, **SECTION VIEW** option.

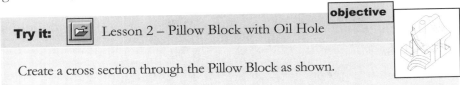

**Try it:** Lesson 2 – Pillow Block with Oil Hole

**objective**

Create a cross section through the Pillow Block as shown.

***STEP 1 -*** Click **VIEW, DISPLAY, SECTION VIEW**.

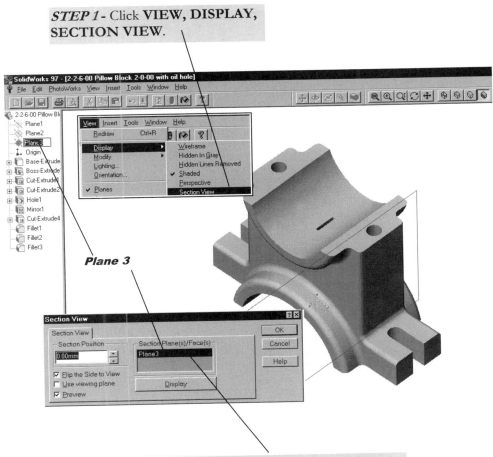

Plane 3

***STEP 2 -*** In the pop-up dialog, select a plane to use as the **"first section-cutting plane."**  Click on **Plane 3** in the FeatureManager.

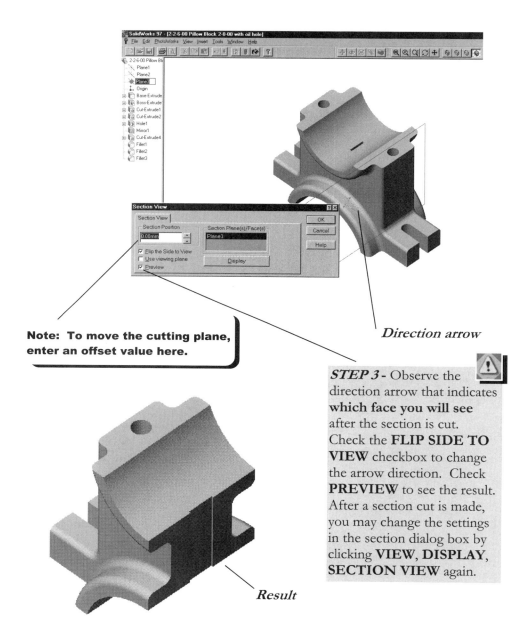

Note: To move the cutting plane, enter an offset value here.

*Direction arrow*

**STEP 3 -** Observe the direction arrow that indicates **which face you will see** after the section is cut. Check the **FLIP SIDE TO VIEW** checkbox to change the arrow direction. Check **PREVIEW** to see the result. After a section cut is made, you may change the settings in the section dialog box by clicking **VIEW, DISPLAY, SECTION VIEW** again.

*Result*

Figure 3.19 – Section Cut Using One Cutting Plane

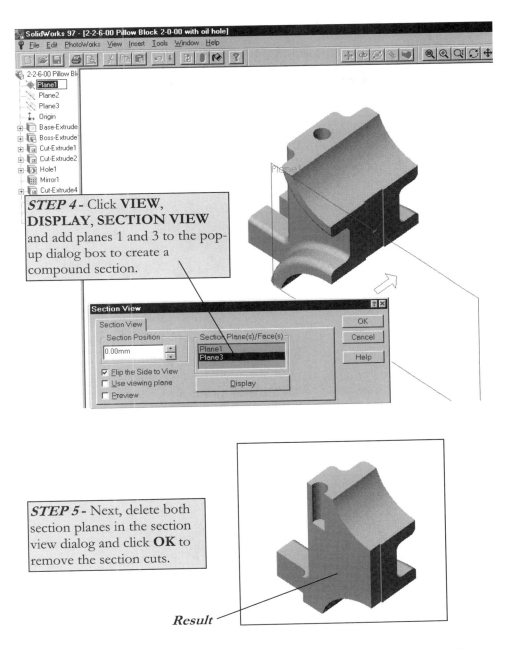

**STEP 4 -** Click **VIEW, DISPLAY, SECTION VIEW** and add planes 1 and 3 to the pop-up dialog box to create a compound section.

**STEP 5 -** Next, delete both section planes in the section view dialog and click **OK** to remove the section cuts.

*Result*

Figure 3.20 – Section Cut Using Two Cutting Planes

*Isometric view*

*Viewing plane section of isometric view*

**STEP 6 -** Finally, create a section relative to the display screen by rotating the part and choosing **USE VIEWING PLANE from the** SECTION VIEW **dialog box**. Experiment with the **SECTION POSITION VALUE** and all of the dialog box buttons to learn what they do. Also, try various viewing plane section cuts before closing the part. When finished, close without saving.

**STEP 7 -** When finished, close without saving.

*Rotated viewing plane section*

## Naming and suppressing features

### Lesson 3.7.1 - Naming Features

You can edit computer-assigned feature names in the FeatureManager by clicking twice on the name and typing the change. This works just like changing file names in Microsoft Explorer.

**Try it:** Lesson 2 – Pillow Block with Oil Hole

Rename the rectangular cut traversing the two diameters to **"OIL PASSAGE."**

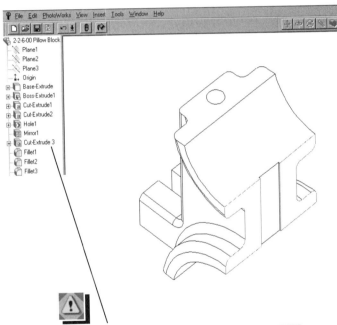

**STEP 1-** Click twice (do not double-click) on **Cut 3** in the FeatureManager and change the feature name to **"Oil Passage."** You may have to hold down your second click momentarily depending on how your cursor double-click speed is set.

**STEP 2-** Save the part.

## Lesson 3.7.2 - Suppressing Features

You can suppress features from the display or show them again.

**Try it:**  Lesson 2 – Pillow Block with Oil Hole

Hide and show the Oil Passage for practice.

*STEP 1 -* Right click **OIL PASSAGE**, click **PROPERTIES**, then check the suppress box and OK.

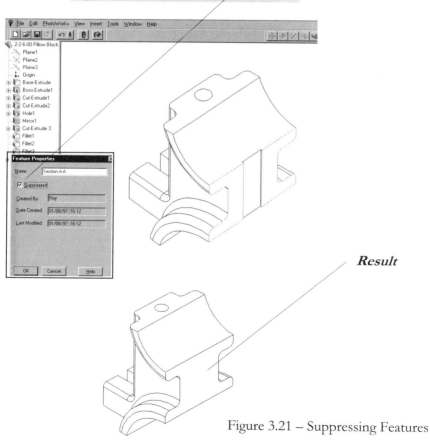

*Result*

Figure 3.21 – Suppressing Features

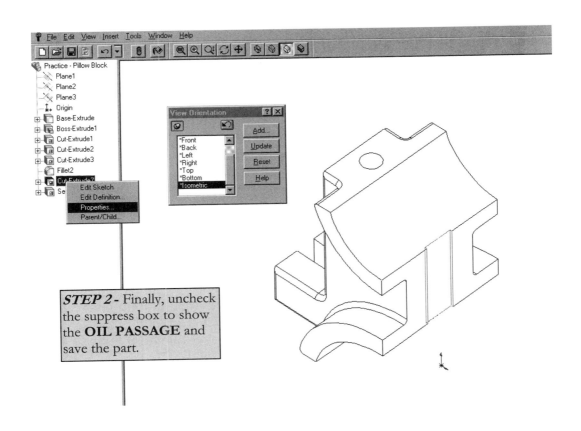

**STEP 2 -** Finally, uncheck the suppress box to show the **OIL PASSAGE** and save the part.

Chapter 4

# Chapter 4 – BASIC PART MODELING

## Extruded shapes and cuts

### Graphical Index

Lessons for the following parts contain the most common procedures for sketching and extruding basic shapes and cuts. The parts and construction techniques shown were selected to provide a logical learning curve starting with very basic procedures to more advanced techniques. To simplify lessons, only pertinent dimensions and constraints are shown. All parts modeled in Chapter 4 are dimensioned in millimeters. When grids are shown, use the grid/units settings shown in Lesson 4.1.1, step 1.

If you are new to SolidWorks, it is recommended that you try each lesson. Immediately review a lesson after you try it and repeat any procedures that you have not mastered before going on to the next lesson. If you are familiar with the software, look at the illustrations to find the type of geometry that you want to create, and try the appropriate lesson. To find commands by name, look them up in the index found in the back of this book.

**Remember to file each part by name and save your work after each step is completed successfully.** Be sure to save each current part before you start a new lesson. The following images show the lessons included in the first section of Chapter 4.

Lesson 4.1.1

Bracket Mount

Lesson 4.1.2

Channel Brace

Lesson 4.1.3

Swivel Connector

Lesson 4.1.4
Guide Clip

Lesson 4.1.5
Guard Bar

Lesson 4.1.6
Hub Support Bracket

Lesson 4.1.7
Hex Cone

Lesson 4.1.8
Shear Blade

Lesson 4.1.9
Lock Plate

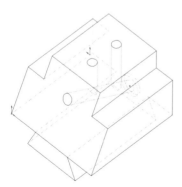

Lesson 4.1.10
Dovetail Wedge

Lesson 4.1.11
Sensor Cover

## Lesson 4.1.1 - Bracket Mount

This lesson gives you practice creating a simple extrusion with cuts and fillets.

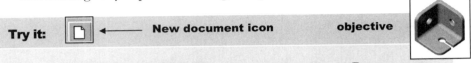

**Try it:** ☐ ← **New document icon** **objective**

Create the **BRACKET MOUNT** by following these steps. Be sure to save your work often. If you make mistakes, use **UNDO** to back out of them. If you make serious mistakes, close the part and reopen at your last good save. **Note: Before creating new parts, you must click on the new document icon, choose "part," and click OK.**

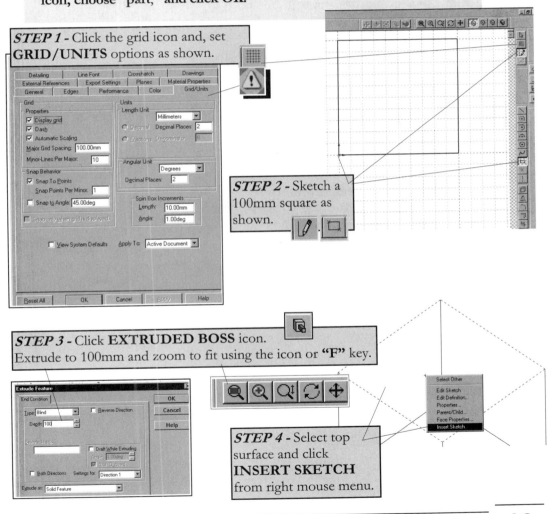

**STEP 1 -** Click the grid icon and, set **GRID/UNITS** options as shown.

**STEP 2 -** Sketch a 100mm square as shown.

**STEP 3 -** Click **EXTRUDED BOSS** icon. Extrude to 100mm and zoom to fit using the icon or **"F"** key.

**STEP 4 -** Select top surface and click **INSERT SKETCH** from right mouse menu.

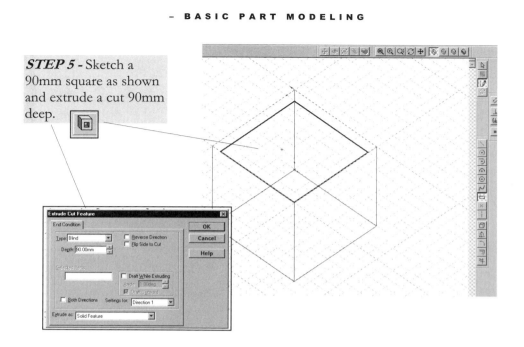

**STEP 5** - Sketch a 90mm square as shown and extrude a cut 90mm deep.

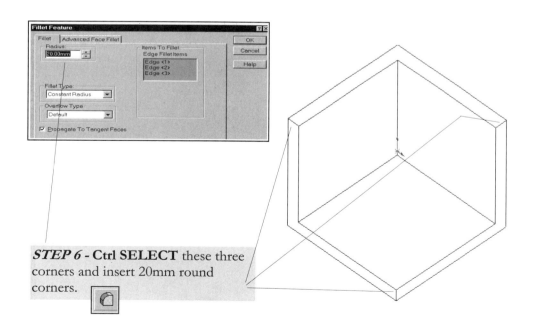

**STEP 6** - **Ctrl SELECT** these three corners and insert 20mm round corners.

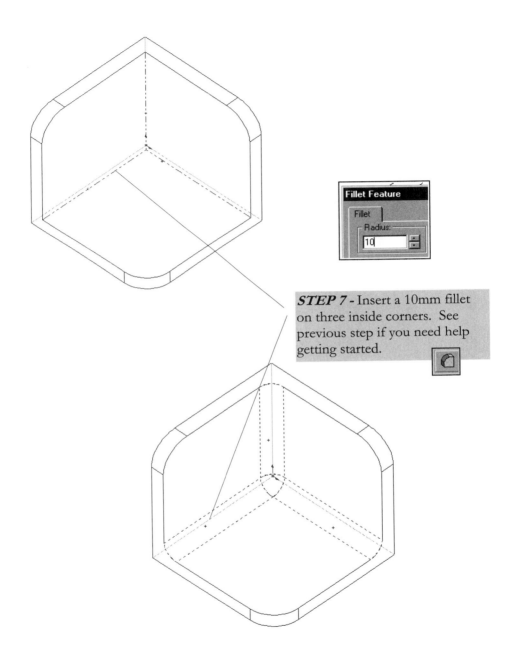

**Fillet Feature**

Fillet

Radius:

10

***STEP 7*** - Insert a 10mm fillet on three inside corners. See previous step if you need help getting started.

*STEP 8* - Click **FACE**, click **SKETCH** icon and sketch a 20mm DIA hole centered on this face. Snap to the center grid point to locate the hole. Click **EXTRUDED CUT ICON**, and extrude **THROUGH ALL** to complete the hole. Repeat this procedure for the other two inside faces as shown.

Note: To place other holes, you may alternately select the cut feature (Hole 1) from the FeatureManager and while depressing the Ctrl key, drag the feature to another location to copy it.

*STEP 9* - Edit sketch of hole shown, change grid spacing to 20 minor lines per major, then sketch the rectangle using grid points as shown. **INSERT, CUT, THROUGH ALL**.

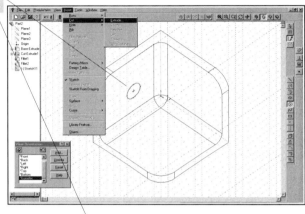

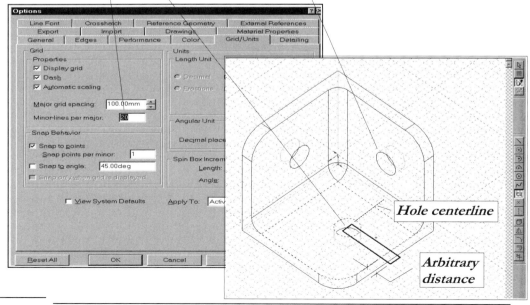

*Hole centerline*

*Arbitrary distance*

**STEP 10 - Ctrl SELECT** three inside faces and insert 3mm fillets to remaining edges.

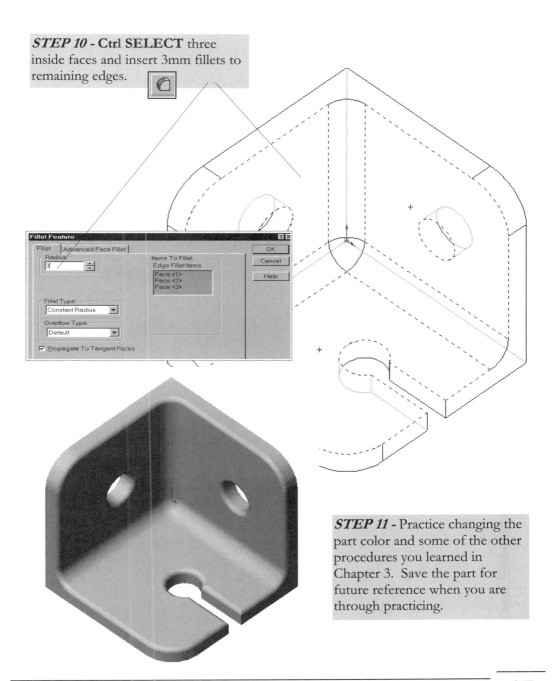

**STEP 11 -** Practice changing the part color and some of the other procedures you learned in Chapter 3. Save the part for future reference when you are through practicing.

### Lesson 4.1.2 - Channel Brace

This lesson gives you practice with dimensioning and using the offset tool. In this lesson, you will see that using the offset tool is the fastest way to create the sketch for the channel cut, even though you will delete the offset relation and modify the offset sketch.

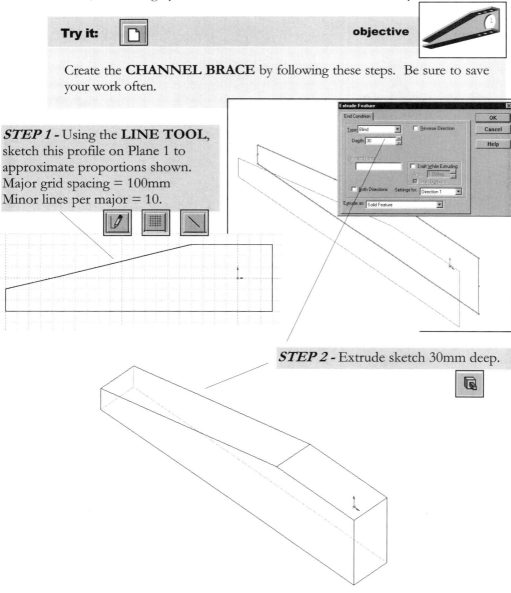

**Try it:**                                                         **objective**

Create the **CHANNEL BRACE** by following these steps. Be sure to save your work often.

***STEP 1*** - Using the **LINE TOOL**, sketch this profile on Plane 1 to approximate proportions shown.
Major grid spacing = 100mm
Minor lines per major = 10.

***STEP 2*** - Extrude sketch 30mm deep.

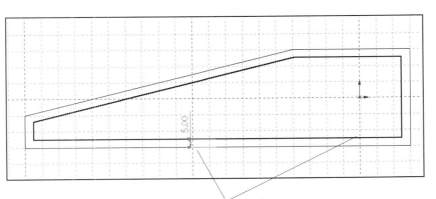

**STEP 3** - In front view, insert a 5mm offset. Click the face, click the **SKETCH TOOL** icon, click the **OFFSET** icon and enter 5mm for the offset dimension.
Be sure the offset is inward by checking the "reverse" checkbox.

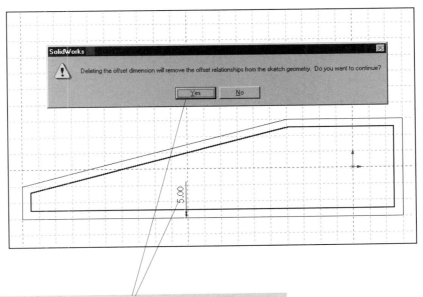

**STEP 4** - In order to modify this sketch, delete the offset dimension and click yes in the pop-up dialog to delete the associated "offset" relationship.

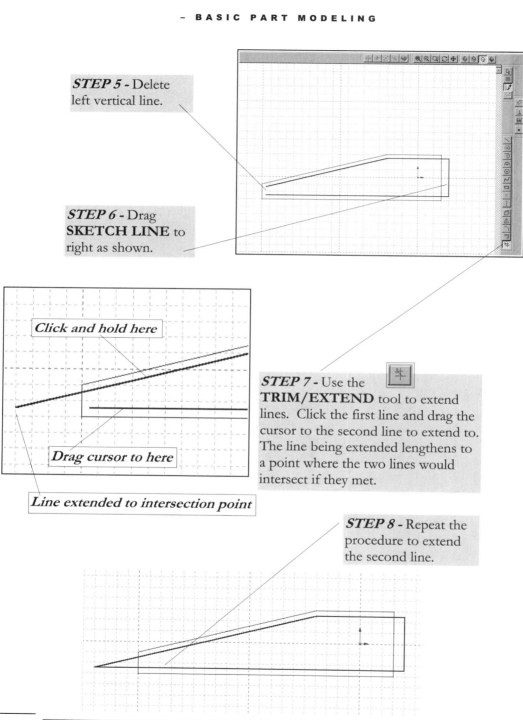

**STEP 5 -** Delete left vertical line.

**STEP 6 -** Drag **SKETCH LINE** to right as shown.

*Click and hold here*

*Drag cursor to here*

*Line extended to intersection point*

**STEP 7 -** Use the **TRIM/EXTEND** tool to extend lines. Click the first line and drag the cursor to the second line to extend to. The line being extended lengthens to a point where the two lines would intersect if they met.

**STEP 8 -** Repeat the procedure to extend the second line.

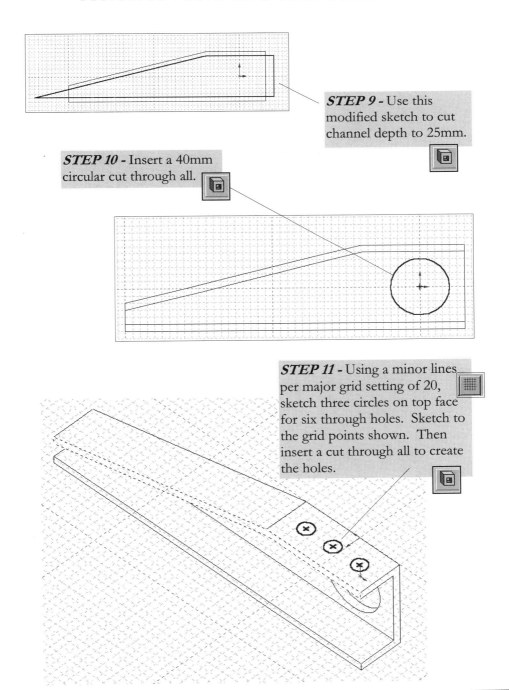

**STEP 9 -** Use this modified sketch to cut channel depth to 25mm.

**STEP 10 -** Insert a 40mm circular cut through all.

**STEP 11 -** Using a minor lines per major grid setting of 20, sketch three circles on top face for six through holes. Sketch to the grid points shown. Then insert a cut through all to create the holes.

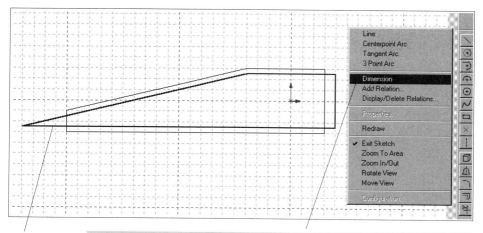

*Sketch of*
*Cut 1*

**STEP 12 - EDIT SKETCH** of **CUT 1**. From the right mouse menu, click **DIMENSION**, then add the dimensions shown below. The design intent is to preserve this spacing when other part geometry changes, and since the offset relation was deleted, you must now enter these dimensions manually.

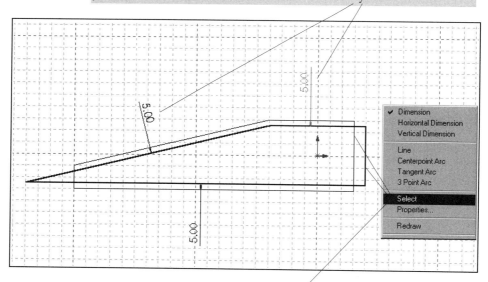

**STEP 13 -** Choose **SELECT** from the right mouse menu and **Ctrl SELECT** the two vertical lines. The next step will constrain these lines to keep the cut in the right place on the base extrusion even if the base extrusion shape is modified.

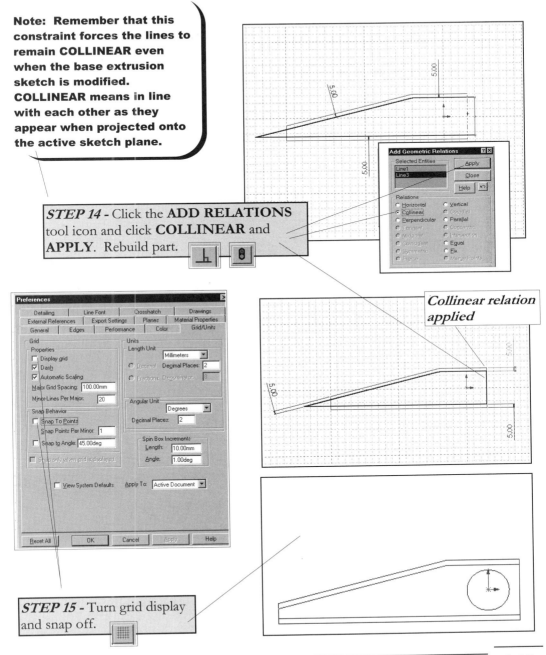

**Note: Remember that this constraint forces the lines to remain COLLINEAR even when the base extrusion sketch is modified. COLLINEAR means in line with each other as they appear when projected onto the active sketch plane.**

*STEP 14* - Click the **ADD RELATIONS** tool icon and click **COLLINEAR** and **APPLY**. Rebuild part.

*Collinear relation applied*

*STEP 15* - Turn grid display and snap off.

*Be sure to pick this surface*

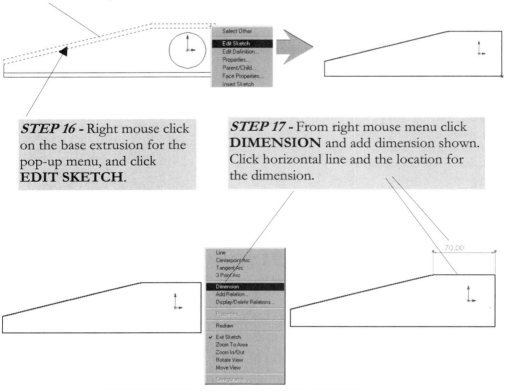

**STEP 16 -** Right mouse click on the base extrusion for the pop-up menu, and click **EDIT SKETCH**.

**STEP 17 -** From right mouse menu click **DIMENSION** and add dimension shown. Click horizontal line and the location for the dimension.

**STEP 18 -** From right mouse menu click **SELECT** and double-click this dimension to modify it. Next, add the rest of the dimensions and modify them as shown in the following illustrations.

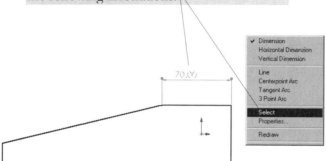

**Note:** Since the right edge was constrained collinear with the channel cut sketch, this corner will move when the dimension shown is modified.

Modify
93

93.00

60.00

230.00

*Holes located by grid spacing in previous step*

**Hole dimensions**

55.00

35.00

15.00

63.00

42.00

21.00

*Was*

*Is*

**Note:** To get a better understanding of the COLLINEAR constraint, try this lesson again without the constraint to see what happens when dimensions are modified.

*Finished part*

**Note:** Be sure to save your finished parts.

**4-15**

### Lesson 4.1.3 - Swivel Connector

This lesson gives you practice extruding bosses and cuts in two directions at once from midplanes. Using the **MIDPLANE** option keeps the part origin in the center of the part, and because default planes can be used for most of the part construction, the need to create additional sketch construction planes is minimized.

**Try it:**     **objective**

Model the **SWIVEL CONNECTOR** following these steps.

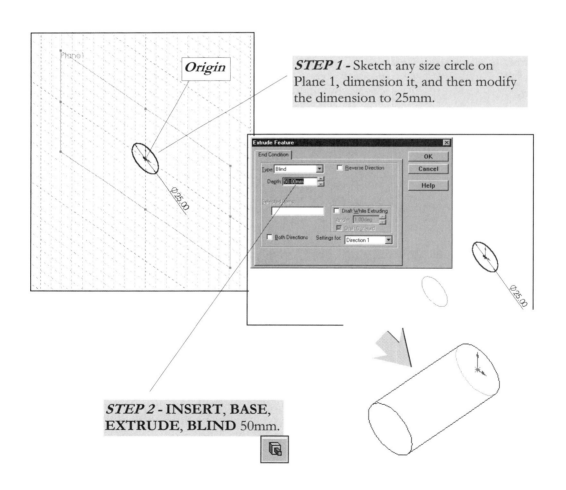

*Origin*

**STEP 1** - Sketch any size circle on Plane 1, dimension it, and then modify the dimension to 25mm.

**STEP 2** - INSERT, BASE, EXTRUDE, BLIND 50mm.

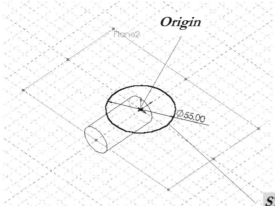

*Origin*

Plane2

⌀55.00

**STEP 3** - On Plane 2, sketch a circle and **DIMENSION** it to 55mm diameter.

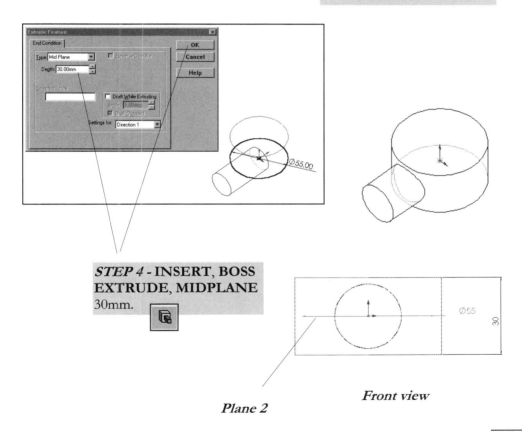

**STEP 4** - INSERT, BOSS EXTRUDE, MIDPLANE 30mm.

*Plane 2*

*Front view*

⌀55

30

**4-17**

*Observe cut direction with dynamic preview.*
*Click reverse box to change direction.*

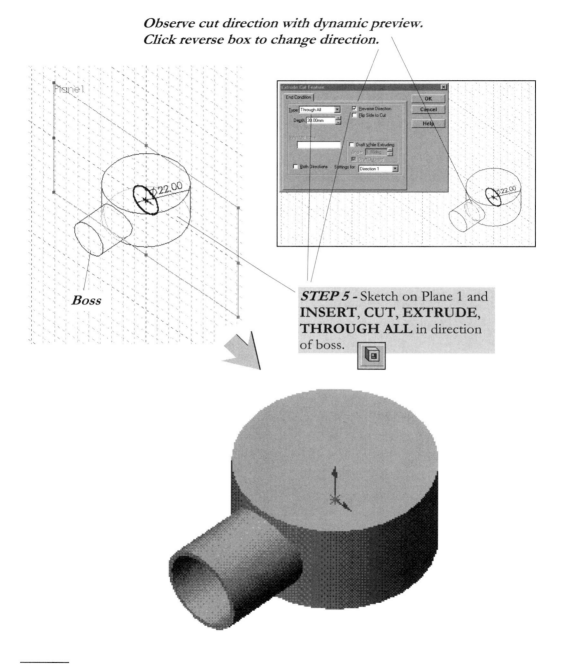

Boss

**STEP 5 -** Sketch on Plane 1 and
**INSERT, CUT, EXTRUDE,
THROUGH ALL** in direction
of boss.

**STEP 6** - Set grid to 10mm spacing (10 minor lines per major when major grid spacing = 100mm). Check grid snap on. Sketch a 40mm diameter circle **on top surface** and **INSERT, CUT, EXTRUDE, THROUGH ALL.**

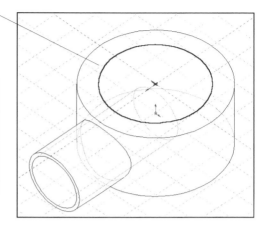

Note: Note that it is preferable to construct this sketch on the top surface and not a default plane. Because the sketch will always remain on the surface (even if the surface moves due to a revised extrusion depth), the design intent of a "through-hole" will always remain intact.

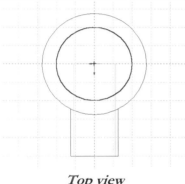

*Top view*

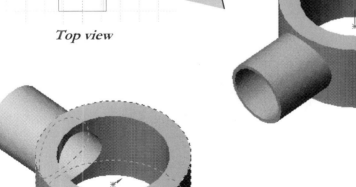

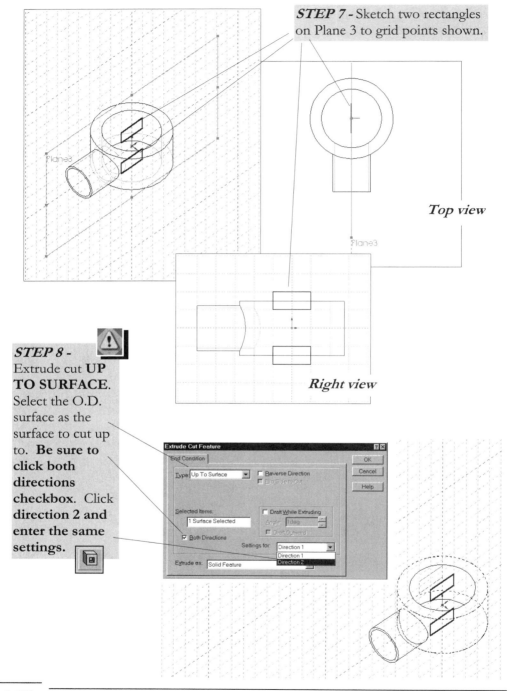

**STEP 7 -** Sketch two rectangles on Plane 3 to grid points shown.

*Top view*

*Right view*

**STEP 8 -** Extrude cut **UP TO SURFACE**. Select the O.D. surface as the surface to cut up to. **Be sure to click both directions checkbox.** Click direction 2 and enter the same settings.

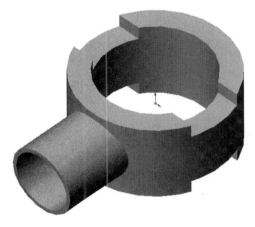

*Finished model*

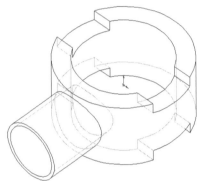

### Lesson 4.1.4 - Guide Clip

This lesson introduces the power of thin-feature extruding from single line sketches. It also reinforces the advantages of strategically locating part origins so that the default planes can be used productively for sketching and extruding features.

**Try it:** 📄                         **objective**

Model the **GUIDE CLIP** base feature with a **THIN FEATURE** extrusion. Also, locate the part relative to the part origin so that default planes can be used for all construction.

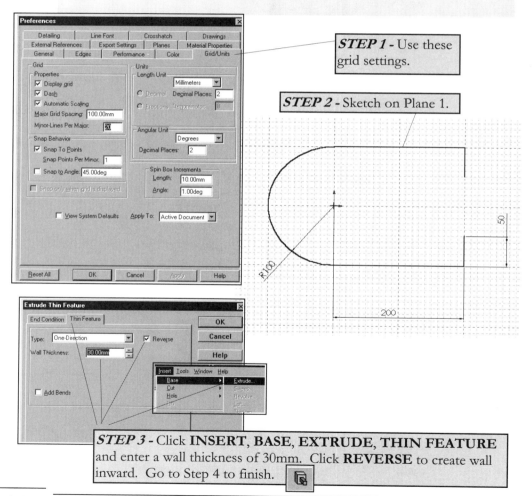

*STEP 1* - Use these grid settings.

*STEP 2* - Sketch on Plane 1.

*STEP 3* - Click **INSERT, BASE, EXTRUDE, THIN FEATURE** and enter a wall thickness of 30mm. Click **REVERSE** to create wall inward. Go to Step 4 to finish.

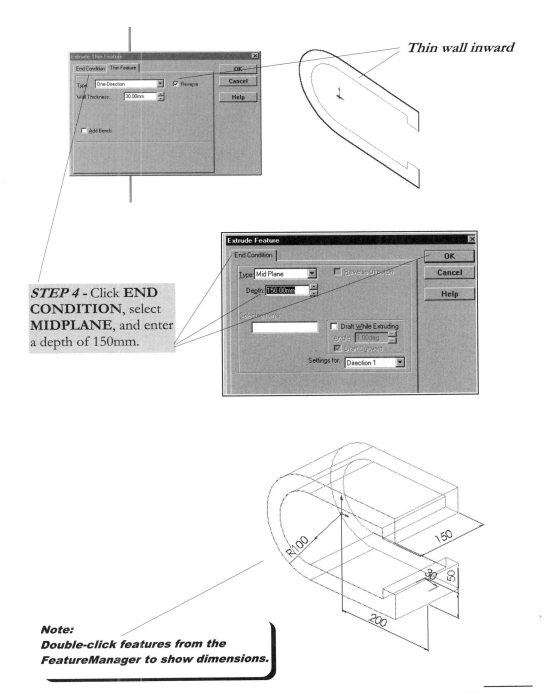

*Thin wall inward*

**STEP 4** - Click **END CONDITION**, select **MIDPLANE**, and enter a depth of 150mm.

**Note:**
**Double-click features from the FeatureManager to show dimensions.**

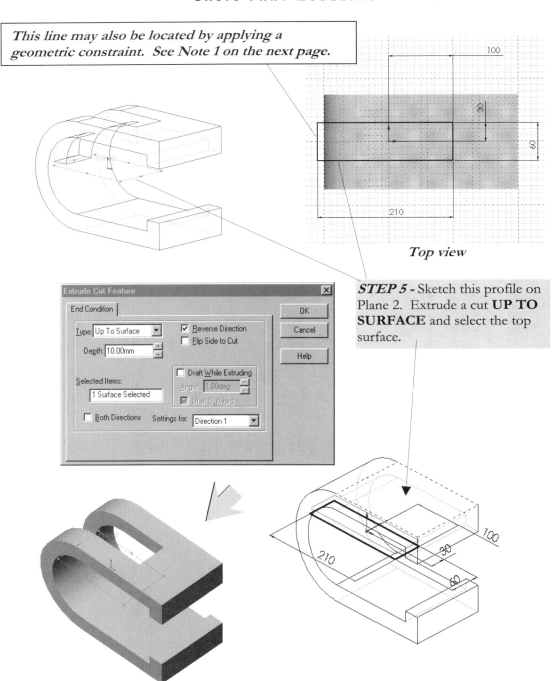

*This line may also be located by applying a geometric constraint. See Note 1 on the next page.*

*Top view*

**Extrude Cut Feature**

End Condition

Type: Up To Surface

Depth: 10.00mm

Reverse Direction

Flip Side to Cut

Selected Items:
1 Surface Selected

Draft While Extruding
Angle: 1.00deg
Draft Outward

Both Directions    Settings for: Direction 1

OK
Cancel
Help

**STEP 5** - Sketch this profile on Plane 2. Extrude a cut **UP TO SURFACE** and select the top surface.

*Plane 2*

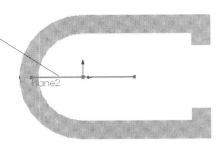

**STEP 6** - Sketch this profile on Plane 2 and extrude cut downward as shown in following illustrations. Extrude a cut **UP TO SURFACE** and select the bottom surface. (See the next page for illustration.)

*This line may also be located by applying a geometric constraint. See Note 1 below.*

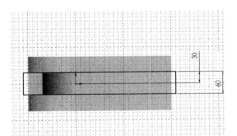

Top view

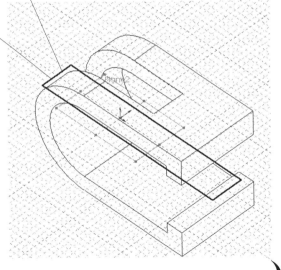

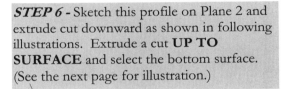

Front view

Note 1: You can preserve the "design intent" that the cuts will always extend through the guide clip outside surfaces even when the surface diameter is increased. Adding a collinear relation between the outside surface diameter and the line indicated for each cut does this.

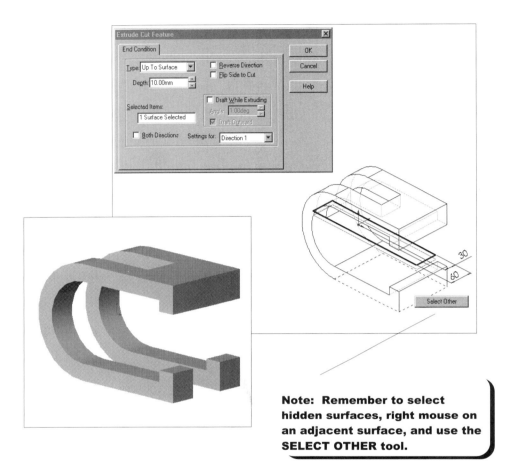

**Note: Remember to select hidden surfaces, right mouse on an adjacent surface, and use the SELECT OTHER tool.**

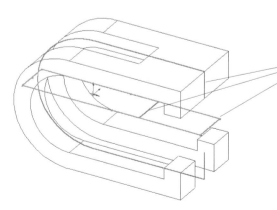

*Remember that you can select any sketch from the FeatureManager to superimpose it on the part. This can be a helpful technique to visualize complex designs in progress.*

### Lesson 4.1.5 - Guard Bar

This lesson shows another example of how to use thin-line extruding to increase productivity. It also introduces the use of construction geometry and simple shelling.

**Try it:** objective

Model the **GUARD BAR** starting with a single line sketch profile.

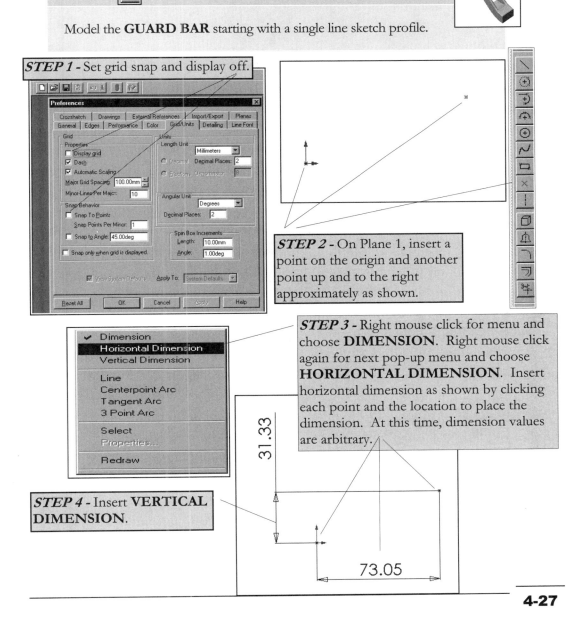

*STEP 1 -* Set grid snap and display off.

*STEP 2 -* On Plane 1, insert a point on the origin and another point up and to the right approximately as shown.

*STEP 3 -* Right mouse click for menu and choose **DIMENSION**. Right mouse click again for next pop-up menu and choose **HORIZONTAL DIMENSION**. Insert horizontal dimension as shown by clicking each point and the location to place the dimension. At this time, dimension values are arbitrary.

*STEP 4 -* Insert **VERTICAL DIMENSION**.

31.33

73.05

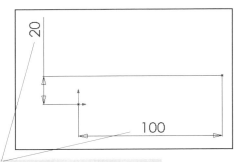

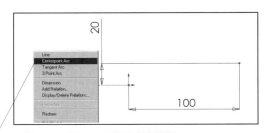

***STEP 5 -*** Modify the dimensions to these values.

***STEP 6 -*** Right mouse for **CENTERPOINT ARC** tool.

***STEP 7 -*** Draw **CENTERPOINT ARC** from origin and add tangent line approximately as shown. Use cursor inferencing to place line tangent to arc.

*Start point is exactly above origin. Use cursor inferencing to place endpoint vertical above origin.*

*Drag endpoint to optimum position for placing second arc (see note).*

*Origin*

**Note: In SolidWorks, sketches are usually "roughed-in" with approximate proportions to the shape you are designing. Then sketch elements can be moved by dragging or dimensioning them.**

***STEP 8 -*** Right mouse for **CENTERPOINT ARC** tool, sketch second arc using dimensioned centerpoint, and constrain the arc tangent to the line using the **ADD RELATIONS** tool.

***STEP 9 -*** Choose **DIMENSION** tool from right mouse menu, and add arc dimensions shown. To dimension an arc, click the arc and click a location for the dimension.

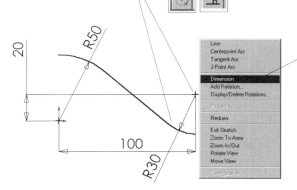

**4-28**

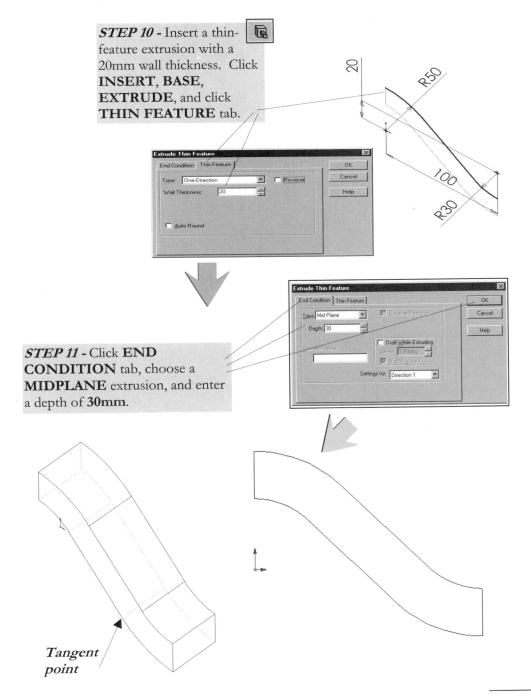

**STEP 10 -** Insert a thin-feature extrusion with a 20mm wall thickness. Click **INSERT, BASE, EXTRUDE,** and click **THIN FEATURE** tab.

**STEP 11 -** Click **END CONDITION** tab, choose a **MIDPLANE** extrusion, and enter a depth of **30mm**.

*Tangent point*

**4-29**

Note: Remember to
save your work often!

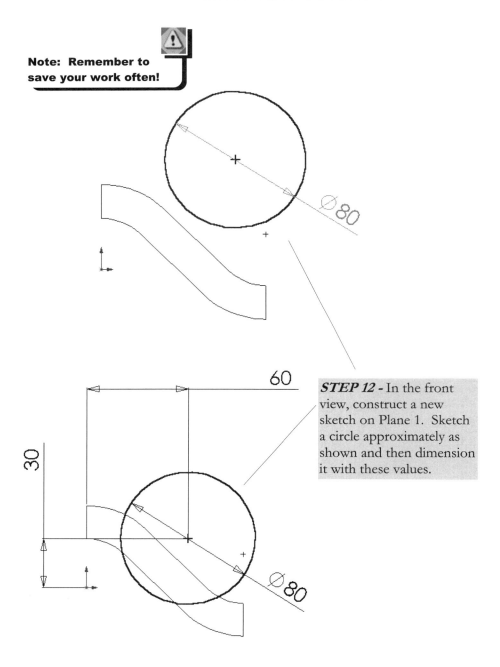

60

30

STEP 12 - In the front
view, construct a new
sketch on Plane 1. Sketch
a circle approximately as
shown and then dimension
it with these values.

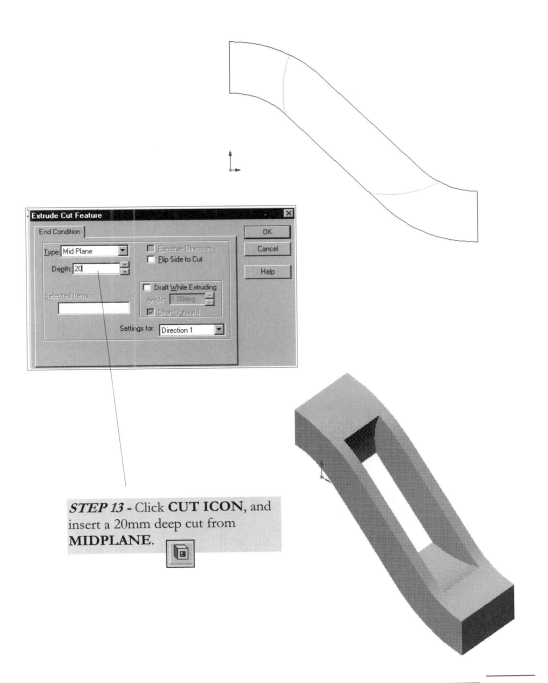

**Extrude Cut Feature**

End Condition

Type: Mid Plane

Depth: 20

Selected Items:

□ Reverse Direction
□ Flip Side to Cut

□ Draft While Extruding
Angle: 1.00deg
☑ Draft Outward

Settings for: Direction 1

OK
Cancel
Help

*STEP 13 -* Click **CUT ICON**, and insert a 20mm deep cut from **MIDPLANE**.

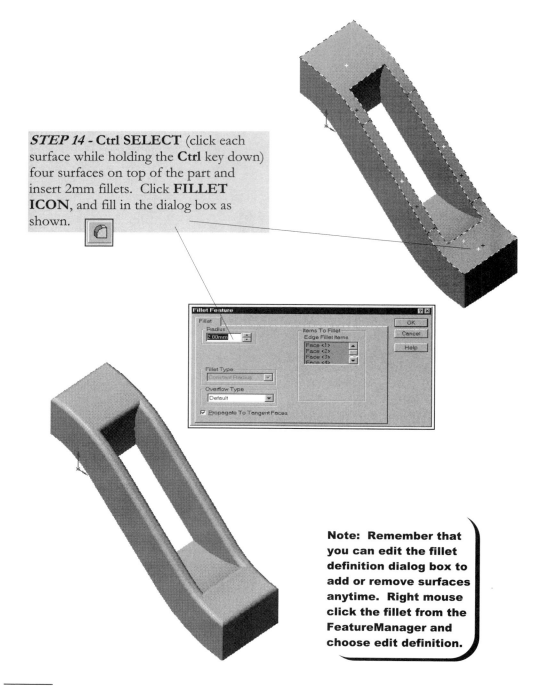

*STEP 14* - **Ctrl SELECT** (click each surface while holding the **Ctrl** key down) four surfaces on top of the part and insert 2mm fillets. Click **FILLET ICON**, and fill in the dialog box as shown.

Note: Remember that you can edit the fillet definition dialog box to add or remove surfaces anytime. Right mouse click the fillet from the FeatureManager and choose edit definition.

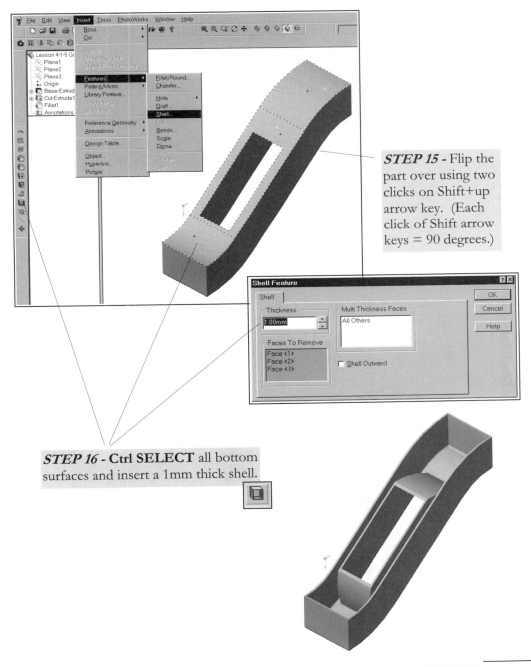

*STEP 15* - Flip the part over using two clicks on Shift+up arrow key. (Each click of Shift arrow keys = 90 degrees.)

*STEP 16* - **Ctrl SELECT** all bottom surfaces and insert a 1mm thick shell.

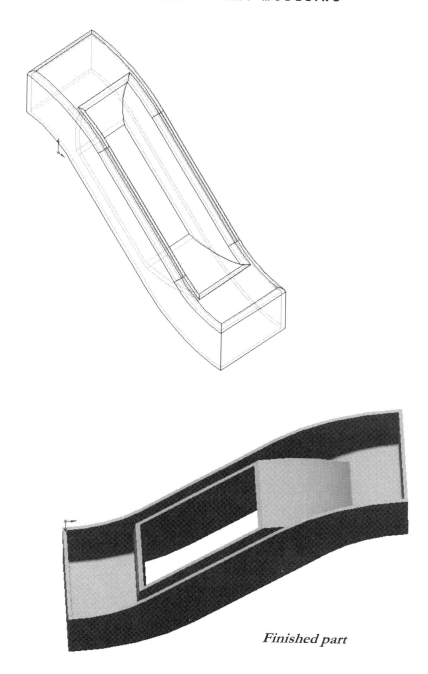

*Finished part*

## Lesson 4.1.6 - Hub Support Bracket

This lesson will give you experience working with an auxiliary face and additional constraint options. Remember that constraints are used to capture design intent. For example, in the objective part, geometric relations can be added so that the hub and hole through it will always remain concentric even if other part features change. Also, the two holes in the auxiliary face can be constrained to remain the same diameter. Geometry can be constrained automatically when sketching by dimensioning or by applying geometric relations with other part geometry.

**Try it:**    🗋                                                            **objective**

Model the **HUB SUPPORT BRACKET** using thin-wall extrusion. Apply constraints to capture the geometric relationships and design intent described below. For this lesson, be sure that the grid snap and grid display are turned off.

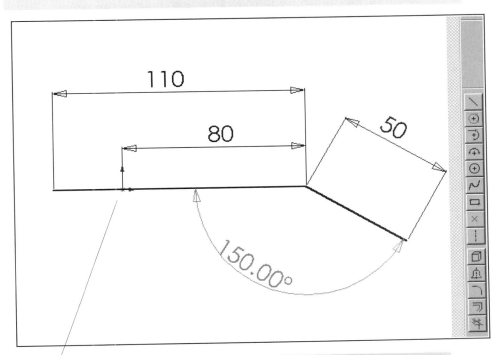

*STEP 1* - On Plane 1, sketch this profile through the part origin and dimension. Single lines can be dimensioned by clicking the line and a placement for the dimension.

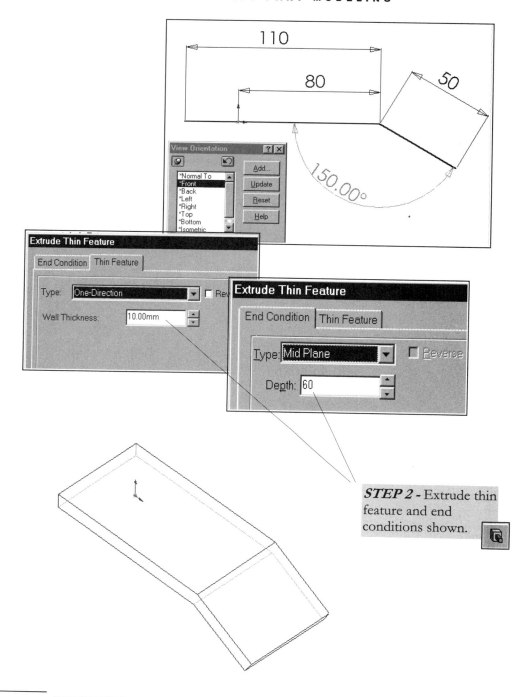

STEP 2 - Extrude thin feature and end conditions shown.

**STEP 3** - On top surface, sketch **CENTERPOINT ARC** tangent to plate edges and insert cut as shown.

**STEP 4** - Sketch circle on top surface.

**STEP 5** - **CTRL SELECT** circle and edge, click **ADD RELATIONS** icon and choose **CONCENTRIC** from dialog box. Click **APPLY**. Now the boss will always remain concentric to the outer edge even if the radius or centerpoint location changes.

**STEP 6** - Extrude boss 20mm deep. To modify depth, access the **EDIT DEFINITION** dialog from the FeatureManager by right mouse clicking the feature.

**STEP 7** - Sketch circle on top of boss and constrain concentric to boss edge.

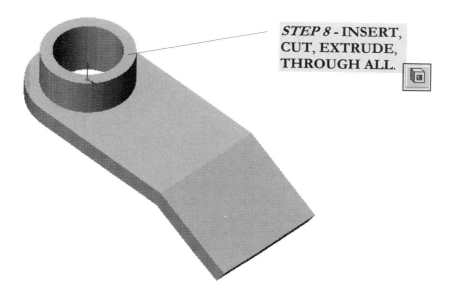

***STEP 8* - INSERT, CUT, EXTRUDE, THROUGH ALL.**

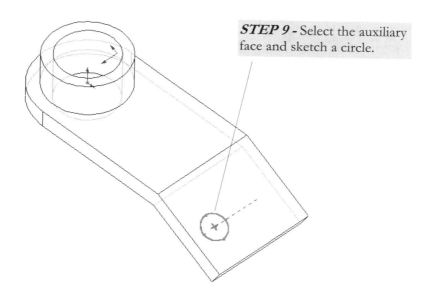

***STEP 9* -** Select the auxiliary face and sketch a circle.

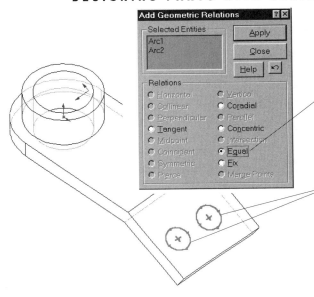

**STEP 10** - Sketch a second circle, **Ctrl SELECT** both circles and constrain **EQUAL**. This constraint will ensure that the circles will always remain the same diameter even if one of them is modified.

**STEP 11** - Constrain the circles **VERTICAL**. Ctrl **SELECT** each circle centerpoint and choose **VERTICAL** in the add relations dialog box. This constraint will insure that the holes will always remain in-line vertically (in relation to the orthographic projection of the view).

*Add relations icon*

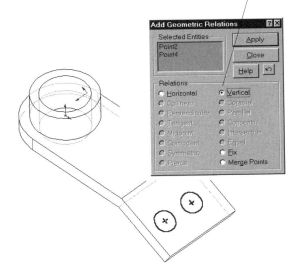

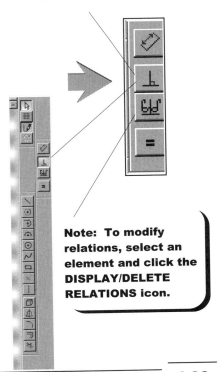

**Note: To modify relations, select an element and click the DISPLAY/DELETE RELATIONS icon.**

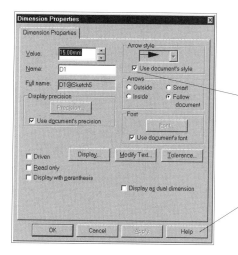

Note: To change dimension properties such as arrowhead location, right mouse click a DIMENSION, and choose PROPERTIES from the pop-up dialog. Unclick "Use documents style" and choose another listed option (such as font). Study some of the other options in this dialog box using SolidWorks help.

*STEP 12* - Dimension the circles, then insert through-holes using the **CUT ICON**.

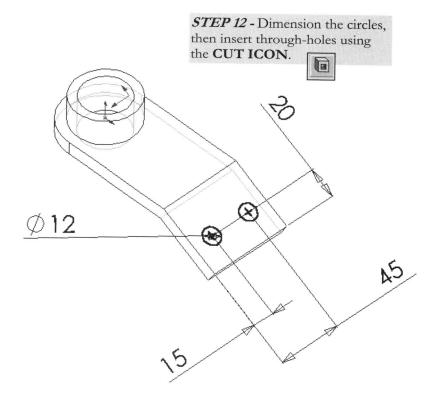

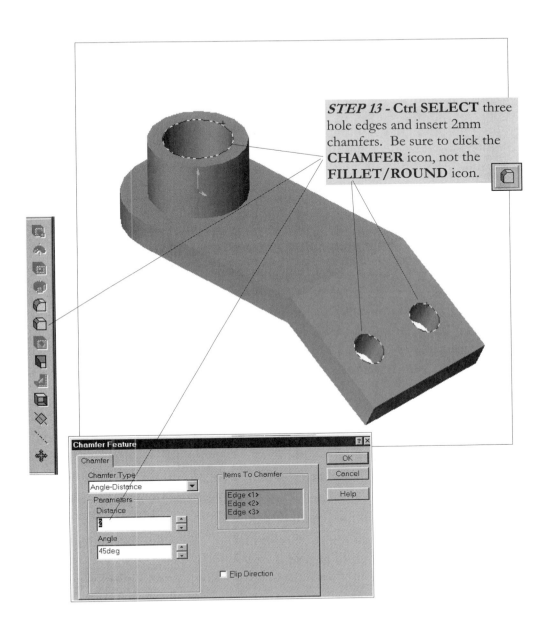

STEP 13 - Ctrl SELECT three hole edges and insert 2mm chamfers. Be sure to click the **CHAMFER** icon, not the **FILLET/ROUND** icon.

**Chamfer Feature**

Chamfer

Chamfer Type
Angle-Distance

Parameters
Distance
2

Angle
45deg

Items To Chamfer
Edge <1>
Edge <2>
Edge <3>

OK
Cancel
Help

☐ Flip Direction

STEP 14 - **Ctrl SELECT** edges shown and insert 3mm fillet/rounds. Be sure to round off the entire edge shown in dashed lines.

*STEP 15* - Add a 3mm fillet/round to these edges.

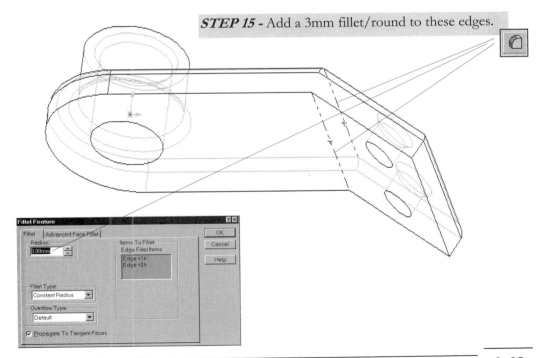

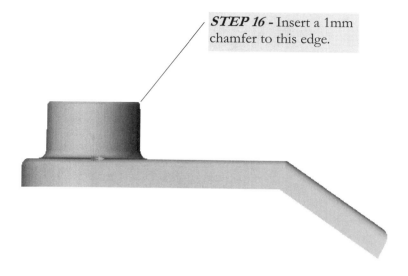

**STEP 16 -** Insert a 1mm chamfer to this edge.

*Finished part*

## Lesson 4.1.7 - Hex Cone

This lesson introduces simple draft extrusions and more constraint tools and tips. The hexagonal sketch will be constrained tangent to the inscribed circle in such a way that simply changing the distance across flats will regenerate a new hexagon. This sketch can be saved separately and reused anywhere that a hexagonal shape is required.

**Try it:** 

**objective**

Model the **HEX CONE** using a **"HEXAGON MASTER"** sketch that you will create.

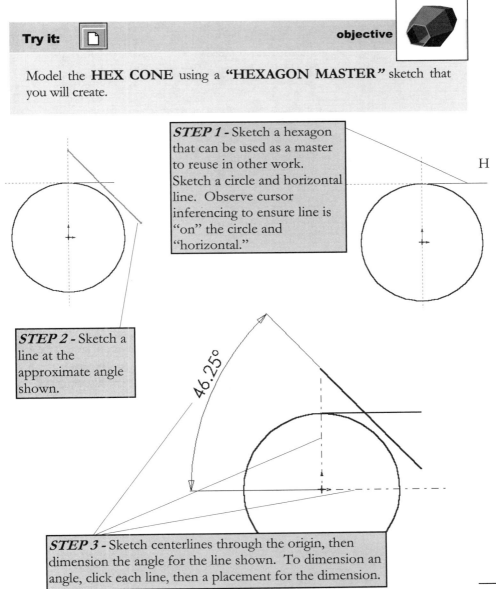

**STEP 1 -** Sketch a hexagon that can be used as a master to reuse in other work. Sketch a circle and horizontal line. Observe cursor inferencing to ensure line is "on" the circle and "horizontal."

H

**STEP 2 -** Sketch a line at the approximate angle shown.

46.25°

**STEP 3 -** Sketch centerlines through the origin, then dimension the angle for the line shown. To dimension an angle, click each line, then a placement for the dimension.

**STEP 4 -** Change the angle to 60 degrees.

**STEP 5 - *Ctrl SELECT*** the circle and the horizontal line, and click **ADD RELATION** icon. From dialog box constrain **TANGENT**. Also constrain the circle and 60-degree line tangent.

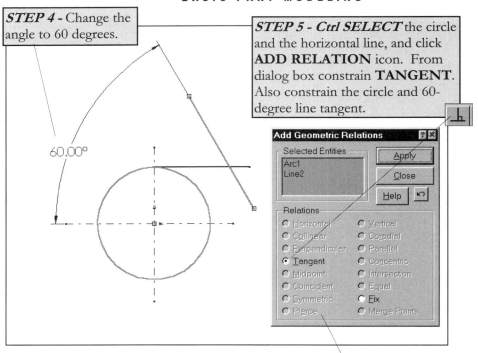

60.00°

**Add Geometric Relations**

Selected Entities
Arc1
Line2

Apply
Close
Help

Relations

○ Horizontal    ○ Vertical
○ Collinear     ○ Coradial
○ Perpendicular ○ Parallel
● Tangent       ○ Concentric
○ Midpoint      ○ Intersection
○ Coincident    ○ Equal
○ Symmetric     ○ Fix
○ Pierce        ○ Merge Points

**STEP 6 -** Trim the horizontal and 60-degree lines to the centerlines and to each other as shown.

**Note: Relations not applicable to the sketch elements selected are grayed out.**

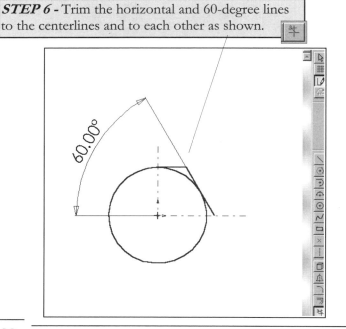

60.00°

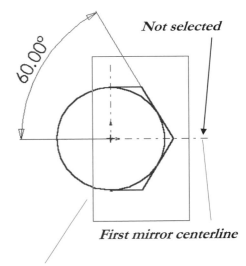

*This centerline is not selected*

**Note: Remember that elements must be totally in a box to be selected. If any part of an element is outside of the box, it won't be selected.**

*Not selected*

***STEP 7* - BOX SELECT** as shown to capture only horizontal centerline and two sketch lines. To **BOX SELECT**, hold down the left mouse button while you drag a diagonal across the box.

*First mirror centerline*

***STEP 8* - MIRROR** selections. Then **MIRROR** result about vertical centerline.

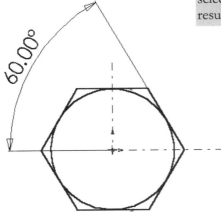

*Original sketch mirrored twice*

**STEP 9 -** Right mouse click circle for
pop-up menu. Choose **PROPERTIES**.

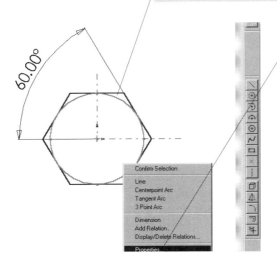

**STEP 10 -** Click **CONSTRUCTION ARC
BOX** to make circle construction geometry.
**CONSTRUCTION GEOMETRY** remains
with a sketch as a reference entity.

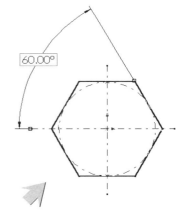

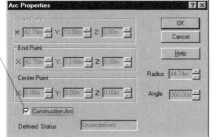

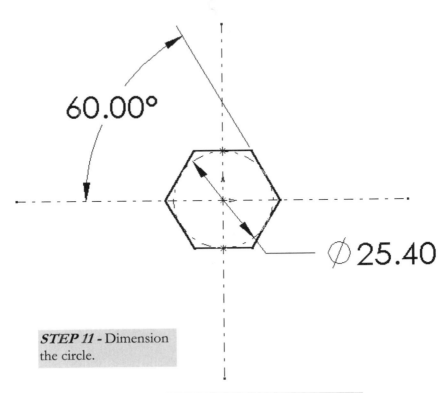

60.00°

⌀ 25.40

**STEP 11** - Dimension the circle.

**STEP 12** - Save as **HEXMASTER SKETCH**. Save again with current part name, **HEX CONE**.

Note: Because the circle is tangent to the HEX PROFILE, the circle diameter is the same as the dimension "across flats" on the hexagon. Therefore, to change the hex dimension across flats, simply modify the circle diameter. Use the HEXMASTER SKETCH in any new part that has a hexagon in it.

Note: For a better understanding of how to manage constraints, change the dimensions of the circle in the **HEX SKETCH** with the tangency relationships removed. Observing how the sketch reacts without the constraints will give you a better understanding of what the constraints do when they are applied.

     To remove the tangency constraints on a line, select the line and click the **DISPLAY/DELETE RELATIONS** icon from the toolbar. Click "delete all" from the pop-up dialog box. Be sure to restore the constraints before going on to the next step.

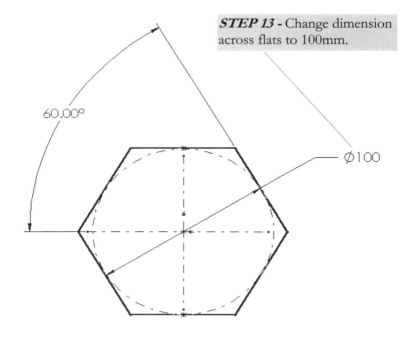

*STEP 13* - Change dimension across flats to 100mm.

60.00°

Ø100

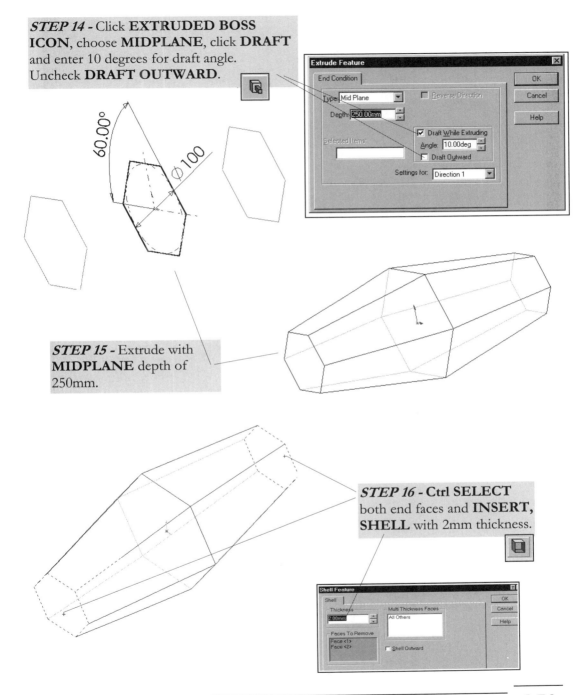

**STEP 14 -** Click **EXTRUDED BOSS ICON**, choose **MIDPLANE**, click **DRAFT** and enter 10 degrees for draft angle. Uncheck **DRAFT OUTWARD**.

**STEP 15 -** Extrude with **MIDPLANE** depth of 250mm.

**STEP 16 - Ctrl SELECT** both end faces and **INSERT, SHELL** with 2mm thickness.

**4-51**

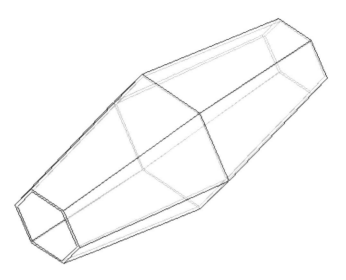

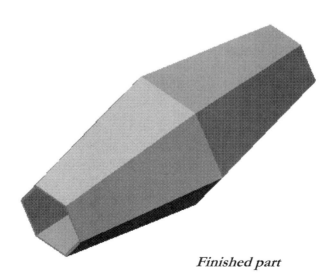

*Finished part*

## Lesson 4.1.8 - Shear Blade

This lesson shows how to create a compound-angled cut like the cutting edge of the shear blade. To create the cut, a construction plane will have to be inserted at the correct angle. The cut profile will be sketched on this new plane and extruded into the shear blade.

**Try it:**    **objective**

Model the **SHEAR BLADE** base feature by extruding the sketch shown below, then extrude a cut to create the blade edge.

**Note: In SolidWorks, create a rough sketch first. Drag sketch elements to resize them if necessary, then dimension the sketch. Add or remove constraints as necessary to get the shape you want, and to preserve design intent.**

***STEP 1 -*** On Plane 1, sketch and dimension this profile. Use the right mouse menu to access the sketch and dimension tools needed. Use 3-point arc tool for arc.

**Note: Create a rough sketch of this profile with approximate proportions shown. While sketching, use the value displayed at the cursor to establish approximate height and width of sketch. The sketch will take on the exact shape as you dimension it. Start with the largest dimensions first and work your way in. When sketch elements become fully defined, they turn black.**

*Always place the origin at the location of your primary datum selection.*

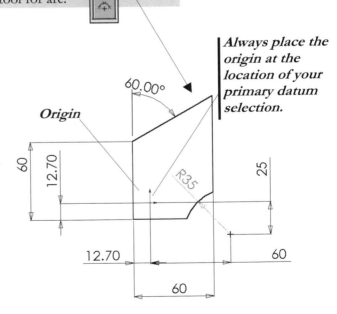

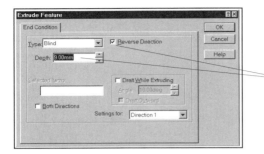

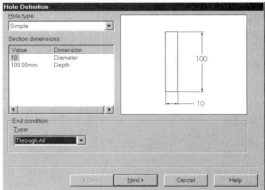

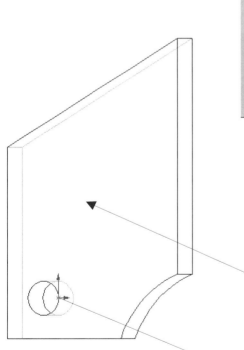

*STEP 2 -* Extrude to depth of 9mm.  Click **REVERSE DIRECTION** so the origin is on the front face.

*STEP 3 -* Click front face and **INSERT, FEATURES, HOLE, WIZARD**.  In the Wizard, change the diameter to **10mm**, and choose **THROUGH HOLE**.  Click **NEXT**, then drag the hole centerpoint to the part origin and click **FINISH**.

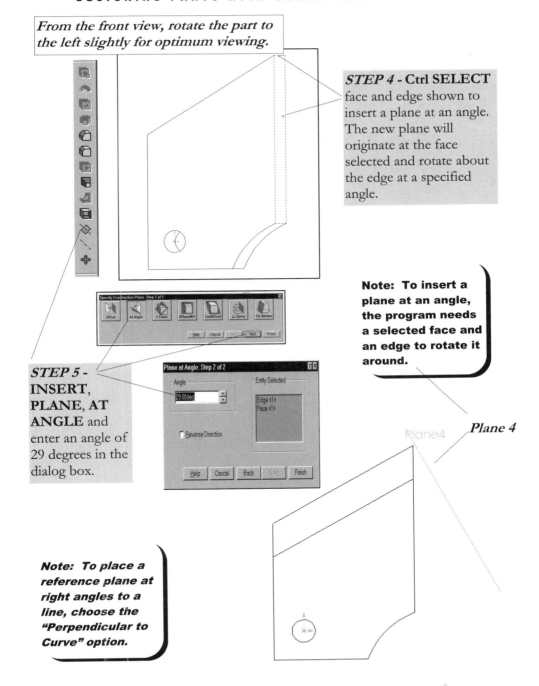

*From the front view, rotate the part to the left slightly for optimum viewing.*

**STEP 4 - Ctrl SELECT** face and edge shown to insert a plane at an angle. The new plane will originate at the face selected and rotate about the edge at a specified angle.

Note: To insert a plane at an angle, the program needs a selected face and an edge to rotate it around.

*STEP 5 -* **INSERT, PLANE, AT ANGLE** and enter an angle of 29 degrees in the dialog box.

Specify Construction Plane, Step 1 of 2
Offset | At Angle | 3 Points | 1/Plane@Pt | Line&Point | ⊥ Curve | On Surface
Help | Cancel | Back | Next | Finish

Plane at Angle: Step 2 of 2
Angle
29.00deg
☐ Reverse Direction
Entity Selected
Edge <1>
Face <1>
Help | Cancel | Back | Next | Finish

Plane4    *Plane 4*

Note: To place a reference plane at right angles to a line, choose the "Perpendicular to Curve" option.

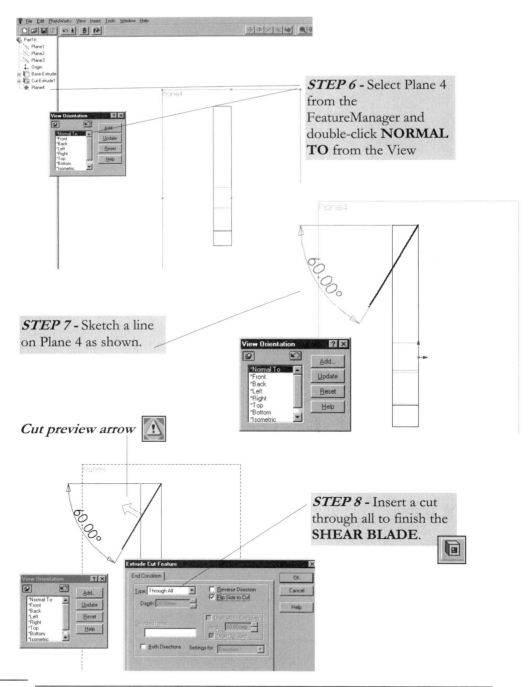

**STEP 6 -** Select Plane 4 from the FeatureManager and double-click **NORMAL TO** from the View

**STEP 7 -** Sketch a line on Plane 4 as shown.

*Cut preview arrow*

**STEP 8 -** Insert a cut through all to finish the **SHEAR BLADE**.

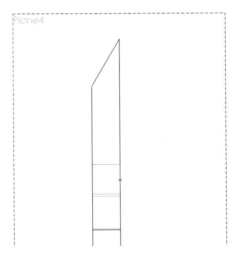

*View normal to Plane 4*

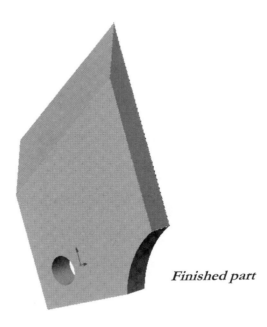

*Finished part*

### Lesson 4.1.9 - Lock Plate

This lesson introduces the **CONVERT ENTITIES** sketch tool and circular patterning procedures. The **CONVERT ENTITIES** tool converts a projection of existing model edges into sketch elements on the active sketch plane.

**Try it:** □                  **objective**

Model the **LOCK PLATE** following these steps.

**STEP 1 -** Sketch a 20mm diameter circle on Plane 1 and extrude 6mm deep. Right mouse click a dimension to change properties such as arrow head location and dimension font.

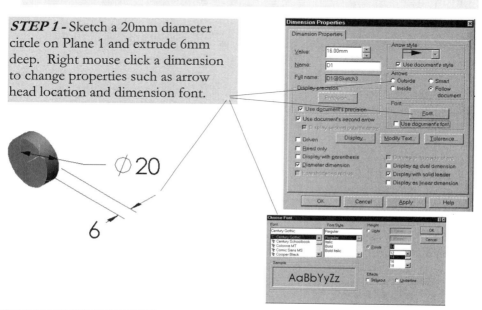

**STEP 2 -** Click the front face and **INSERT SKETCH**. Sketch a 16mm diameter circle <u>on the front face</u> of the extrusion and add other geometry as shown. Sketch one angular line and mirror it about the 30-degree centerline. Change arrowheads and font to look like the sketch at the right.

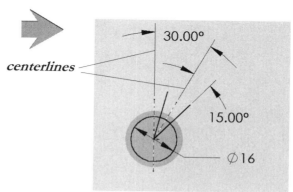

*Front view*

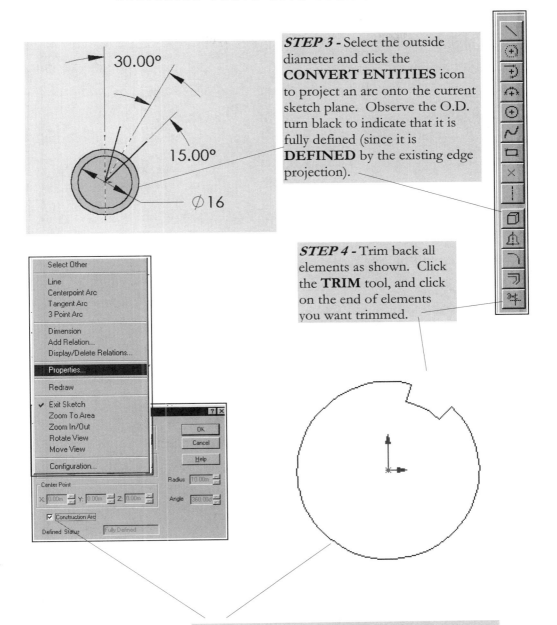

**STEP 3** - Select the outside diameter and click the **CONVERT ENTITIES** icon to project an arc onto the current sketch plane. Observe the O.D. turn black to indicate that it is fully defined (since it is **DEFINED** by the existing edge projection).

30.00°

15.00°

Ø16

**STEP 4** - Trim back all elements as shown. Click the **TRIM** tool, and click on the end of elements you want trimmed.

Select Other

Line
Centerpoint Arc
Tangent Arc
3 Point Arc

Dimension
Add Relation...
Display/Delete Relations...

Properties...

Redraw

✓ Exit Sketch
Zoom To Area
Zoom In/Out
Rotate View
Move View

Configuration...

OK
Cancel
Help

Radius 10.00m

Angle 360.00d

Center Point
X 0.00m  Y 0.00m  Z 0.00m

✓ Construction Arc

Defined Status    Fully Defined

**STEP 5** - Right mouse click the outer (20mm) diameter arc and choose **PROPERTIES** from the pop-up menu. Click the **CONSTRUCTION ARC** box to convert it to construction geometry.

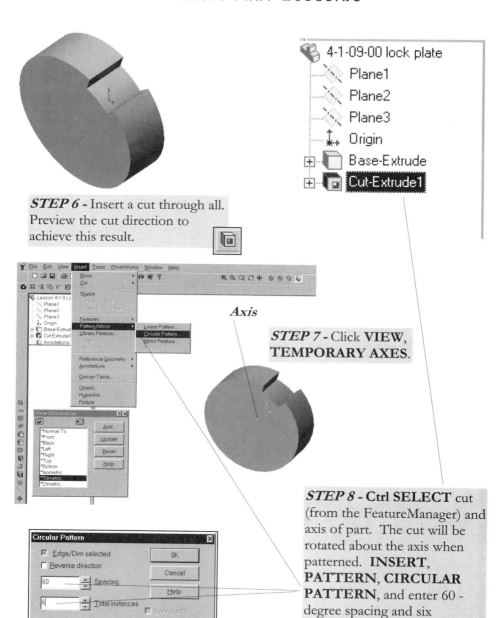

4-1-09-00 lock plate
- Plane1
- Plane2
- Plane3
- Origin
- Base-Extrude
- Cut-Extrude1

**STEP 6 -** Insert a cut through all. Preview the cut direction to achieve this result.

*Axis*

**STEP 7 -** Click **VIEW, TEMPORARY AXES**.

**STEP 8 - Ctrl SELECT** cut (from the FeatureManager) and axis of part. The cut will be rotated about the axis when patterned. **INSERT, PATTERN, CIRCULAR PATTERN,** and enter 60 - degree spacing and six instances in the pop-up dialog.

Circular Pattern
- ☑ Edge/Dim selected
- ☐ Reverse direction
- 60 ▲ Spacing
- 6 ▲ Total instances
- ☐ Vary sketch
- ☐ Geometry pattern
- Items to copy: Cut-Extrude1
- Instances deleted:
- OK
- Cancel
- Help

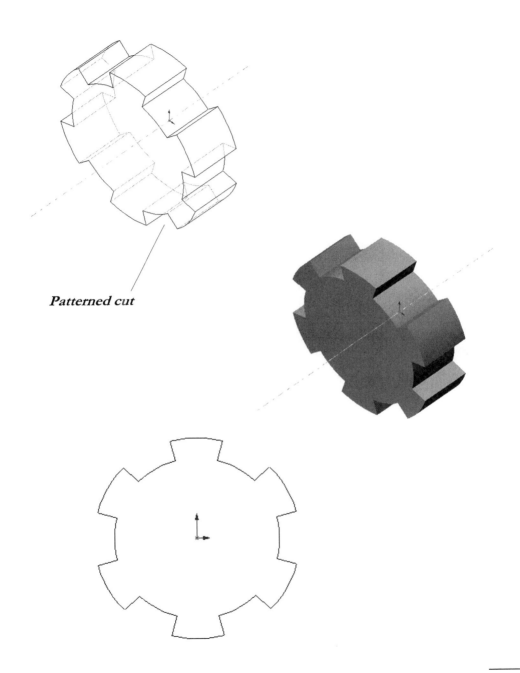

Patterned cut

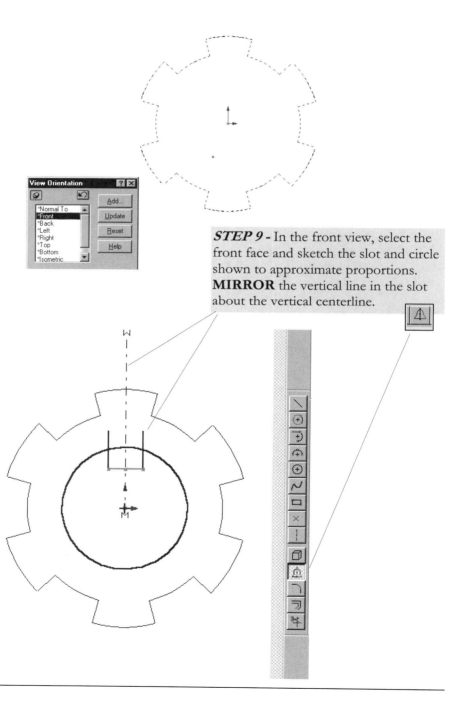

**STEP 9 -** In the front view, select the front face and sketch the slot and circle shown to approximate proportions. **MIRROR** the vertical line in the slot about the vertical centerline.

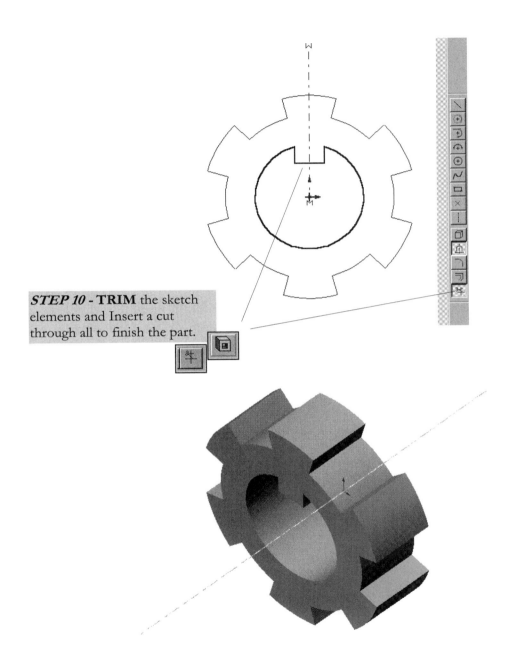

*STEP 10* - **TRIM** the sketch elements and Insert a cut through all to finish the part.

## Lesson 4.1.10 - Dovetail Wedge

**Try it:** objective

Model the **DOVETAIL WEDGE**. This lesson demonstrates how to work with auxiliary surfaces, how to inference geometry between surfaces, and how to measure between points on surfaces.

*STEP 1* - Sketch the profile shown on the front plane and extrude 100mm deep in reverse direction (see next page). Use grid points as an aid in sketching. Sketch and mirror about a centerline if you prefer.

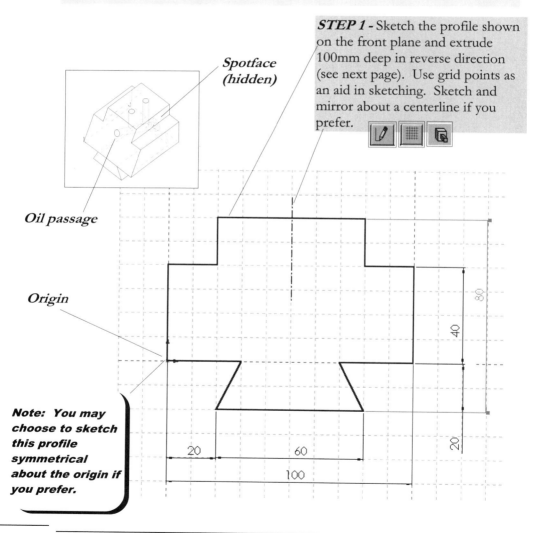

*Spotface (hidden)*

*Oil passage*

*Origin*

**Note: You may choose to sketch this profile symmetrical about the origin if you prefer.**

20    60

100

80

40

20

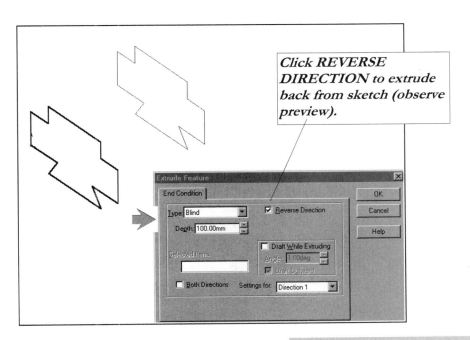

**Click REVERSE DIRECTION** *to extrude back from sketch (observe preview).*

**STEP 2 -** Sketch on right face and extrude a cut through all.

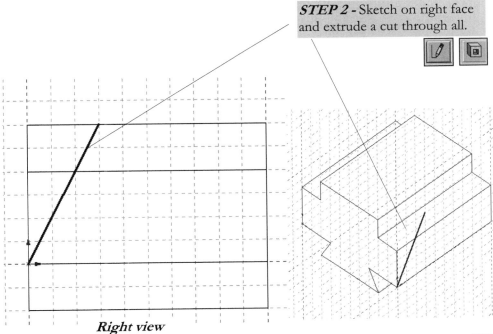

*Right view*

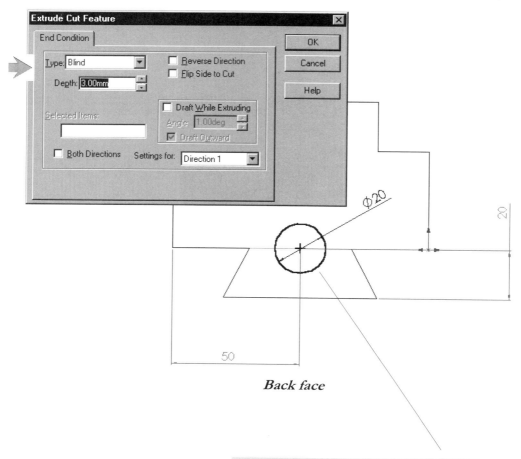

**Extrude Cut Feature**

End Condition

Type: Blind

Depth: 3.00mm

☐ Reverse Direction
☐ Flip Side to Cut

☐ Draft While Extruding
Angle: 1.00deg
☑ Draft Outward

Selected Items:

☐ Both Directions    Settings for: Direction 1

OK
Cancel
Help

Φ20

20

50

*Back face*

**STEP 3 -** On the back face, extrude a 20mm diameter cut – 3 mm deep.

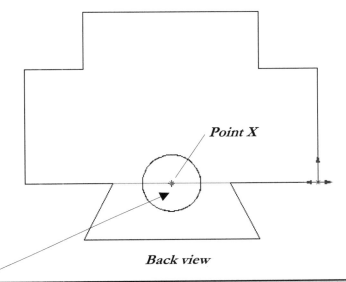

*Point X*

*Back view*

**STEP 4 -** Select the bottom surface of the **SPOTFACE, INSERT SKETCH**, and sketch a Point X at the center of the circle. **EXIT SKETCH**.

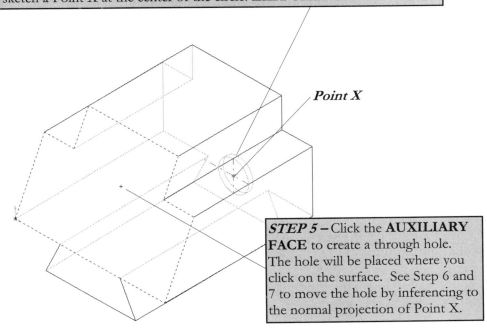

*Point X*

**STEP 5 –** Click the **AUXILIARY FACE** to create a through hole. The hole will be placed where you click on the surface. See Step 6 and 7 to move the hole by inferencing to the normal projection of Point X.

**STEP 6 -** Double-click **NORMAL TO**. The auxiliary face is normal (perpendicular) to the viewer's "line of sight." Click **INSERT, FEATURES, HOLE, SIMPLE** from the top menu bar.

*Point X as it appears projected normal to the auxiliary face.*

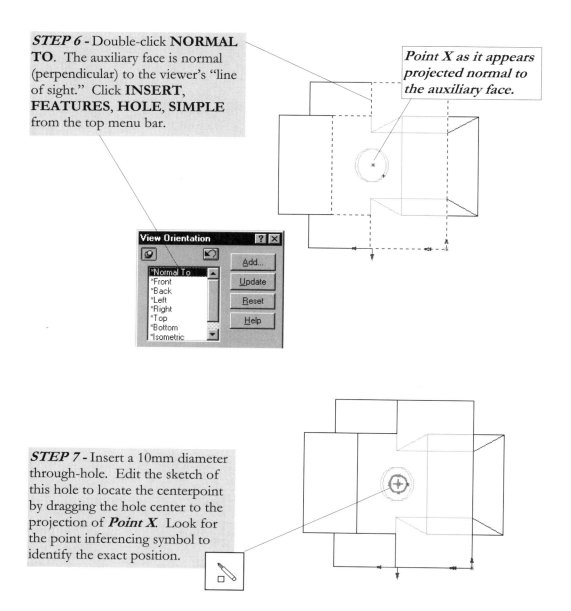

**STEP 7 -** Insert a 10mm diameter through-hole. Edit the sketch of this hole to locate the centerpoint by dragging the hole center to the projection of **Point X**. Look for the point inferencing symbol to identify the exact position.

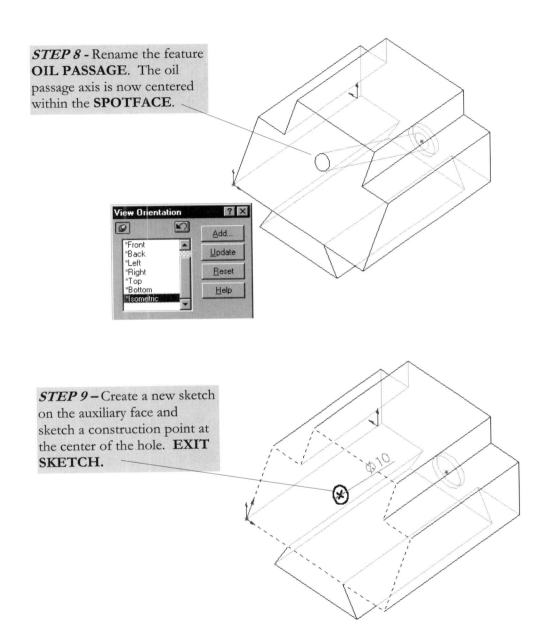

*STEP 8* - Rename the feature **OIL PASSAGE**. The oil passage axis is now centered within the **SPOTFACE**.

*STEP 9* – Create a new sketch on the auxiliary face and sketch a construction point at the center of the hole. **EXIT SKETCH.**

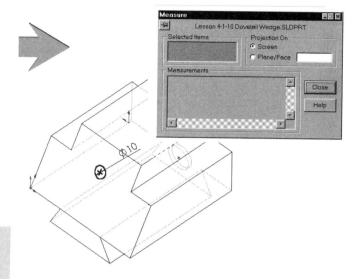

***STEP 10*** - Click **TOOLS**, **MEASURE** to activate the measuring tool.

*Push pin to keep dialog box visible.*

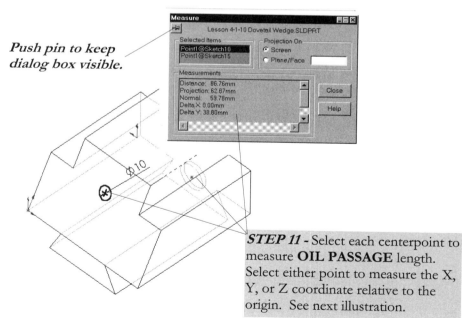

***STEP 11*** - Select each centerpoint to measure **OIL PASSAGE** length. Select either point to measure the X, Y, or Z coordinate relative to the origin. See next illustration.

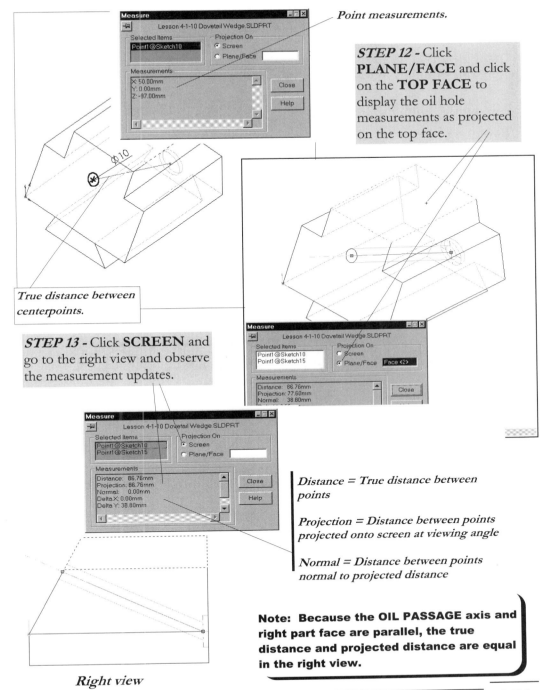

*Point measurements.*

**Measure**
Lesson 4-1-10 Dovetail Wedge SLDPRT
Selected Items
Point1@Sketch10
Projection On
○ Screen
○ Plane/Face
Measurements
X: 50.00mm
Y: 0.00mm
Z: -97.00mm
Close
Help

**STEP 12 -** Click **PLANE/FACE** and click on the **TOP FACE** to display the oil hole measurements as projected on the top face.

*True distance between centerpoints.*

**STEP 13 -** Click **SCREEN** and go to the right view and observe the measurement updates.

**Measure**
Lesson 4-1-10 Dovetail Wedge SLDPRT
Selected Items
Point1@Sketch10
Point1@Sketch15
Projection On
○ Screen
○ Plane/Face  Face <2>
Measurements
Distance: 86.76mm
Projection: 77.60mm
Normal: 38.80mm
Close

**Measure**
Lesson 4-1-10 Dovetail Wedge SLDPRT
Selected Items
Point1@Sketch10
Point1@Sketch15
Projection On
○ Screen
○ Plane/Face
Measurements
Distance: 86.76mm
Projection: 86.76mm
Normal: 0.00mm
Delta X: 0.00mm
Delta Y: 38.80mm
Close
Help

*Distance = True distance between points*

*Projection = Distance between points projected onto screen at viewing angle*

*Normal = Distance between points normal to projected distance*

**Note: Because the OIL PASSAGE axis and right part face are parallel, the true distance and projected distance are equal in the right view.**

*Right view*

4-71

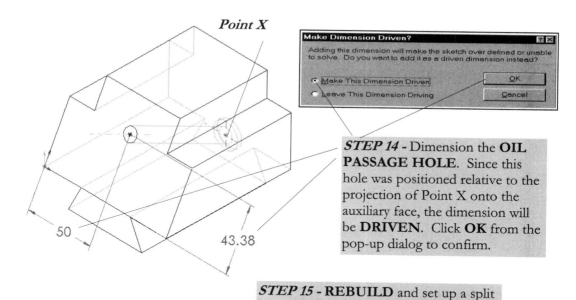

Point X

**Make Dimension Driven?**

Adding this dimension will make the sketch over defined or unable to solve. Do you want to add it as a driven dimension instead?

○ Make This Dimension Driven
○ Leave This Dimension Driving

OK
Cancel

**STEP 14** - Dimension the **OIL PASSAGE HOLE**. Since this hole was positioned relative to the projection of Point X onto the auxiliary face, the dimension will be **DRIVEN**. Click **OK** from the pop-up dialog to confirm.

50
43.38

**STEP 15** - **REBUILD** and set up a split screen display of the part as shown.

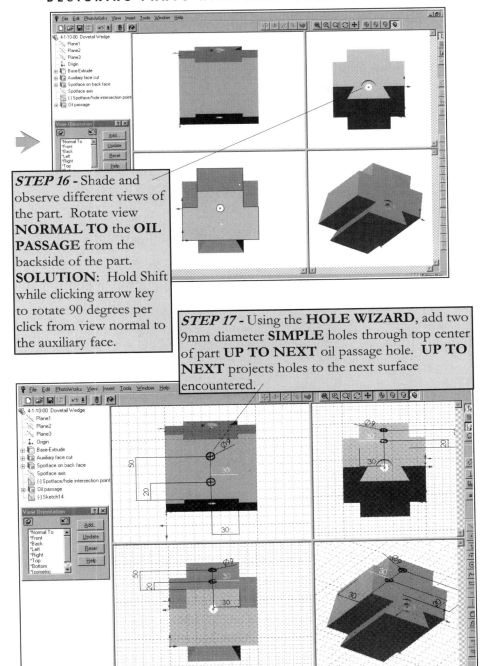

**STEP 16 -** Shade and observe different views of the part. Rotate view **NORMAL TO** the **OIL PASSAGE** from the backside of the part. **SOLUTION**: Hold Shift while clicking arrow key to rotate 90 degrees per click from view normal to the auxiliary face.

**STEP 17 -** Using the **HOLE WIZARD**, add two 9mm diameter **SIMPLE** holes through top center of part **UP TO NEXT** oil passage hole. **UP TO NEXT** projects holes to the next surface encountered.

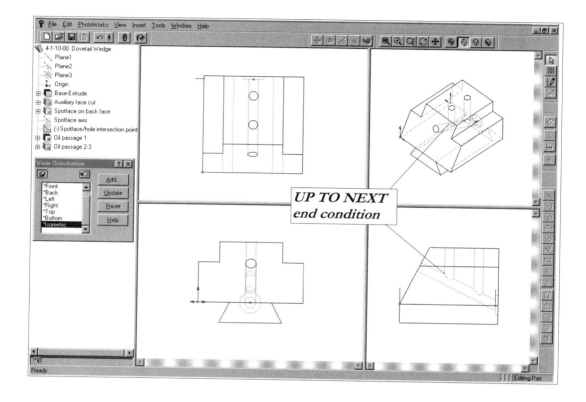

*Finished part*

*STEP 18 -* Save the part, then modify the top surface holes. Right mouse click a hole from the FeatureManager, choose **EDIT DEFINITION**, and experiment with modifying the hole types and the hole dimensions. If you save your modifications, do not overwrite the original part.

### Lesson 4.1.11 - Sensor Cover

This lesson introduces the rib tool. The rib tool simplifies the insertion of ribs into a part. It adds a rib of specified thickness and direction between a contour that you sketch and the surrounding part.

**Try it:** objective

Model the **Sensor Cover** and add ribs as shown.

 *Checked*

***STEP 1*** - On Plane 2 (top view), sketch a 200mm-diameter circle. Extrude with 10-degree draft as indicated in the dialog box.

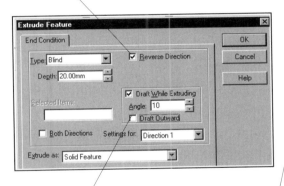

**Note: Click TOOLS, OPTIONS, REFERENCE GEOMETRY if you would like to rename the default planes to orthographic planes. Rename Plane 1 to Front, Plane 2 to Top, and Plane 3 to Right. Optionally, you may click twice on a plane from the FeatureManager to change its name.**

 *Not checked*

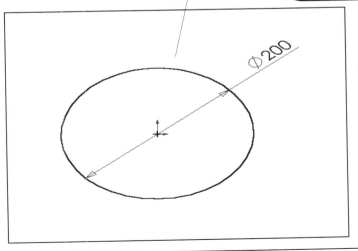

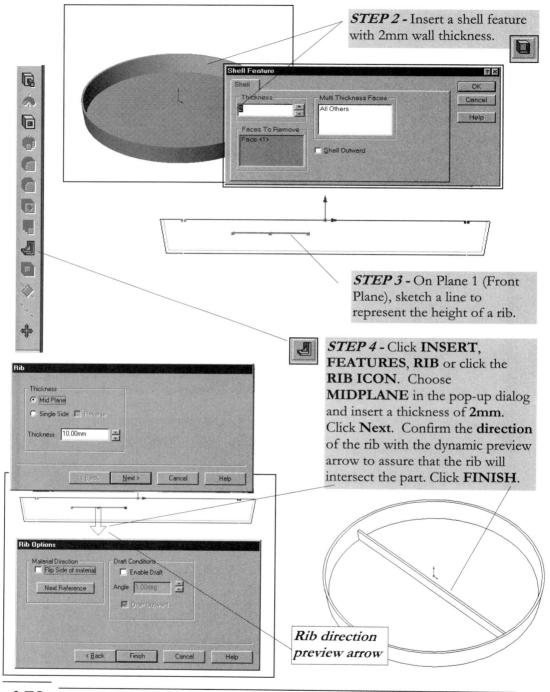

**STEP 2 -** Insert a shell feature with 2mm wall thickness.

**STEP 3 -** On Plane 1 (Front Plane), sketch a line to represent the height of a rib.

**STEP 4 -** Click **INSERT**, **FEATURES**, **RIB** or click the **RIB ICON**. Choose **MIDPLANE** in the pop-up dialog and insert a thickness of **2mm**. Click **Next**. Confirm the **direction** of the rib with the dynamic preview arrow to assure that the rib will intersect the part. Click **FINISH**.

*Rib direction preview arrow*

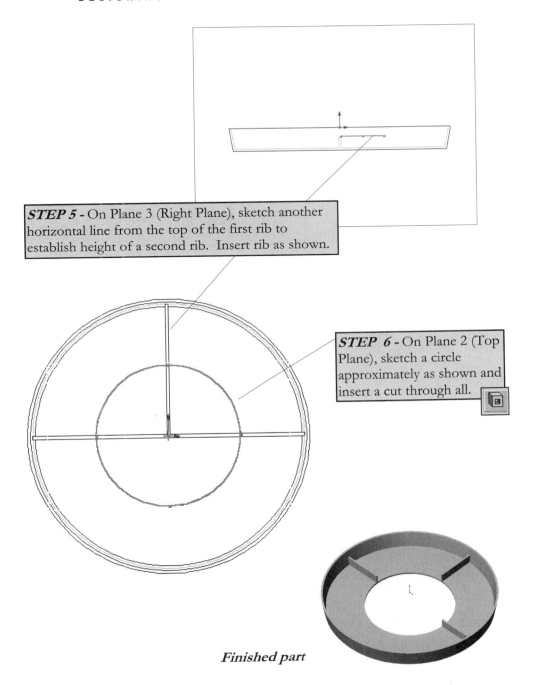

**STEP 5 -** On Plane 3 (Right Plane), sketch another horizontal line from the top of the first rib to establish height of a second rib.  Insert rib as shown.

**STEP 6 -** On Plane 2 (Top Plane), sketch a circle approximately as shown and insert a cut through all.

*Finished part*

## Revolved shapes and cuts

### Graphical Index

These illustrations represent the types of parts that can be made with revolutions. Revolved features have an axis of symmetry, as if they were turned on a lathe. Revolved features may be combined with extruded, swept, and lofted features to create sophisticated parts.

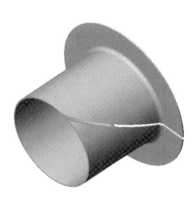

Lesson 4.2.1
Nyliner Bushing

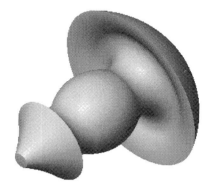

Lesson 4.2.2
Grommet

Lesson 4.2.3
Head – Steering Box

Lesson 4.2.4
Helmet

## Lesson 4.2.1 - Nyliner Bushing

This lesson demonstrates how to create and work with revolved shapes. Two separate cuts are required to create the slit in the bushing. The longitudinal cut profile is sketched on a default construction plane and projected through the revolved body, and the flange cut is sketched on the flange itself. Notice how existing geometry is used to create each sketch.

**Try it:**    **objective**

Model the **Nyliner Bushing** base feature by revolving the sketch shown below, then extrude a cut to create the slit through the bushing.

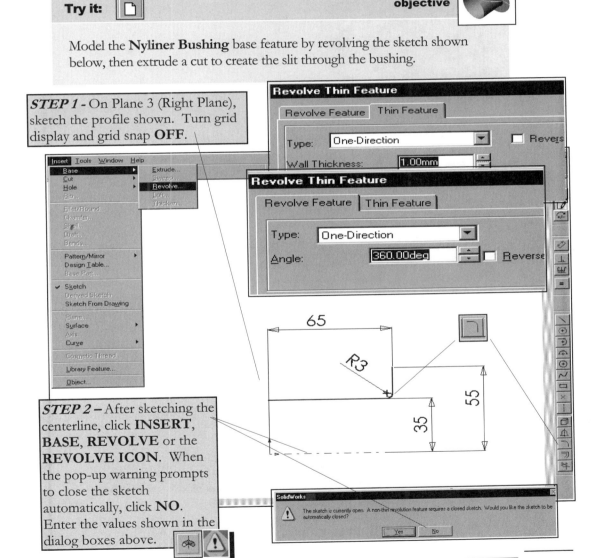

**STEP 1** - On Plane 3 (Right Plane), sketch the profile shown. Turn grid display and grid snap **OFF**.

**STEP 2** – After sketching the centerline, click **INSERT**, **BASE**, **REVOLVE** or the **REVOLVE ICON**. When the pop-up warning prompts to close the sketch automatically, click **NO**. Enter the values shown in the dialog boxes above.

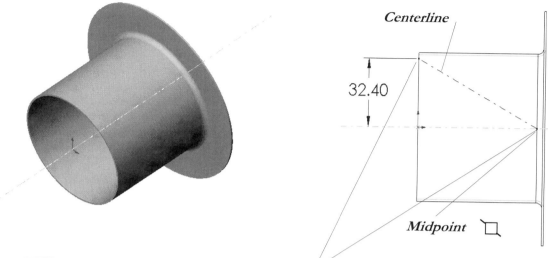

Centerline

32.40

Midpoint

**STEP 3 -** On Right Plane, sketch a centerline with endpoints terminating at the midpoint and dimension shown.

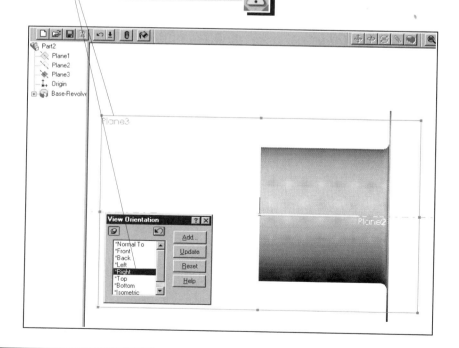

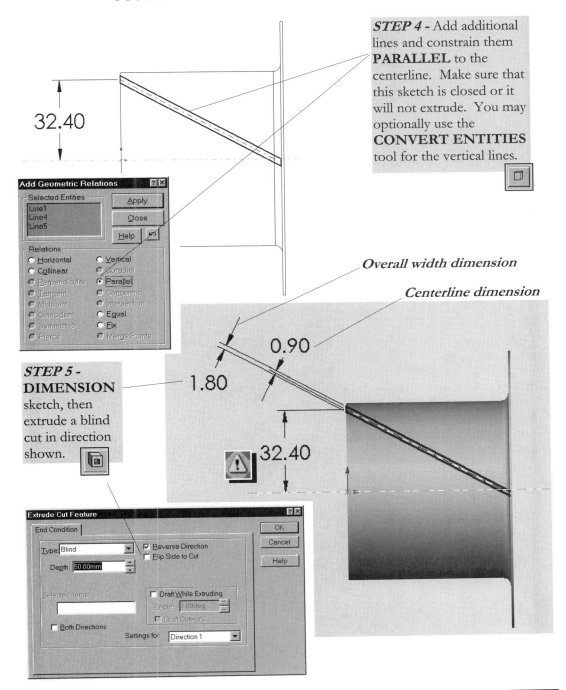

**STEP 4 -** Add additional lines and constrain them **PARALLEL** to the centerline. Make sure that this sketch is closed or it will not extrude. You may optionally use the **CONVERT ENTITIES** tool for the vertical lines.

32.40

**Add Geometric Relations**

Selected Entities
Line1
Line4
Line5

Apply
Close
Help

Relations
- Horizontal
- Collinear
- Perpendicular
- Tangent
- Midpoint
- Coincident
- Symmetric
- Pierce
- Vertical
- Coradial
- ● Parallel
- Concentric
- Intersection
- Equal
- Fix
- Merge Points

*Overall width dimension*

*Centerline dimension*

**STEP 5 -
DIMENSION** sketch, then extrude a blind cut in direction shown.

0.90

1.80

32.40

**Extrude Cut Feature**

End Condition

OK
Cancel
Help

Type: Blind
☑ Reverse Direction
☐ Flip Side to Cut

Depth: 50.00mm

Selected Items:

☐ Draft While Extruding
Angle: 1.00deg
☐ Draft Outward

☐ Both Directions

Settings for: Direction 1

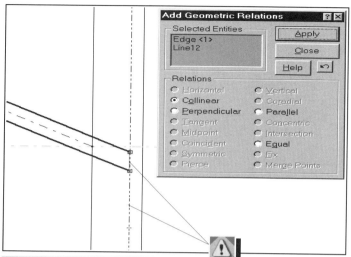

**STEP 6 –** If you did not use the **CONVERT ENTITIES** option for the vertical lines, **EDIT SKETCH** of cut and constrain **LINE** and **EDGE COLLINEAR**. (Now the cut's orientation will be preserved with the part even if the base revolution dimensions are modified.) Reminder: Fully defined sketch elements turn black. Also remember that the Convert Entities tool automatically adds an **ON EDGE** (collinear) constraint.

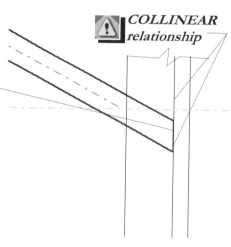

*COLLINEAR relationship*

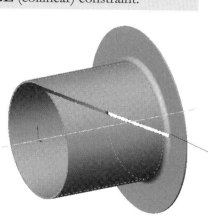

**STEP 7 -** Rebuild the part and verify that your cut looks like this.

*STEP 8* - Select the bottom face.

*STEP 9* - Sketch a rectangle and insert a cut through the top flange as shown.

**Note: For additional help positioning this sketch, see the next page.**

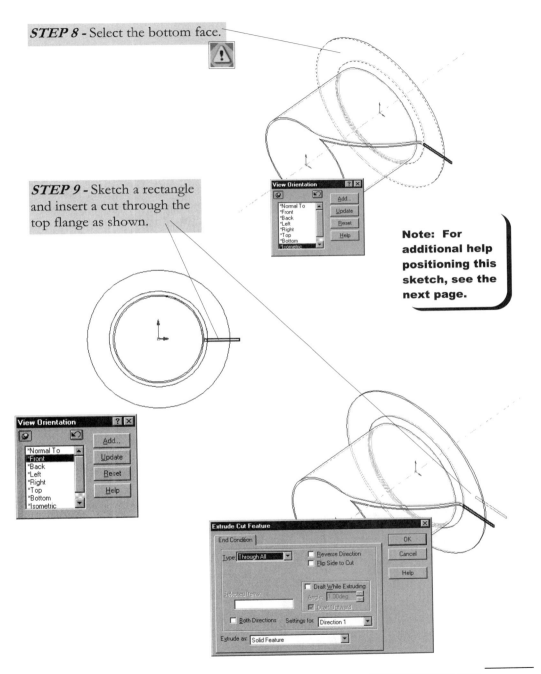

**STEP 10 -** To begin this sketch, **CONVERT ENTITY** of existing cut for a starting point. Be sure to use the edge on the surface indicated in order to capture the outermost projection of t[⚠]st cut.

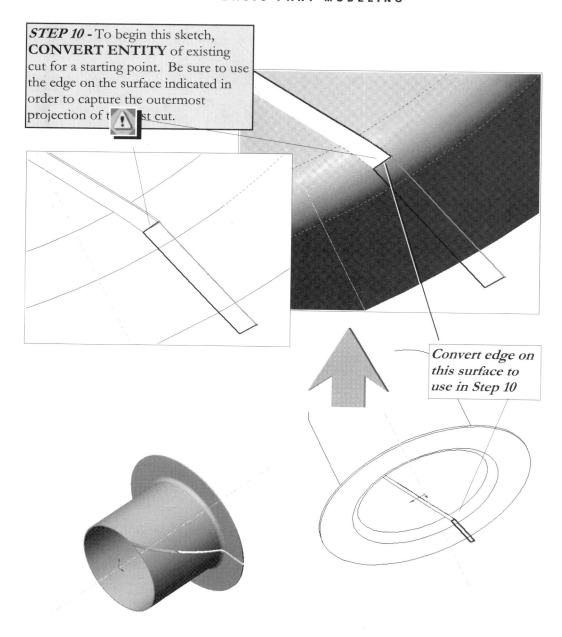

Convert edge on this surface to use in Step 10

*Finished part*

## Lesson 4.2.2 - Grommet

This lesson provides more instruction on the use of sketch constraints and revolved features. It also introduces the **MODIFY SKETCH TOOL**. This tool makes it possible to move, rotate, or resize a sketch within a model.

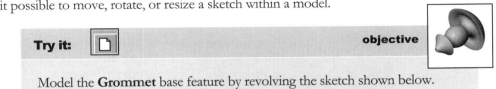

**Try it:** objective

Model the **Grommet** base feature by revolving the sketch shown below.

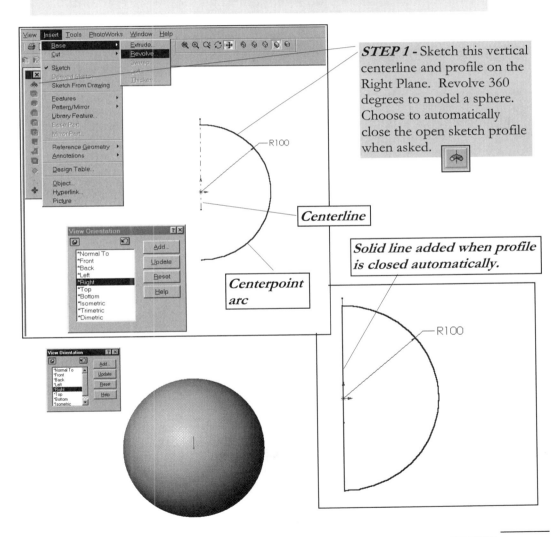

*STEP 1* - Sketch this vertical centerline and profile on the Right Plane. Revolve 360 degrees to model a sphere. Choose to automatically close the open sketch profile when asked.

*Centerline*

*Centerpoint arc*

*Solid line added when profile is closed automatically.*

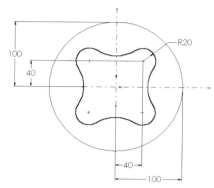

*Completed sketch reference*

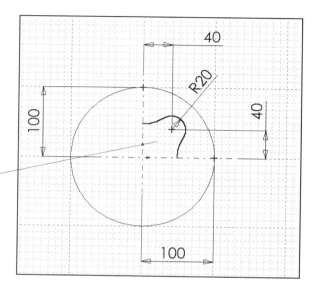

**STEP 2 -** On the Right Plane, sketch and dimension this profile, which you will mirror to complete the sketch. Be sure that the arc endpoints end up <u>on the centerlines before</u> the mirror operations are performed. See steps 2a to 2g for detailed instructions on how to create this sketch. Be sure to dimension to centerlines.

**STEP 2a -** Select the Right Plane, **INSERT SKETCH**, and go to the Right View. Turn grid snap and display **ON** and use 100mm major grid spacing with 10 minor lines per major.

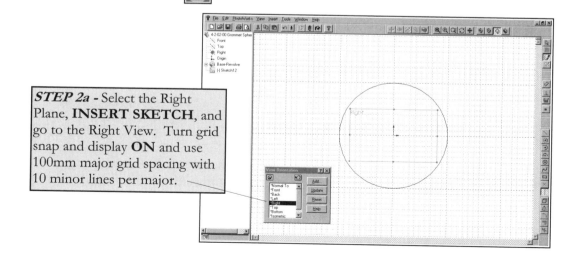

**STEP 2b -** Sketch a horizontal and vertical centerline through the origin as shown.

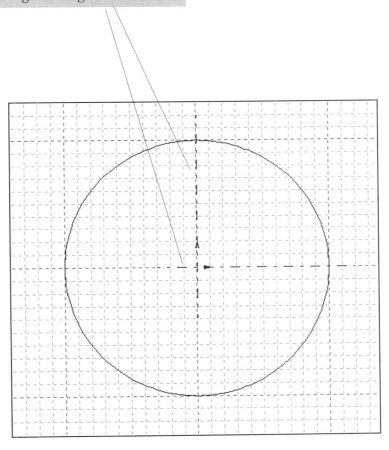

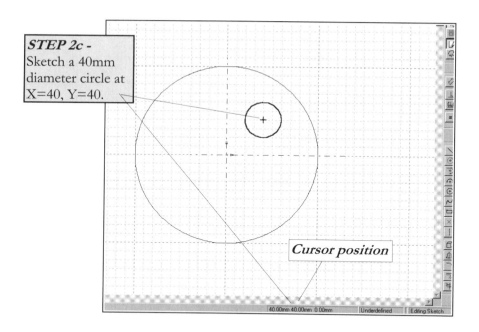

**STEP 2c -** Sketch a 40mm diameter circle at X=40, Y=40.

*Cursor position*

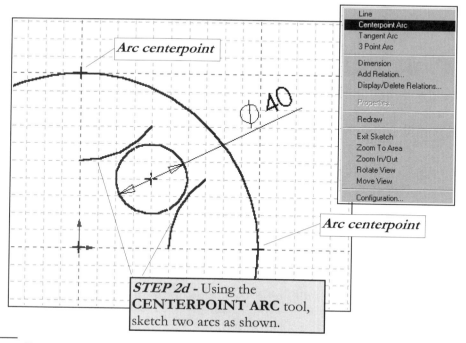

*Arc centerpoint*

Line
Centerpoint Arc
Tangent Arc
3 Point Arc

Dimension
Add Relation...
Display/Delete Relations...

Properties...

Redraw

Exit Sketch
Zoom To Area
Zoom In/Out
Rotate View
Move View

Configuration...

*Arc centerpoint*

**STEP 2d -** Using the **CENTERPOINT ARC** tool, sketch two arcs as shown.

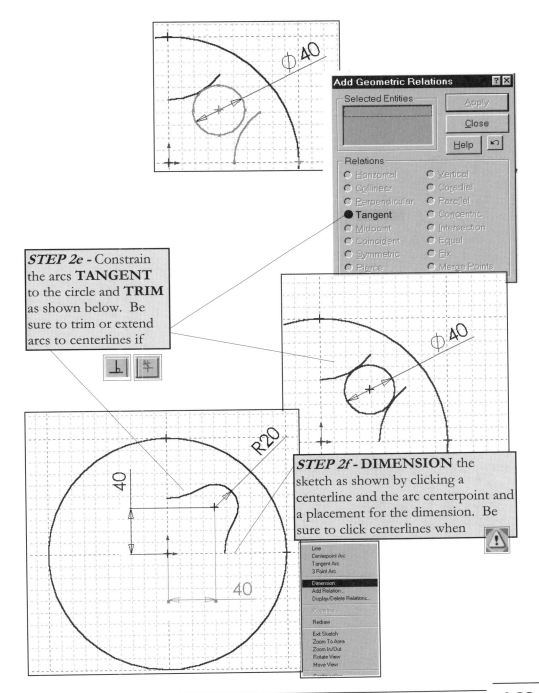

**Add Geometric Relations**

Selected Entities

Apply

Close

Help

Relations

- ○ Horizontal    ○ Vertical
- ○ Collinear     ○ Coradial
- ○ Perpendicular ○ Parallel
- ● Tangent       ○ Concentric
- ○ Midpoint      ○ Intersection
- ○ Coincident    ○ Equal
- ○ Symmetric     ○ Fix
- ○ Pierce        ○ Merge Points

**STEP 2e -** Constrain the arcs **TANGENT** to the circle and **TRIM** as shown below. Be sure to trim or extend arcs to centerlines if

**STEP 2f - DIMENSION** the sketch as shown by clicking a centerline and the arc centerpoint and a placement for the dimension. Be sure to click centerlines when

Line
Centerpoint Arc
Tangent Arc
3 Point Arc
Dimension
Add Relation...
Display/Delete Relations...
Properties...
Redraw
Exit Sketch
Zoom To Area
Zoom In/Out
Rotate View
Move View

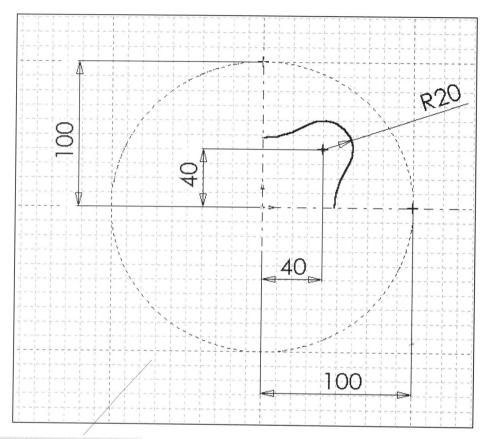

**STEP 2g -** Complete the dimensioning as shown. Notice that sketch elements turn black when they become **FULLY DEFINED**.

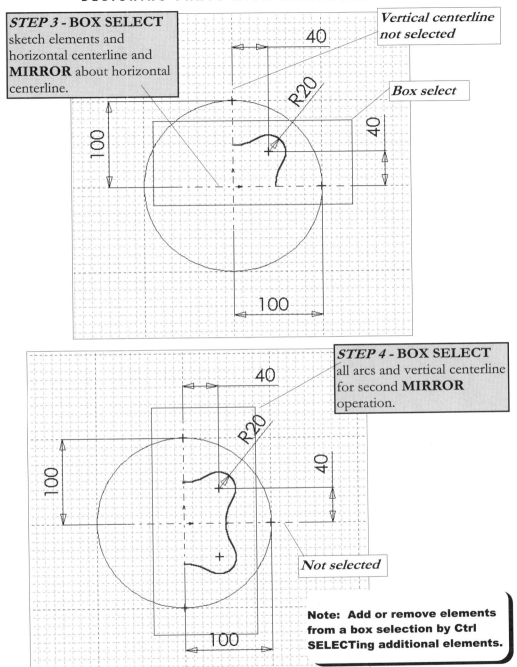

**STEP 3 - BOX SELECT** sketch elements and horizontal centerline and **MIRROR** about horizontal centerline.

Vertical centerline not selected

Box select

40

R20

100

40

100

**STEP 4 - BOX SELECT** all arcs and vertical centerline for second **MIRROR** operation.

40

R20

100

40

Not selected

100

Note: Add or remove elements from a box selection by Ctrl SELECTing additional elements.

*STEP 5* - From right mouse menu, **EXIT SKETCH**, then click twice (hold the second click momentarily) on the sketch name in the FeatureManager and you will be able to edit the name of the sketch. Rename the sketch **SPROCKET SKETCH**.

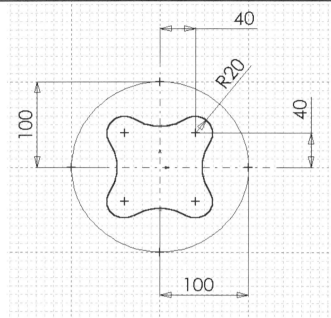

*STEP 6* - Rebuild and **SAVE THE PART**. Then **EDIT** the **SPROCKET SKETCH** and make some modifications to it. Change some dimensions. Then delete some dimensions and drag sketch elements to see how the sketch reacts with different levels of constraints. Try a few modifications and then click the **UNDO** icon to back out of your changes. When you are done learning, close the **part without saving your sketch changes**. Then reload the part with the good sketch to continue with the next step.

Note: Because of the mirror operations used to finish this sketch profile, the sketch will remain symmetrical when sketch elements are modified.

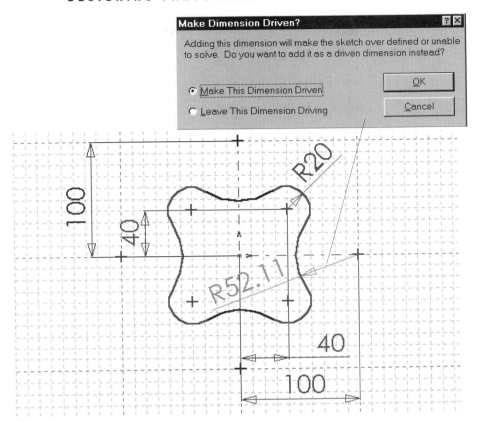

**STEP 7 - EDIT** the Sprocket Sketch. Add the R52.11mm dimension and notice that the sketch becomes **OVER DEFINED** and dimensions turn red. In this state the sketch has redundant dimensions or constraints (in this case the 100mm dimensions "drive" the arc radius). You can make the R52.11mm dimension a "driven dimension" because it is a result of the 100mm dimension and other sketch constraints, and allow it to be displayed, or you can delete the 52.11mm dimension to return the sketch to a **FULLY DEFINED** state. At this time, **DELETE the 52.11R dimension**.

Note: Steps 8-17 on the following pages will give you extra practice modifying sketches, and will help you to create the optional part variations shown at the end of this section. Remember that proficiency comes with practice, so retake the parts of this lesson that you are not confident with.

**STEP 8 -** While still in **EDIT SKETCH** mode, you must delete sketch "external references" to the part model so that you can move the sketch within the model. Delete all **COINCIDENT RELATIONS** for the horizontal and vertical centerlines. This will break the constraints the sketch has to the part origin.

*Scroll to next relation*

**STEP 9 -** Click **TOOLS, SKETCH TOOLS, MODIFY** and notice that the sketch has its own origin separate from the part origin.

**STEP 10 -** Click on the sketch origin with the left mouse button and hold down while dragging the sketch origin to a new position in the center of the sketch.

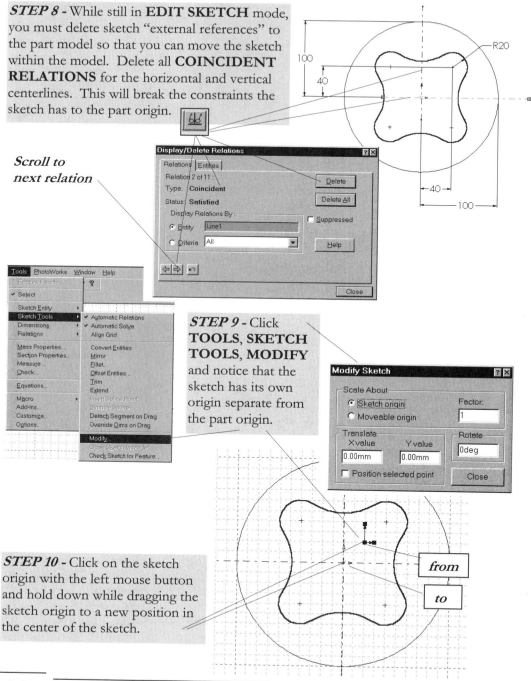

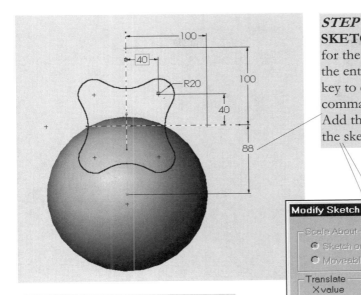

*STEP 11* - In the **MODIFY SKETCH BOX**, enter **88mm** for the **Y VALUE**, and press the enter key. Press the **ESC** key to end the modify command, or click **CLOSE**. Add the 88mm dimension to the sketch as shown.

*STEP 12* - Save the part now. Do not save it again until after you insert a revolved cut at Step 20.

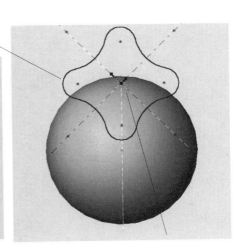

**NOTE: In the next four screenshots, dimensions are not shown for clarity.**

*STEP 13* - **Delete the 88mm dimension** to break external reference to the part. Modify the sketch again (see Step 9). Move the sketch origin and sketch as shown. Rotate the sketch by right mouse dragging any existing sketch element around the sketch origin. The sketch origin is the axis of rotation for the sketch. Optionally, you can enter a value in the rotation angle box.

*STEP 14* - Left mouse drag the origin to a new location and practice rotating the sketch again, by dragging the sketch with the right mouse key depressed.

**Note: The sketch rotates about its own origin.**

**4-95**

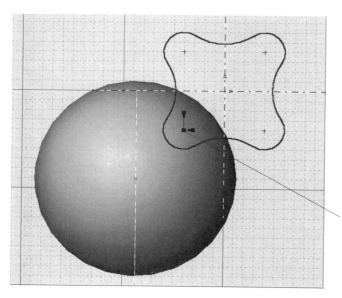

*STEP 15* - Using the left mouse key, drag the sketch and the sketch origin to this approximate location and try rotating the sketch around the sketch origin again, using the right mouse key to rotate.

*STEP 16* - Move the sketch origin back to the center of the sketch and move the sketch to this position, then resize the sketch by changing the scale factor to 1.5 and pressing the enter key.

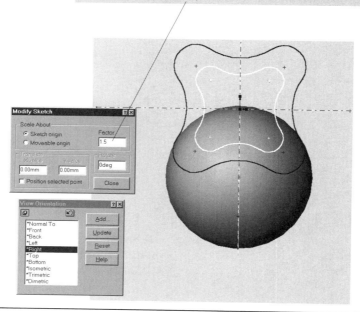

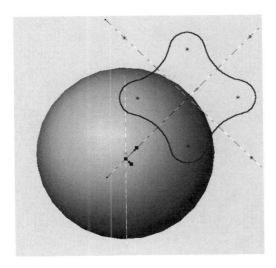

*STEP 17* - Click the undo icon to undo Step 16, then drag the sketch origin to the center of the sphere. Next, revolve the sketch around the center of the sphere using a right mouse drag or by entering a value in the **ROTATE BOX** of the **MODIFY SKETCH** dialog.

Note: The MODIFY SKETCH tool makes it easy to reuse existing sketches in new parts because you can move, rotate, or resize the existing sketch as required. Refer to SolidWorks program help for more information on the MODIFY SKETCH command.

*STEP 18* - Close and **do not save** the part now. Reopen the part previously saved (Step 11).

*STEP 19* - Edit the **SPROCKET SKETCH**. Add a horizontal centerline through the sphere origin.

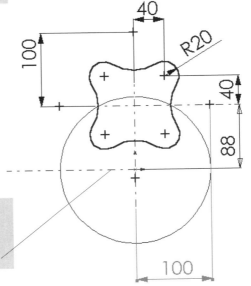

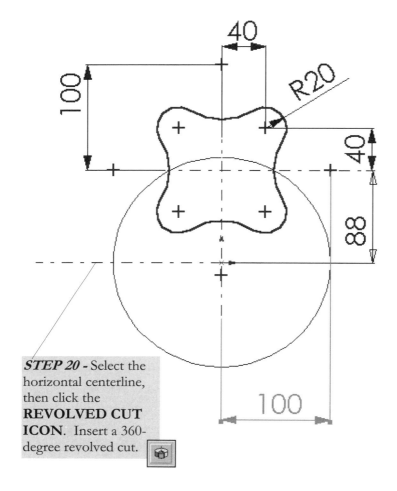

40

R20

100

40

88

100

**STEP 20 -** Select the horizontal centerline, then click the **REVOLVED CUT ICON**. Insert a 360-degree revolved cut.

Note: There are many ways to reuse and modify sketches in the same part or in other parts. You may COPY and PASTE sketches, or you may delete a part feature and use its sketch to create a new feature. For example, to use the SPROCKET SKETCH for an EXTRUDED CUT, delete the REVOLVED CUT feature from the FeatureManager. Then edit the SPROCKET SKETCH from the FeatureManager and insert an EXTRUDED CUT. Be sure to save the old part before experimenting, and reload it before going on to the next step. Save any new models you create with a unique name.

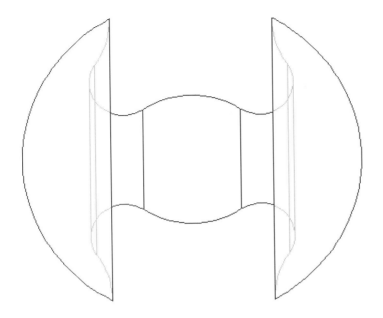

*Result of revolved cut*

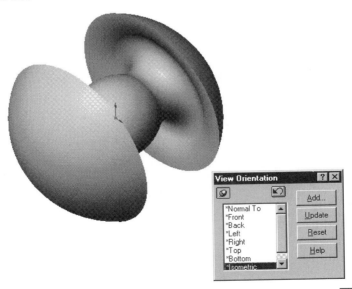

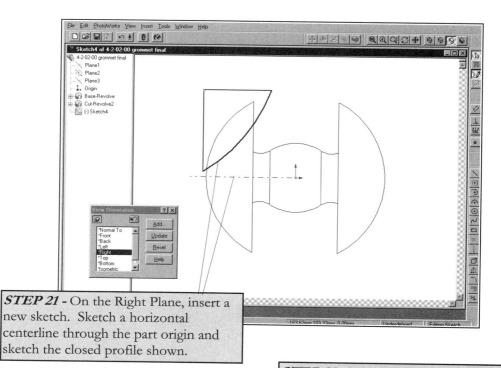

**STEP 21** - On the Right Plane, insert a new sketch. Sketch a horizontal centerline through the part origin and sketch the closed profile shown.

**STEP 22** - Insert a **REVOLVED CUT** 360 degrees around the horizontal centerline to finish the part. Be sure to save the part now.

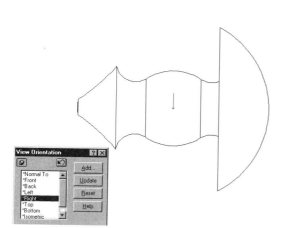

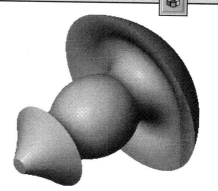

*Finished part*

Note: Try to model some variations of the part by modifying the sketch for the revolved cut and rebuilding the part with the new sketch. Save each part you create with a unique name. When modifying sketches, don't forget that you can modify or delete constraints as well as modify dimensions.

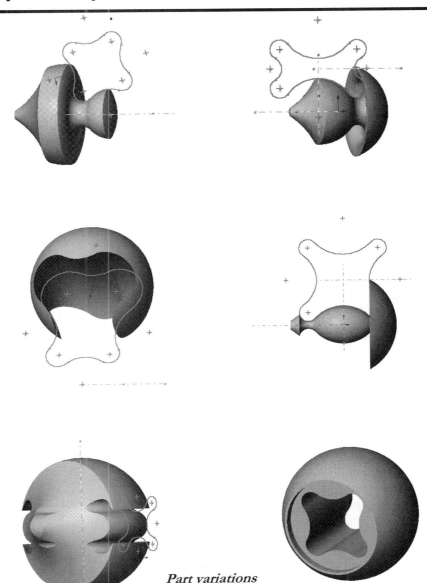

*Part variations*

### Lesson 4.2.3 - Head - Steering Box

This lesson gives more practice with sketching, dimensioning and revolutions, and provides a general review of some of the previous lessons.

**Try it:** 🖵                                    **objective**

Model the **STEERING BOX HEAD** base feature by revolving the sketch profile shown below.

***STEP 1*** - On Plane 2 (Top Plane), sketch and dimension the profile shown, then revolve it around the vertical centerline to create a base revolution. A larger view of the sketch profile is shown on the next page.

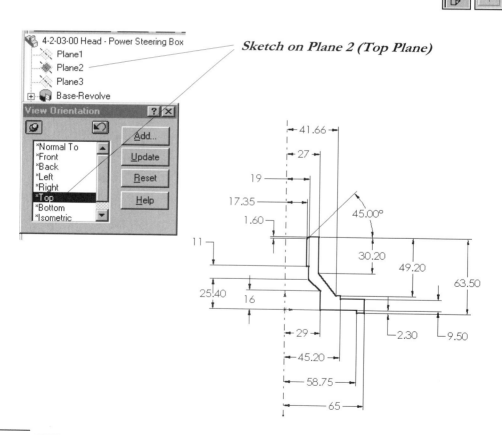

*Sketch on Plane 2 (Top Plane)*

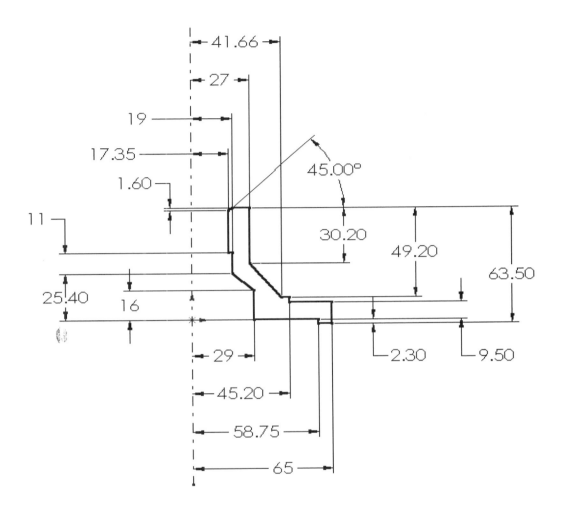

**Notes:**
1. Remember to right mouse click on a dimension for its **PROPERTIES** sheet, then change arrowheads to outside if required. Also, you can change the dimension precision and font from within the property box.
2. Click and drag dimensions to position them as shown.
3. Notice when elements become fully dimensioned (**DEFINED**), they turn black.

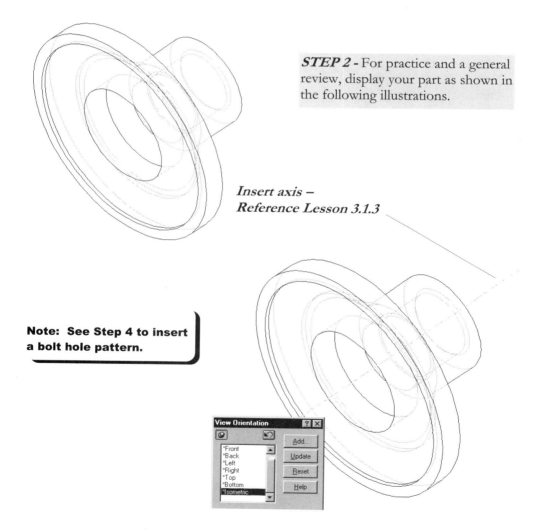

**STEP 2 -** For practice and a general review, display your part as shown in the following illustrations.

*Insert axis –*
*Reference Lesson 3.1.3*

**Note: See Step 4 to insert a bolt hole pattern.**

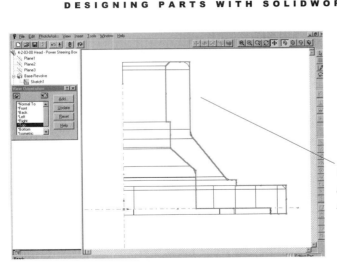

*Create some
section cuts –
Reference Lesson 3.6.1*

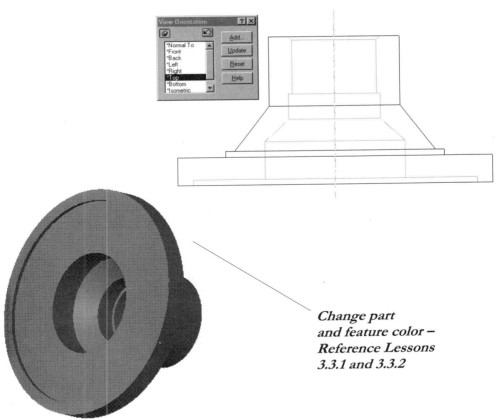

*Change part
and feature color –
Reference Lessons
3.3.1 and 3.3.2*

*Revolve the part and save as a named view –*
*Reference Lesson 3.5.4*

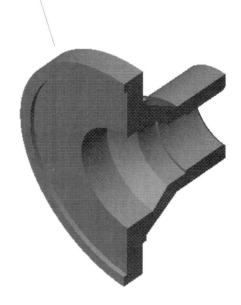

**STEP 3 -** Add some fillets, rounds, and chamfers – Reference Lesson 2.1.6.

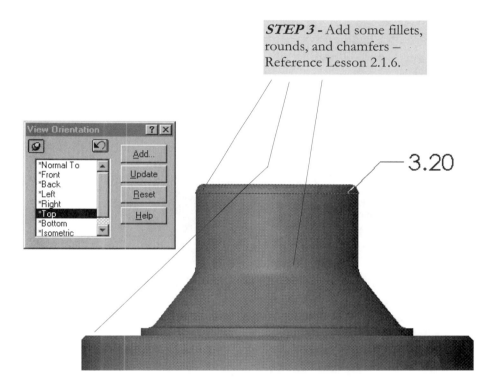

3.20

***STEP 4 -*** Insert eight through-holes equally spaced using the **CIRCULAR PATTERN** tool. First insert one hole on a vertical or horizontal centerline and use it to pattern with. Remember that you must select the part axis to pattern around – Reference Lesson 4.1.9.

**Note:** Try to create this section after adding the holes – Reference Lesson 3.6.1.

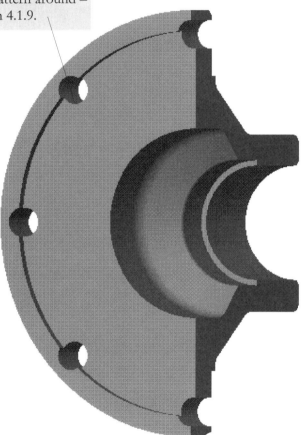

**Note:** To insert a linear pattern, click **INSERT, PATTERN/MIRROR, LINEAR PATTERN**, and fill in the dialog box.

## Lesson 4.2.4 – Helmet

This lesson shows how complex shapes can be made using simple revolved features combined with other techniques you have already learned.

**Try it:** **objective**

Model the **HELMET** base feature by revolving the sketch shown below to create a sphere. Add additional features and shell the part as depicted in the following instructions.

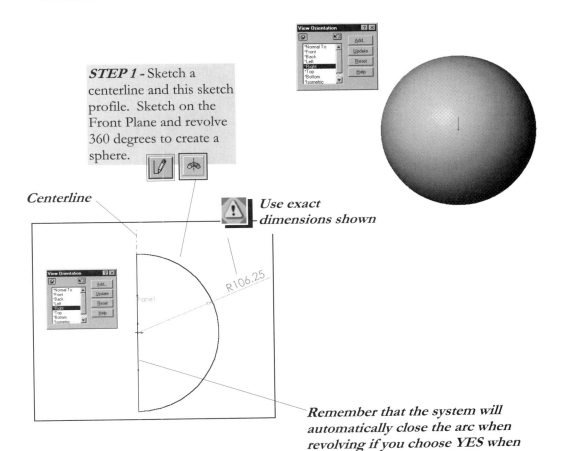

**STEP 1** - Sketch a centerline and this sketch profile. Sketch on the Front Plane and revolve 360 degrees to create a sphere.

*Centerline*

*Use exact dimensions shown*

R106.25

*Remember that the system will automatically close the arc when revolving if you choose YES when prompted in the pop-up dilaog box.*

**STEP 2** - Sketch on the Right Plane and extrude the profile as a **CUT**, **THROUGH ALL** in **BOTH DIRECTIONS**. Use the **TANGENT ARC** option from the right mouse pop-up menu to sketch the round corners. **Note:** Start the sketch with a horizontal centerline, rough-in the sketch to approximate proportions, but ensure that the lines are not horizontal, vertical, or perpendicular to each other **so that automatic constraints are not applied.** Drag the 12mm radius arc centerpoint on top of the horizontal centerline. Dimension the sketch *using exact dimensions shown. Grid snap should be off.*

*Horizontal centerline through part origin*

Note: Preview the cut direction arrow to cut out the visor area as shown on the next page.

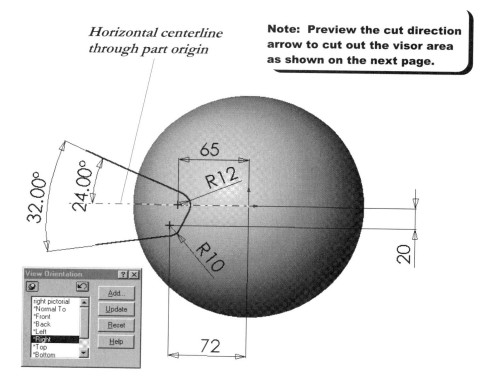

Note: Before adding the angle dimensions, notice that sketch elements defined by dimensions turn black (to indicate that they are "defined"). The angle lines remain blue ("under-defined") until they are dimensioned. Before dimensioning the angle lines, click on their endpoints and drag them to change their angle. Observe how the dimensioned sketch elements remain in place.

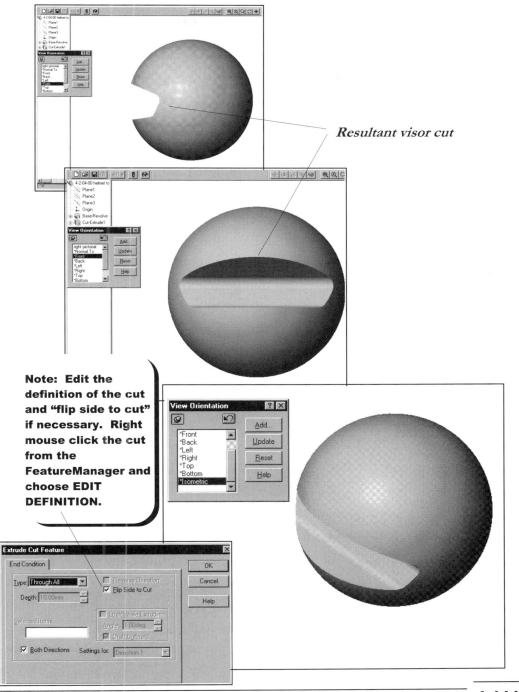

*Resultant visor cut*

**Note: Edit the definition of the cut and "flip side to cut" if necessary. Right mouse click the cut from the FeatureManager and choose EDIT DEFINITION.**

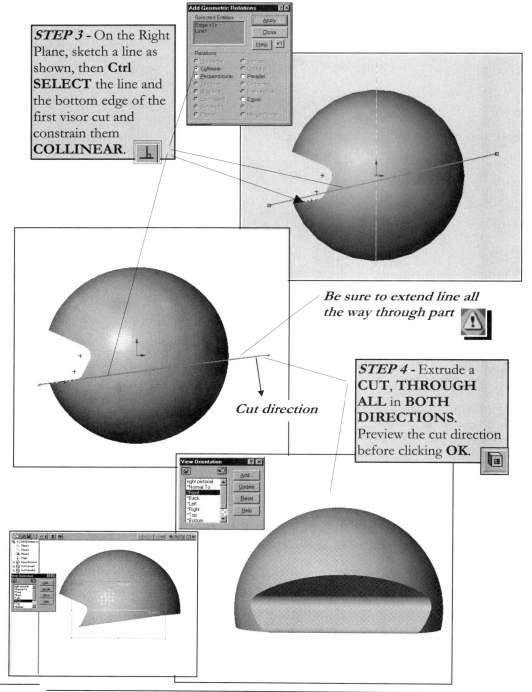

**STEP 3 -** On the Right Plane, sketch a line as shown, then **Ctrl SELECT** the line and the bottom edge of the first visor cut and constrain them **COLLINEAR**.

Add Geometric Relations

Selected Entities
Edge <1>
Line1

Apply
Close
Help

Relations
Horizontal          Vertical
Collinear           Corradial
Perpendicular       Parallel
Tangent             Concentric
Midpoint            Intersection
Coincident          Equal
Symmetric           Fix
Pierce              Merge Points

*Be sure to extend line all the way through part*

*Cut direction*

**STEP 4 -** Extrude a **CUT, THROUGH ALL** in **BOTH DIRECTIONS**. Preview the cut direction before clicking **OK**.

View Orientation

right pictorial
*Normal To
*Front
*Back
*Left
*Right
*Top
*Bottom

Add...
Update
Reset
Help

**4-112**

**STEP 5a -** Select the bottom face, sketch a vertical centerline through the origin, and a **POINT X** on the centerline 20.07mm (toward the front face of the helmet) as shown in the sketch below.

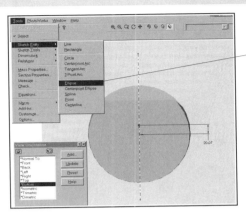

**STEP 5b -** Next, click **TOOLS**, **SKETCH ENTITY**, **ELLIPSE**, and sketch an ellipse using the **POINT X** as its center.

**STEP 5d -** Next drag out minor axis to **POINT Z** from Point X. Drag horizontal to Point X as indicated by the horizontal inferencing line.

**STEP 5c -** To sketch an ellipse, drag out major and minor axes from origin. Start at **POINT X** and drag out major axis toward back of helmet to **POINT Y**.
Be sure to **drag on the vertical centerline** so that the point is constrained to it (see note).

*Helmet front*

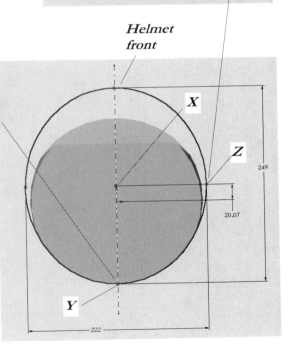

Note: The CONSTRAINTS applied to the ellipse will ensure that it blends properly with the bottom surface so the part will shell. The CONSTRAINTS applied are in this order:
1. 20.07 dimension
2. Point Y on vertical centerline
3. 249 major axis dimension
4. 222 minor axis dimension

**4-113**

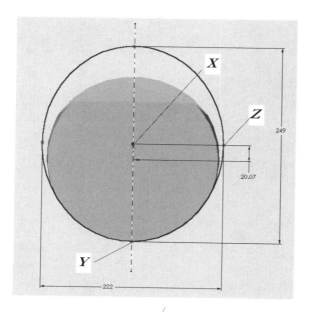

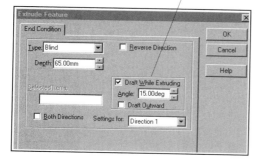

**STEP 6 -** Dimension the ellipse as shown, and extrude the ellipse outward 65mm with a 15-degree inward draft.

**Note: The ellipse sketch and the edge curve of the bottom surface must blend as closely as possible or the helmet will not shell. Use the exact dimensions and procedures given in order to complete this lesson successfully.**

**Note: You can see that by changing dimensions and geometric constraints, you can easily iterate sketches to meet exact requirements.**

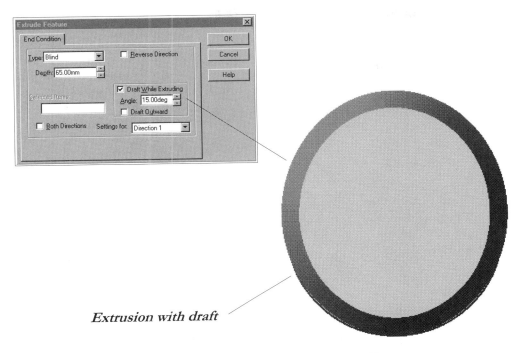

*Extrusion with draft*

*Bottom*

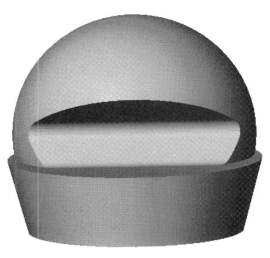

*Front*

**4-115**

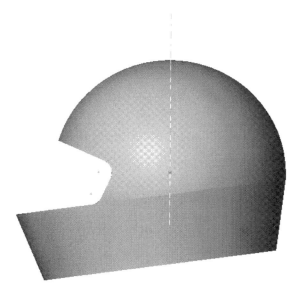

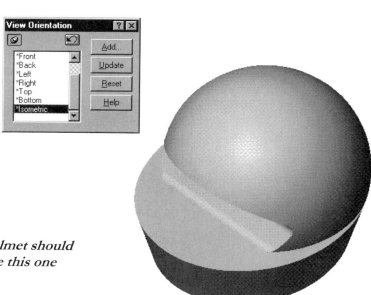

*Your helmet should look like this one*

**STEP 7 -** Create this sketch on Right Plane. Use a **TANGENT ARC** for the 10mm radius. Constrain the sketch **COLLINEAR** where shown.

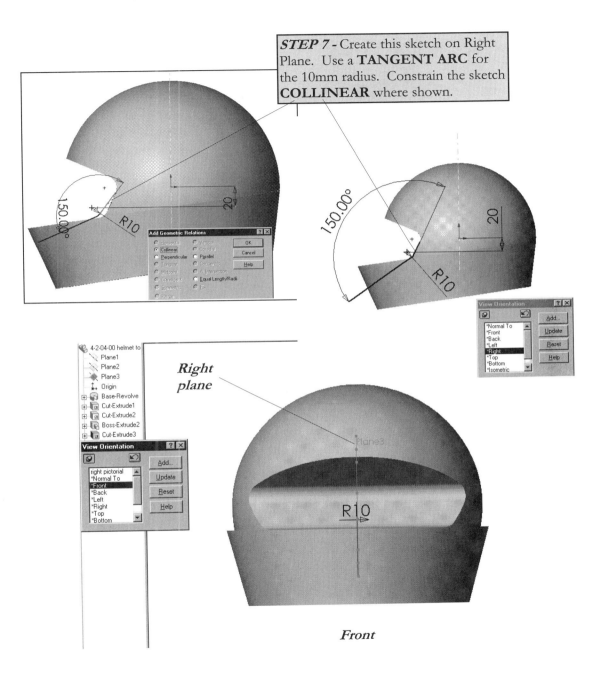

*Right plane*

*Front*

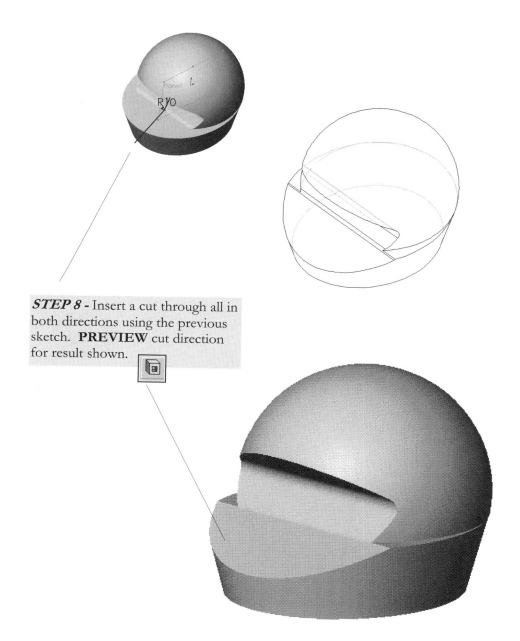

**STEP 8 -** Insert a cut through all in both directions using the previous sketch. **PREVIEW** cut direction for result shown.

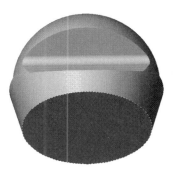

**Shell Feature**

Shell

Thickness
3.00mm

Multi Thickness Faces
All Others

OK

Cancel

Help

Faces To Remove
4 Faces Selected

☐ Shell Outward

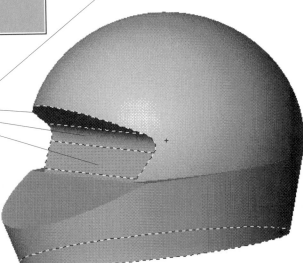

***STEP 9 -*** Select the bottom face and the three faces in the visor area (four faces total), and insert a 3mm **SHELL**. The selected faces will be cut away by the shell function. The remaining bottom surfaces of the visor opening will be removed in the next step by a sketch and cut.

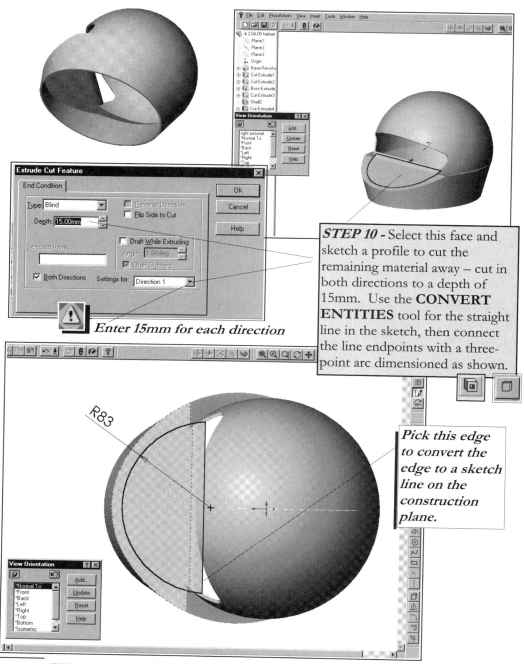

**STEP 10 -** Select this face and sketch a profile to cut the remaining material away – cut in both directions to a depth of 15mm. Use the **CONVERT ENTITIES** tool for the straight line in the sketch, then connect the line endpoints with a three-point arc dimensioned as shown.

*Enter 15mm for each direction*

*Pick this edge to convert the edge to a sketch line on the construction plane.*

R83

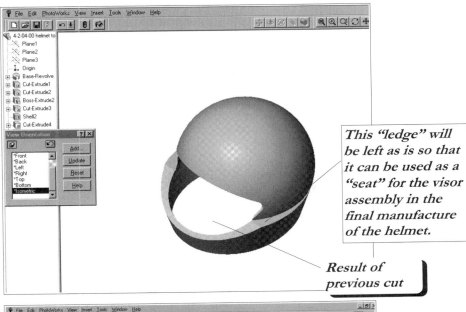

*This "ledge" will be left as is so that it can be used as a "seat" for the visor assembly in the final manufacture of the helmet.*

*Result of previous cut*

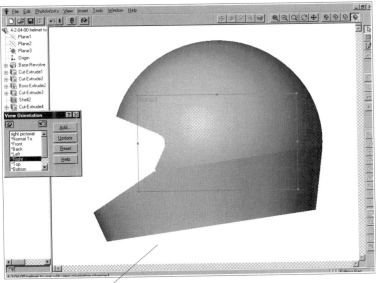

**STEP 11** - Display the right view of the helmet. Note that the bottom of the helmet is not horizontal. To practice some of the view manipulation techniques you have learned, and to get practice with the **SELECT OTHER** tool, see the following steps.

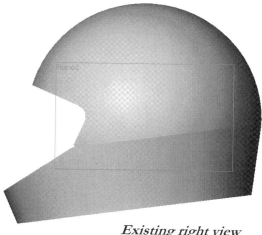

*Existing right view*

**STEP 12 -** Rotate to show the bottom of the helmet. When features are too small to select effectively, you can use the **SELECT OTHER** tool to pick them. To use this tool, click on the edge of the bottom face with the right mouse key. Choose **SELECT OTHER** from the pop-up dialog. Continue to click the right mouse key to toggle through displayed edges and faces until the bottom face highlights. Then choose **YES** by clicking the left mouse key to select the bottom face. This tool also works in sketch mode and makes it easier to select lines that overlap.

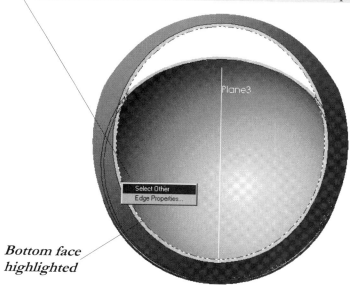

*Bottom face highlighted*

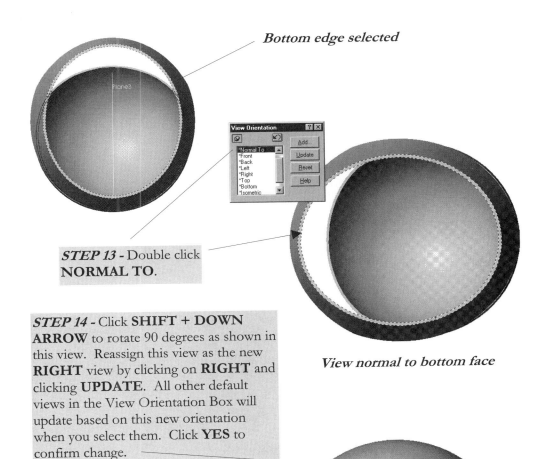

*Bottom edge selected*

*View normal to bottom face*

***STEP 13 -*** Double click **NORMAL TO**.

***STEP 14 -*** Click **SHIFT + DOWN ARROW** to rotate 90 degrees as shown in this view. Reassign this view as the new **RIGHT** view by clicking on **RIGHT** and clicking **UPDATE**. All other default views in the View Orientation Box will update based on this new orientation when you select them. Click **YES** to confirm change.

*New right view of finished part with bottom of helmet horizontal*

## Swept shapes and cuts

### Graphical Index

These parts show the type of geometry that can be modeled by sweeping sketch profiles along a sketch trajectory.

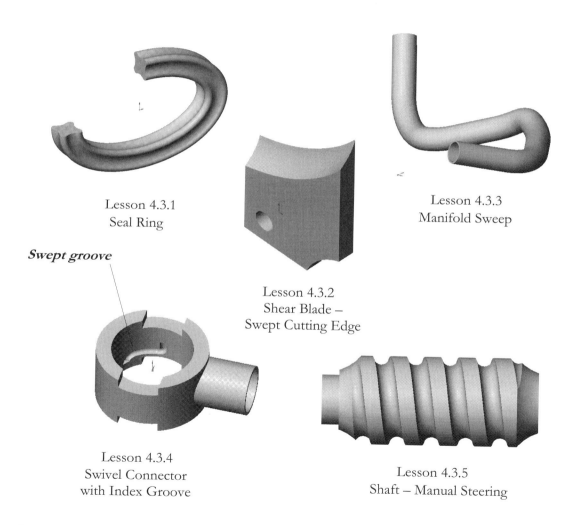

Lesson 4.3.1
Seal Ring

Lesson 4.3.2
Shear Blade –
Swept Cutting Edge

Lesson 4.3.3
Manifold Sweep

*Swept groove*

Lesson 4.3.4
Swivel Connector
with Index Groove

Lesson 4.3.5
Shaft – Manual Steering

### Lesson 4.3.1 - Seal Ring

This lesson gives you practice reusing an existing sketch as a swept profile along a centerpoint ellipse and trajectory. After pasting a sketch into another part, you will probably have to modify its size and position. This can be done by dragging the sketch, dimensioning it, using the Modify Sketch tool, or by constraining sketch elements to other points in the model. For this lesson, you will constrain the **SPROCKET SKETCH** centerpoint to the **ENDPOINT** of the ellipse.

**Try it:**   **objective**

Model the **SEAL RING** base sweep using the **SPROCKET SKETCH** you made in Lesson 4.2.2.

**STEP 1** - Select the Front Plane, and **INSERT SKETCH**. Turn grid display and snap on. Click **TOOLS**, **SKETCH ENTITY**, **CENTERPOINT ELLIPSE**, and sketch this ellipse segment by following the steps on the next page.

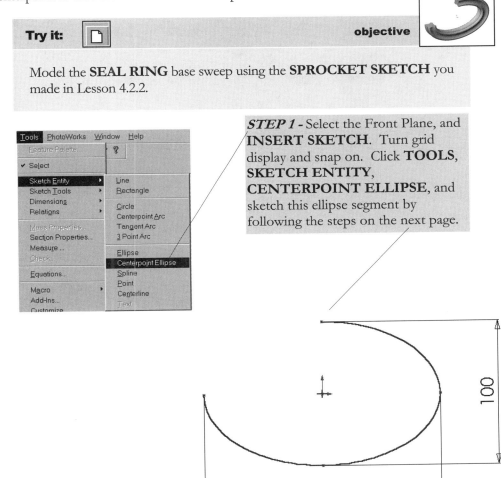

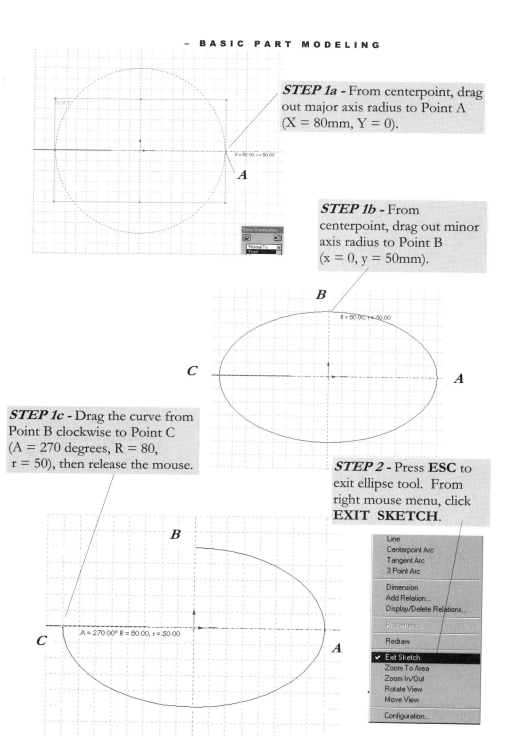

**STEP 1a -** From centerpoint, drag out major axis radius to Point A (X = 80mm, Y = 0).

**STEP 1b -** From centerpoint, drag out minor axis radius to Point B (x = 0, y = 50mm).

**STEP 1c -** Drag the curve from Point B clockwise to Point C (A = 270 degrees, R = 80, r = 50), then release the mouse.

**STEP 2 -** Press **ESC** to exit ellipse tool. From right mouse menu, click **EXIT SKETCH**.

**STEP 3 -** Open the **GROMMET** from lesson 4.2.2. From the FeatureManager, **SELECT** the **SPROCKET SKETCH** and copy it to the clipboard by pressing **EDIT**, **COPY**. Close the **GROMMET** part.

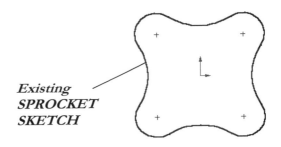

*Existing*
*SPROCKET*
*SKETCH*

**STEP 4 -** Paste the sketch onto the Top Plane. Select the Top Plane from the FeatureManager and click **EDIT**, **PASTE**. Be sure you "exited the sketch" in Step 2.

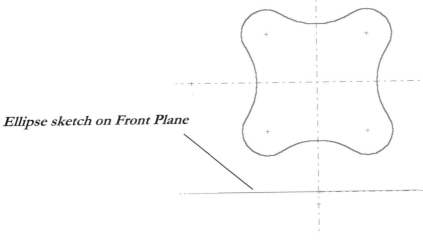

*Ellipse sketch on Front Plane*

*STEP 5 -* Rename Sketch 1 **TRAJECTORY** and Sketch 2 **SPROCKET SKETCH**.

*STEP 6 -* Click the **SPROCKET SKETCH** and the **TRAJECTORY** sketch from the FeatureManager to show both sketches. Your results should look like this. (View rotated and dimensions omitted for clarity.)

*SPROCKET SKETCH*

*TRAJECTORY SKETCH*

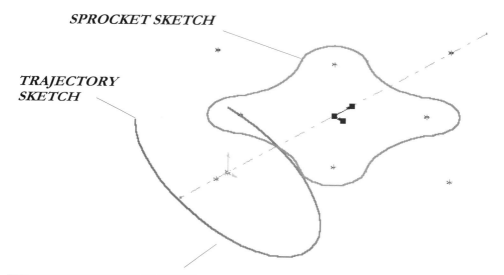

*STEP 7 -* **REBUILD**, go to **TOP VIEW**, then **EDIT SKETCH** of **SPROCKET SKETCH**. Delete all dimensions and construction lines that came from the old sketch when you copied it.

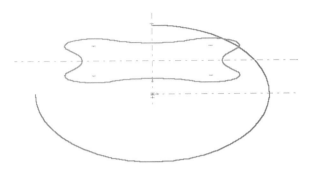

*STEP 8 -* Click **TOOLS**, **SKETCH TOOLS**, **MODIFY**, to modify the **SPROCKET SKETCH**. Change the **SCALE FACTOR TO** 0.2 to reduce the sketch.

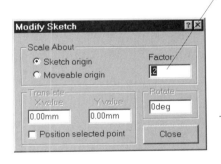

*Results of SPROCKET SKETCH rescaled by a factor of 0.2.*

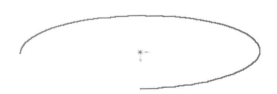

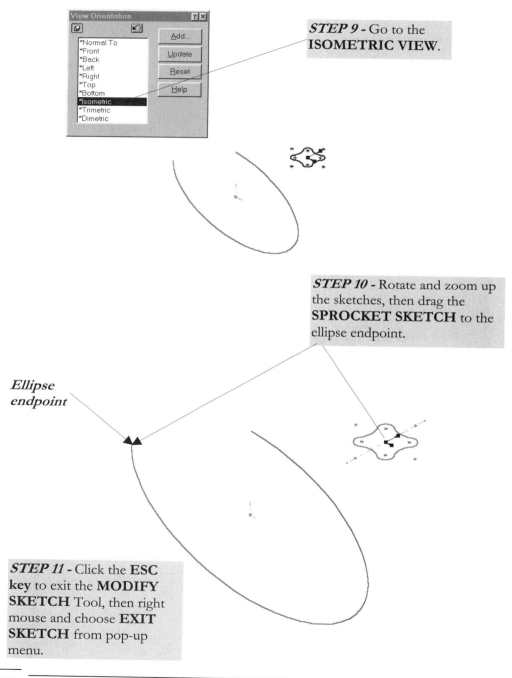

*STEP 9* - Go to the **ISOMETRIC VIEW**.

*STEP 10* - Rotate and zoom up the sketches, then drag the **SPROCKET SKETCH** to the ellipse endpoint.

*Ellipse endpoint*

*STEP 11* - Click the **ESC key** to exit the **MODIFY SKETCH** Tool, then right mouse and choose **EXIT SKETCH** from pop-up menu.

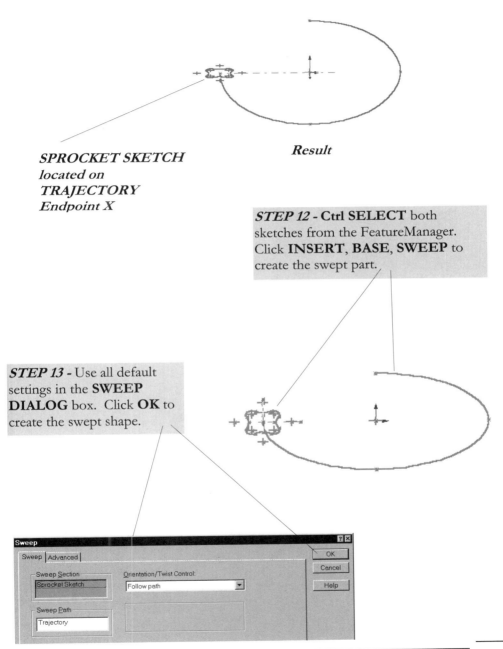

*Result*

*SPROCKET SKETCH*
*located on*
*TRAJECTORY*
*Endpoint X*

*STEP 12 -* **Ctrl SELECT** both sketches from the FeatureManager. Click **INSERT, BASE, SWEEP** to create the swept part.

*STEP 13 -* Use all default settings in the **SWEEP DIALOG** box. Click **OK** to create the swept shape.

Sweep

Sweep | Advanced |

Sweep Section
Sprocket Sketch

Orientation/Twist Control:
Follow path

Sweep Path
Trajectory

OK
Cancel
Help

**4-131**

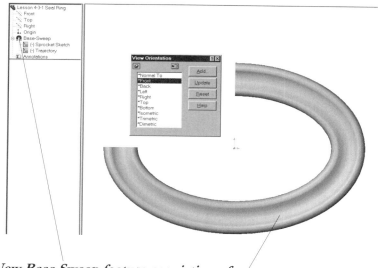

*New Base Sweep feature consisting of*
**SPROCKET SKETCH and TRAJECTORY.**

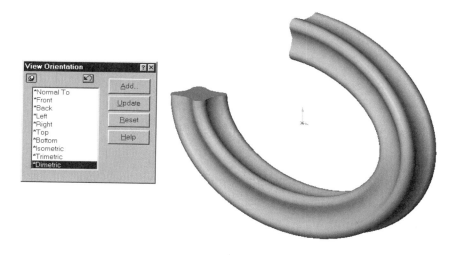

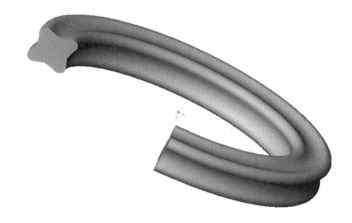

*Finished part*

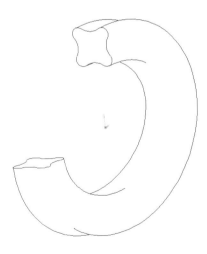

### Lesson 4.3.2 - Shear Blade-Swept Cutting Edge

This lesson demonstrates a swept cut.

**Try it:**  **Shear Blade Lesson 4.1.8**  objective

Open the Existing **SHEAR BLADE** and modify the cutting edge.

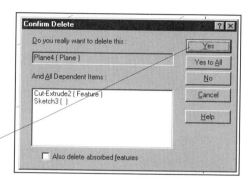

*STEP 1* - On the existing part, delete Plane 4 and the extruded cut. **Ctrl SELECT** from the FeatureManager and press delete key. Click **YES** to confirm deletion.

*STEP 2* - File the part with a new name to preserve the old **SHEAR BLADE**.

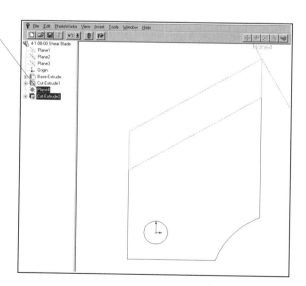

**4-134**

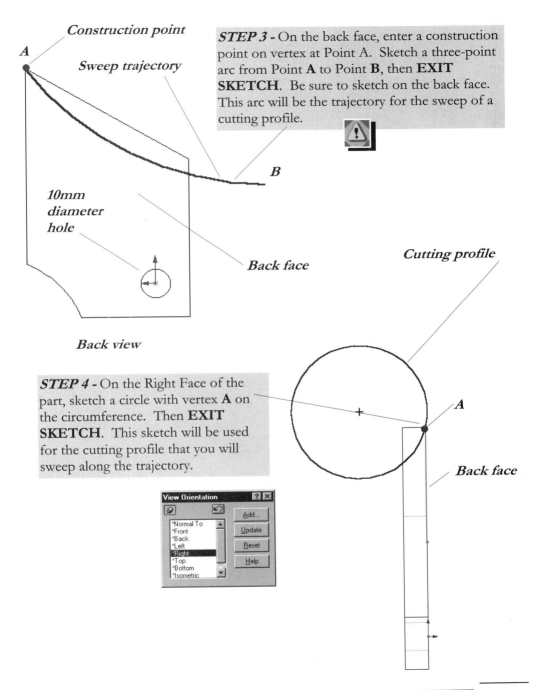

Construction point

**A**

Sweep trajectory

**B**

10mm
diameter
hole

Back face

Back view

**STEP 3 -** On the back face, enter a construction point on vertex at Point A. Sketch a three-point arc from Point **A** to Point **B**, then **EXIT SKETCH**. Be sure to sketch on the back face. This arc will be the trajectory for the sweep of a cutting profile.

Cutting profile

**A**

Back face

**STEP 4 -** On the Right Face of the part, sketch a circle with vertex **A** on the circumference. Then **EXIT SKETCH**. This sketch will be used for the cutting profile that you will sweep along the trajectory.

View Orientation

*Normal To
*Front
*Back
*Left
*Right
*Top
*Bottom
*Isometric

Add...
Update
Reset
Help

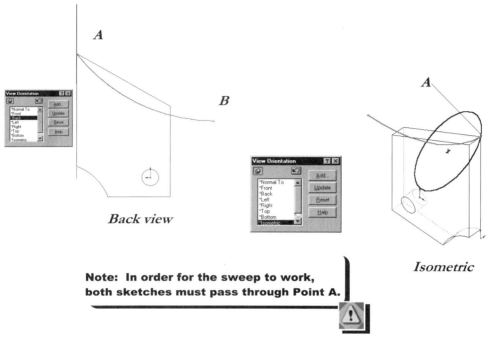

*Back view*

*Isometric*

**Note:  In order for the sweep to work, both sketches must pass through Point A.**

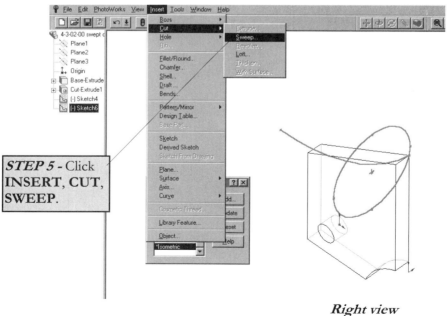

*STEP 5* - Click **INSERT, CUT, SWEEP.**

*Right view*

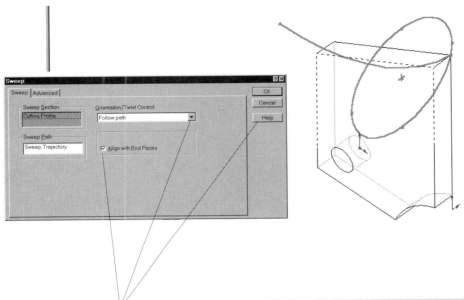

**STEP 6** – Choose **FOLLOW PATH**, and click the **ALIGN WITH END FACES** option in the Sweep dialog box. See note below. Remember to access SolidWorks on-line help for the latest details about the **SWEEP** command.

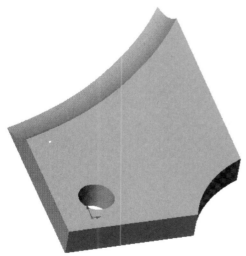

*Finished part*

**Note: Under ORIENTATION/TWIST CONTROL:**

The **FOLLOW PATH** option causes the cutting profile to remain at the same angle with respect to the path (sweep trajectory) at all times.

The **KEEP NORMAL CONSTANT** option causes the cutting profile to remain parallel to the cutting profile sketch plane at all times.

## Lesson 4.3.3 - Manifold Sweep

This lesson shows how to sweep a sketch profile along a 3-D curve. A 3-D curve is the projection of two orthographic sketches that intersect in space. This method of creating a 3-D curve allows the designer to work with orthographic projections that are easy to visualize. For example, to route a manifold pipe around an engine block, simply define the manifold route in two orthographic views by creating a sketch that establishes clearance around other layout components. After defining the clearance sketches in two views, the computer will calculate the actual 3-D path that the manifold will follow.

**Try it:**    **objective**

Model the **MANIFOLD SWEEP** using a 3-D projected curve for the sweep trajectory.

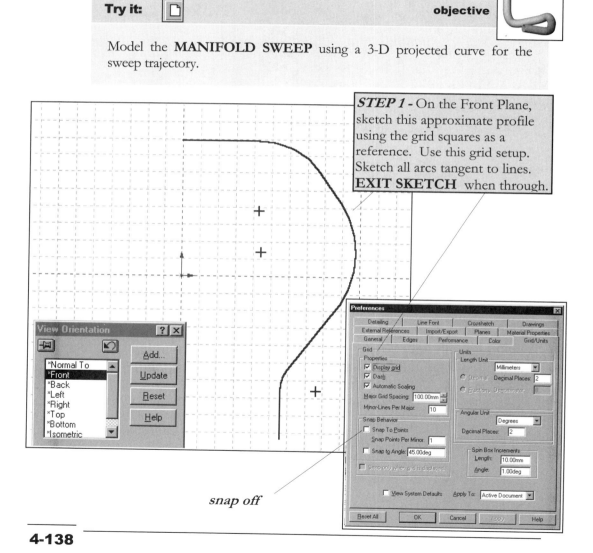

*STEP 1* - On the Front Plane, sketch this approximate profile using the grid squares as a reference. Use this grid setup. Sketch all arcs tangent to lines. **EXIT SKETCH** when through.

*snap off*

**Note:** The view orientation windows below are for reference only. They show Sketch 1 oriented within the part model reference views to graphically illustrate how curves are created from the front and right view (see next page).

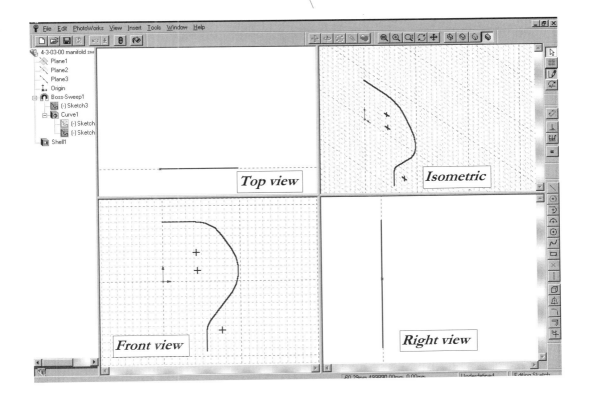

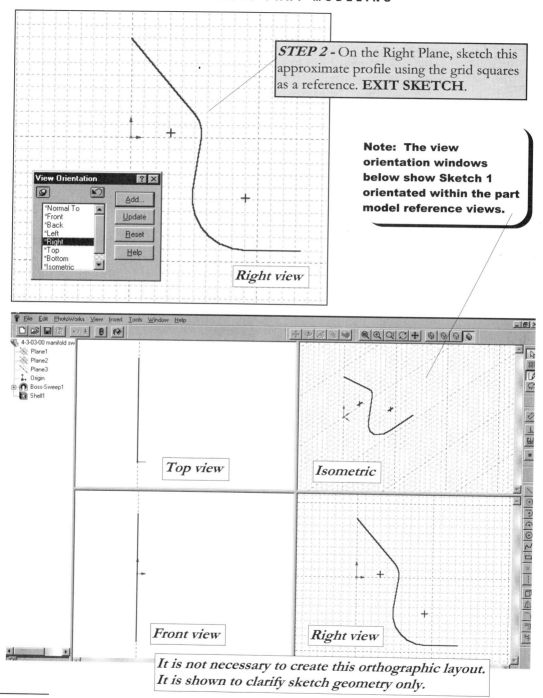

*STEP 2* - On the Right Plane, sketch this approximate profile using the grid squares as a reference. **EXIT SKETCH**.

**Note: The view orientation windows below show Sketch 1 orientated within the part model reference views.**

*Right view*

*Top view*

*Isometric*

*Front view*

*Right view*

*It is not necessary to create this orthographic layout. It is shown to clarify sketch geometry only.*

*STEP 3* - **Ctrl SELECT** Sketches 1 and 2. Click **INSERT**, **REFERENCE GEOMETRY**, **PROJECTED CURVE** to produce the resultant 3-D curve. This projected curve is determined by the spatial intersection of the two orthographic sketches.

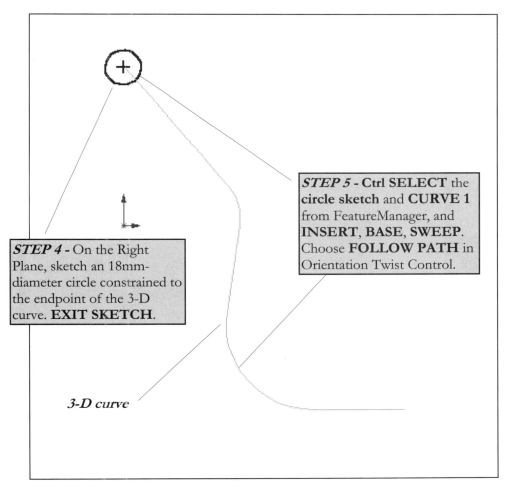

*STEP 5* - **Ctrl SELECT** the **circle sketch** and **CURVE 1** from FeatureManager, and **INSERT, BASE, SWEEP**. Choose **FOLLOW PATH** in Orientation Twist Control.

*STEP 4* - On the Right Plane, sketch an 18mm-diameter circle constrained to the endpoint of the 3-D curve. **EXIT SKETCH**.

*3-D curve*

*Right view*

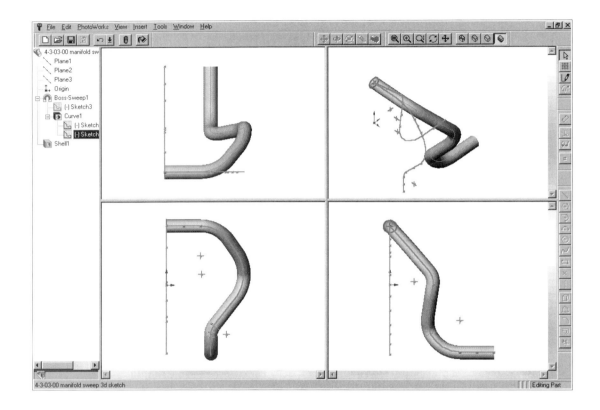

*Sweep showing superimposed orthographic
sketches created on Front and Right Plane.*

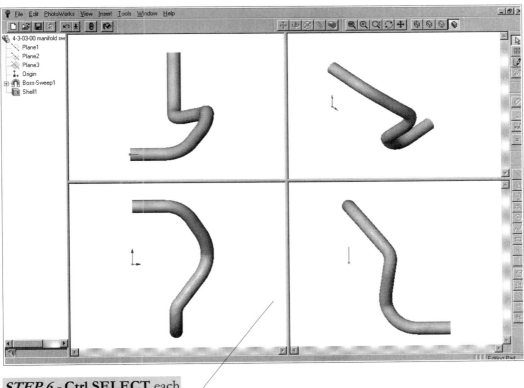

**STEP 6 - Ctrl SELECT** each end of the manifold and insert a 1mm thick shell.

*Finished part*

### Lesson 4.3.4 - Swivel Connector with Index Groove

This lesson shows how to project a 2-D sketch onto a curved surface and use the resultant 3-D curve as a sweep trajectory.

**Try it:**  | **Swivel Connector - Lesson 4.1.3** | **objective**

Open the **SWIVEL CONNECTOR** from Lesson 4.1.3 and model the index groove cut on the inside surface following these steps.

*Index groove cut*

*STEP 1* - On the Right Plane (Plane 3), sketch this approximate profile of the index groove cut. See the next page for a larger detail.

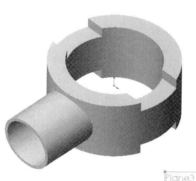

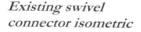

*Existing swivel connector isometric*

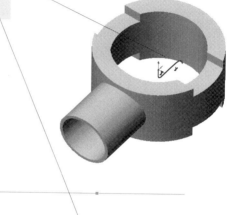

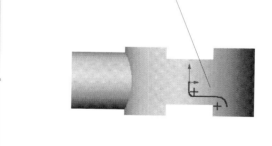

*Be sure to start the endpoint of the sketch exactly at the origin so that the sketch profile to sweep can be easily placed on the sketch endpoint.*

**STEP 2 - EXIT SKETCH**.

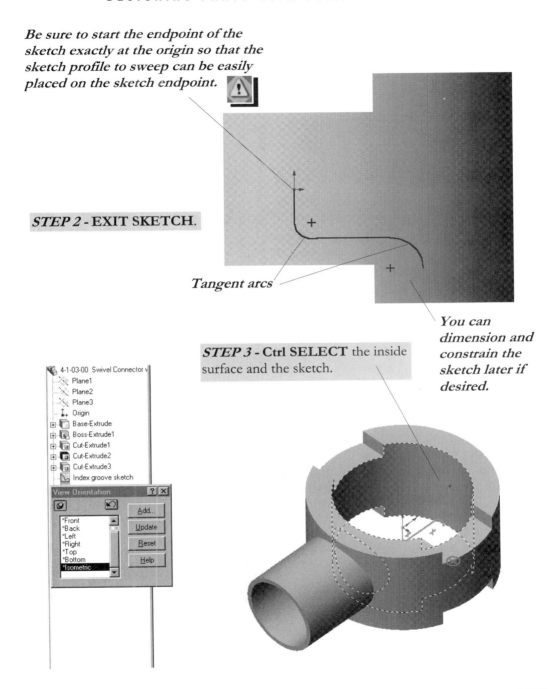

*Tangent arcs*

**STEP 3 - Ctrl SELECT** the inside surface and the sketch.

*You can dimension and constrain the sketch later if desired.*

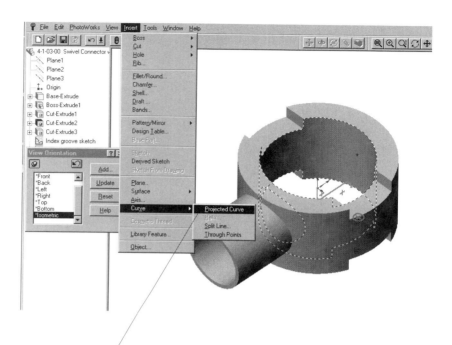

**STEP 4** - Click **INSERT, REFERENCE GEOMETRY, PROJECTED CURVE**.

*Resultant index groove curve projected onto the inside surface*

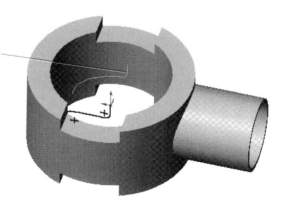

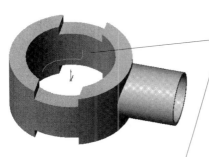

**STEP 5 - SELECT** the Top Plane (Plane 2) and **INSERT SKETCH**. Notice that existing sketch trajectory endpoint lies on the Top Plane because your start point was at the part origin.

*Use this orientation to visualize and sketch the circle*

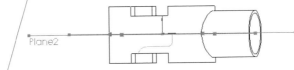

**STEP 6 -** Sketch a circle with the centerpoint on the endpoint of the projected curve. Use the cursor inferencing symbol to snap onto the endpoint. Exit Sketch.

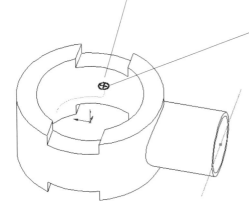

**Note: If this circle is too big, the circle will intersect itself in Step 7 and the sweep will not work. The sweep path radius must be larger than the radius of the circle cut profile. Reduce the circle diameter as required.**

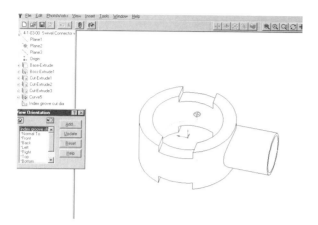

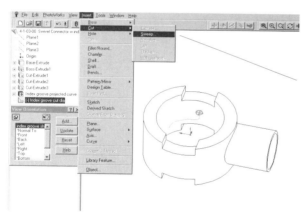

*STEP 7* - **Ctrl SELECT** the **CIRCLE SKETCH** and the **PROJECTED CURVE** from the FeatureManager and **INSERT, CUT, SWEEP.** Choose the **FOLLOW PATH** option from the Orientation/Twist Control dialog box. Rename the cut **INDEX GROOVE.**

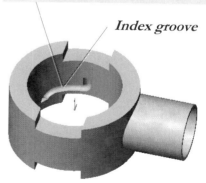

*Index groove*

*Finished part*

## Lesson 4.3.5 - Shaft-Manual Steering

This lesson demonstrates how to model a swept cut using a helix as a trajectory.

**Try it:**                                     **objective**

Model the **MANUAL STEERING SHAFT** below, then sweep the ball groove cut profile along a helix that you will create starting at the end of the shaft.

*Ball groove cut*

**STEP 1 -** On the Right Plane, create this sketch and revolve it around the centerline 360 degrees to create a shaft.

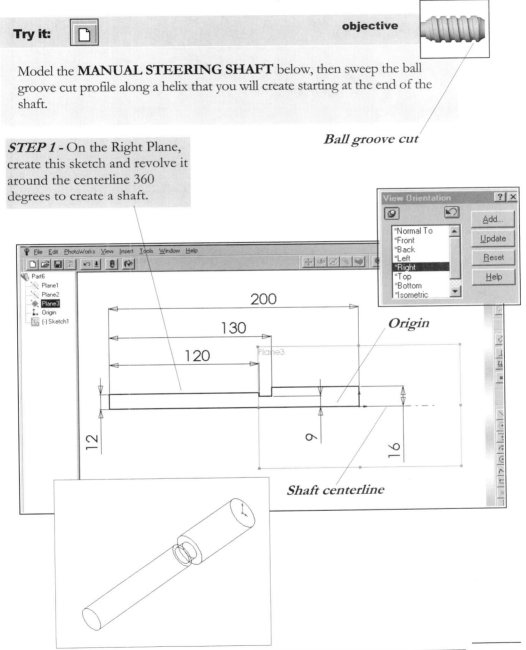

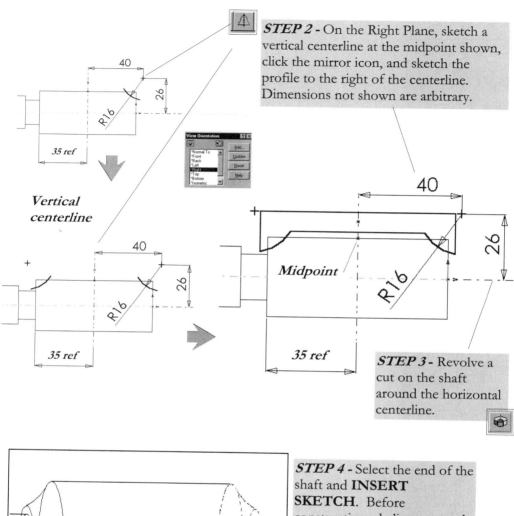

**STEP 2 -** On the Right Plane, sketch a vertical centerline at the midpoint shown, click the mirror icon, and sketch the profile to the right of the centerline. Dimensions not shown are arbitrary.

40

26

R16

35 ref

Vertical centerline

40

26

R16

35 ref

40

26

R16

Midpoint

35 ref

**STEP 3 -** Revolve a cut on the shaft around the horizontal centerline.

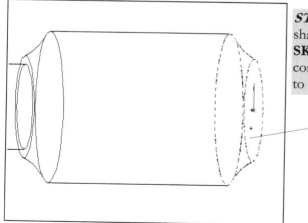

**STEP 4 -** Select the end of the shaft and **INSERT SKETCH**. Before constructing a helix, you need to sketch the helix diameter.

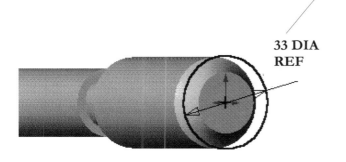

**33 DIA REF**

**STEP 5** - In the next few steps, you will create a helix that will be used as the trajectory to sweep a cut profile on the shaft. Sketch a 33mm-diameter circle as shown to serve as the helix diameter then **EXIT SKETCH**. The **HELIX** function will "uncoil" this circle to parameters you set in the helix dialog box.

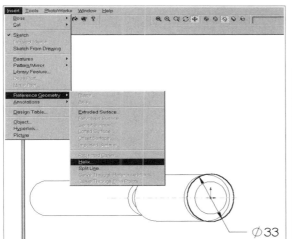

Ø33

**STEP 6** - Select the sketch of the circle, click **INSERT**, **REFERENCE GEOMETRY**, **HELIX** and fill in helix curve dialog box with pitch, revolution, and other parameters as shown below. Notice the helix preview on the shaft end. The preview will change to reflect the opposite direction when you check the **REVERSE DIRECTION** checkbox.

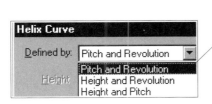

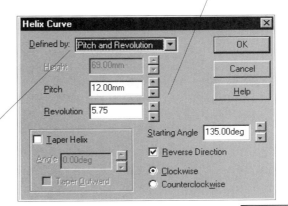

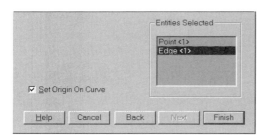

*Resultant helix – If your helix does not look like this in the RIGHT VIEW, right mouse click the HELIX1 in the FeatureManager and choose EDIT DEFINITION. Ensure that the values in the Helix Curve dialog box are the same as shown on the previous page.*

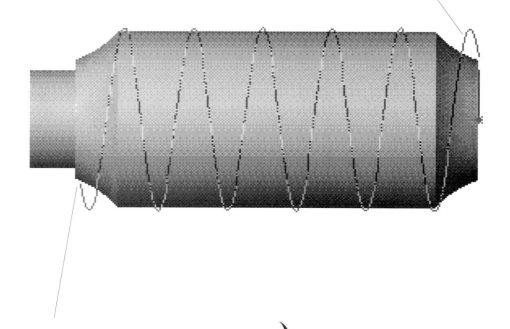

**Note:** To complete the helix cut, you will need to sketch a cut profile on a plane that you will insert at the endpoint of the helix and perpendicular to the curve that defines the helix. (See the next step.)

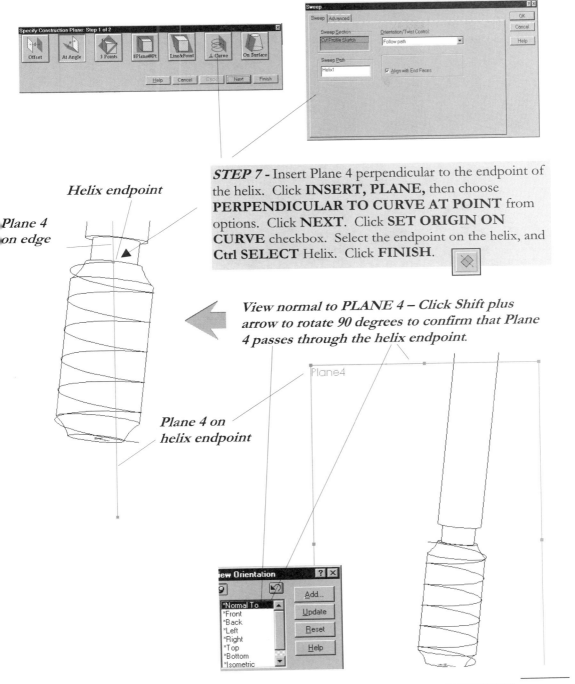

**STEP 7** - Insert Plane 4 perpendicular to the endpoint of the helix. Click **INSERT, PLANE,** then choose **PERPENDICULAR TO CURVE AT POINT** from options. Click **NEXT.** Click **SET ORIGIN ON CURVE** checkbox. Select the endpoint on the helix, and **Ctrl SELECT** Helix. Click **FINISH**.

Helix endpoint

Plane 4 on edge

*View normal to PLANE 4 – Click Shift plus arrow to rotate 90 degrees to confirm that Plane 4 passes through the helix endpoint.*

*Plane 4 on helix endpoint*

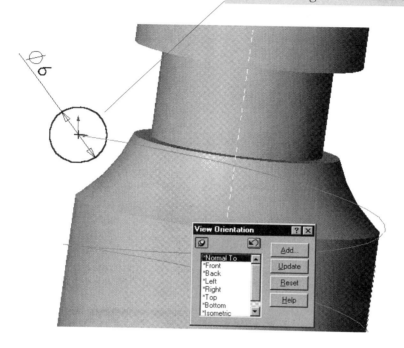

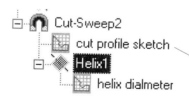

*STEP 9 -* Rename the sketch just constructed to **CUT PROFILE SKETCH** in the FeatureManager.

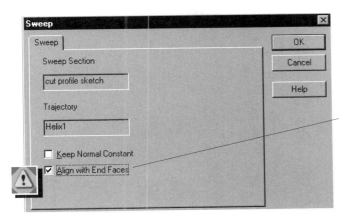

*STEP 10* - **Ctrl SELECT HELIX1** and **CUT PROFILE SKETCH** and **INSERT, CUT, SWEEP.** Click **"FOLLOW PATH"** and **"ALIGN WITH END FACES"** option then click **OK** to sweep cut profile along helix.

*Finished part*

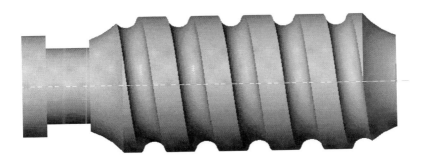

## Lofted shapes and cuts
### Graphical Index

These parts show the type of geometry that can be modeled by lofting between sketch profiles.

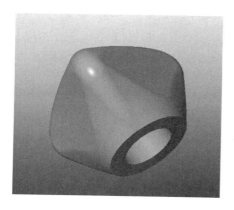

Lesson 4.4.1
Control Knob

Lesson 4.4.2
Shock Mount

## Lesson 4.4.1 - Control Knob

This lesson demonstrates lofting techniques. To create a loft, Ctrl Select two existing sketches to loft between.

**Try it:** 　　　　　　　　　　　　　　　　　　　　　　　　**objective**

Model the **CONTROL KNOB** by creating a loft between a circle and a triangle.

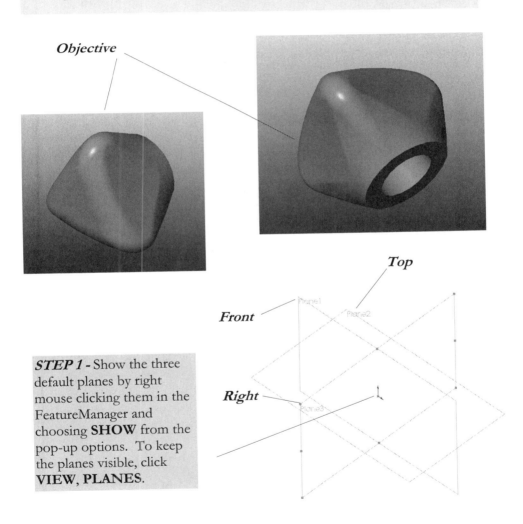

*Objective*

*Top*

*Front*

*Right*

**STEP 1 -** Show the three default planes by right mouse clicking them in the FeatureManager and choosing **SHOW** from the pop-up options. To keep the planes visible, click **VIEW, PLANES**.

*STEP 2 -* Select the Front Plane and sketch a 50mm diameter circle from the origin, and **DIMENSION**. Then **EXIT SKETCH**.

*STEP 3 -* **SELECT** the Front Plane by clicking it (the plane turns green when selected) and insert an offset plane at 40mm. **See the next page for detailed instructions.**

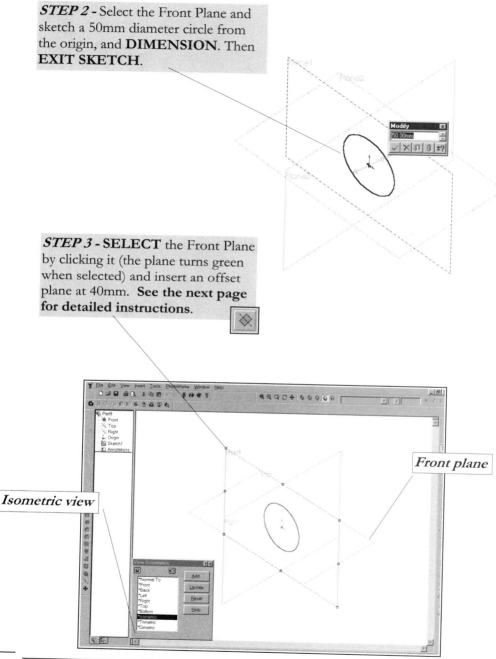

Front plane

Isometric view

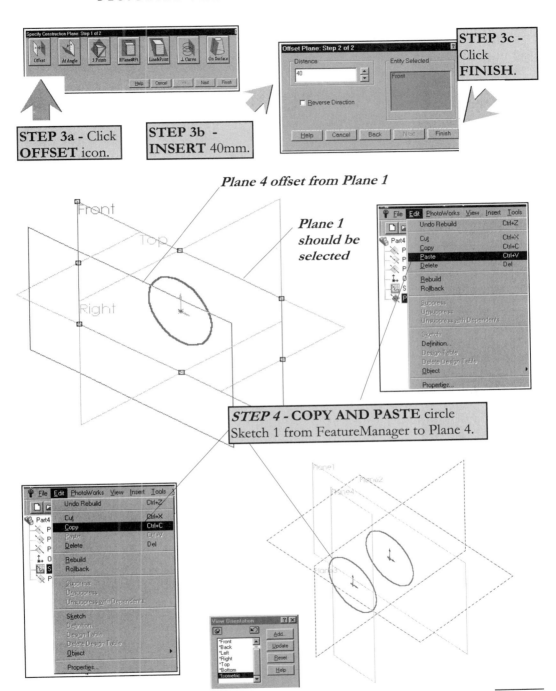

STEP 3c - Click **FINISH**.

**STEP 3a -** Click **OFFSET** icon.

**STEP 3b - INSERT** 40mm.

*Plane 4 offset from Plane 1*

*Plane 1 should be selected*

**STEP 4 - COPY AND PASTE** circle Sketch 1 from FeatureManager to Plane 4.

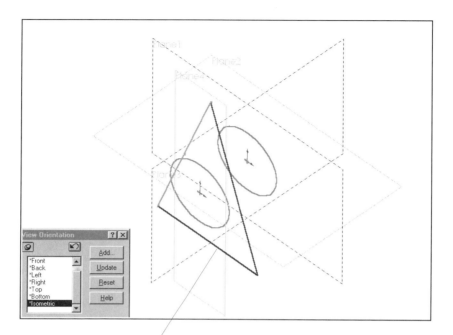

**STEP 5 – EDIT SKETCH** on Plane 4, sketch a rough triangle as shown.

**STEP 6 - Ctrl SELECT** the circle and a side of the triangle and constrain tangent.

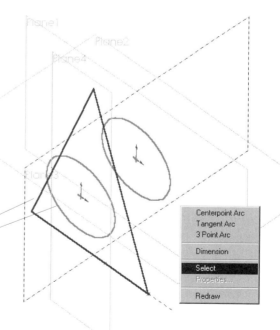

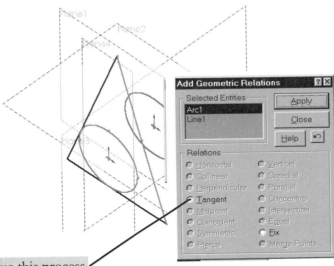

**Add Geometric Relations**

Selected Entities
Arc1
Line1

Apply

Close

Help

Relations
- Horizontal
- Collinear
- Perpendicular
- Tangent
- Midpoint
- Coincident
- Symmetric
- Pierce
- Vertical
- Coradial
- Parallel
- Concentric
- Intersection
- Equal
- Fix
- Merge Points

**STEP 7** - Continue this process until the circle and all three lines are constrained **TANGENT**.

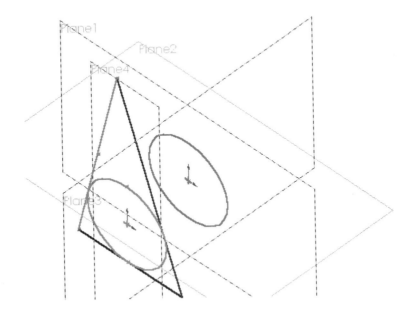

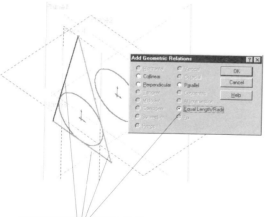

*STEP 8* - **Ctrl SELECT** all three lines and constrain **EQUAL LENGTH**.

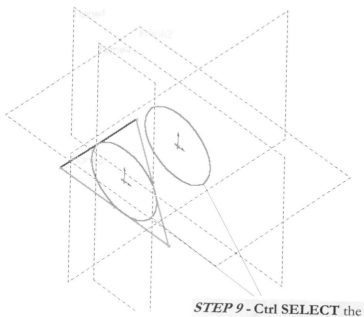

*STEP 9* - **Ctrl SELECT** the two circles and constrain **CONCENTRIC**.

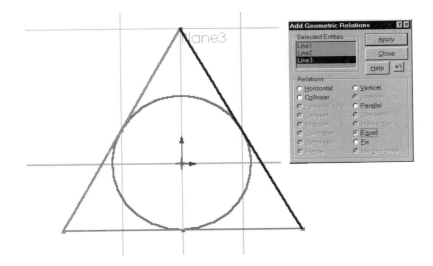

*All lines constrained tangent and equal
and circles constrainted concentric*

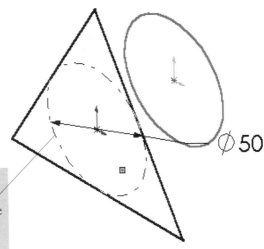

⌀50

**STEP 10 -** Right mouse click the circle for **PROPERTIES**, and click the construction box to make the circle a **CONSTRUCTION ARC**. **EXIT SKETCH**.

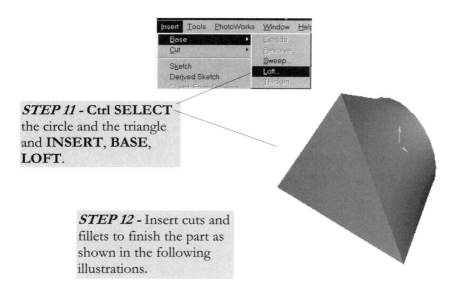

**STEP 11 - Ctrl SELECT** the circle and the triangle and **INSERT, BASE, LOFT**.

**STEP 12 -** Insert cuts and fillets to finish the part as shown in the following illustrations.

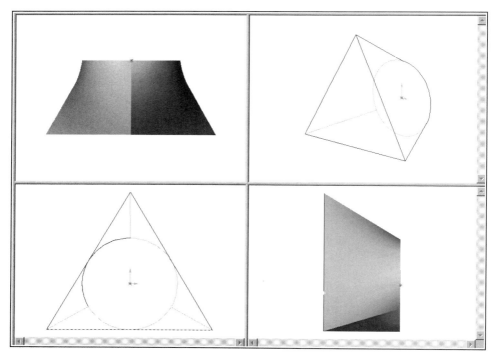

**STEP 12a -** Select the front face and insert 10mm rounds.

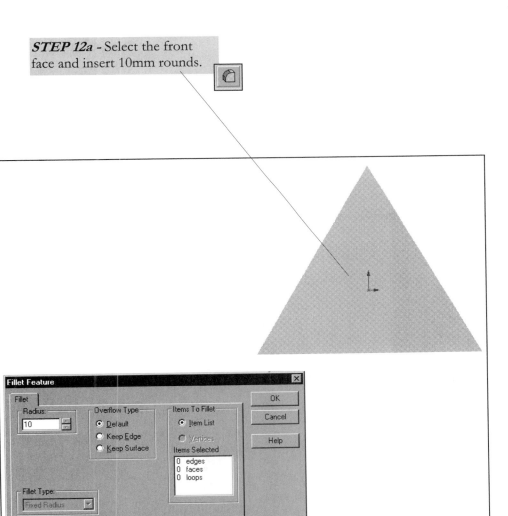

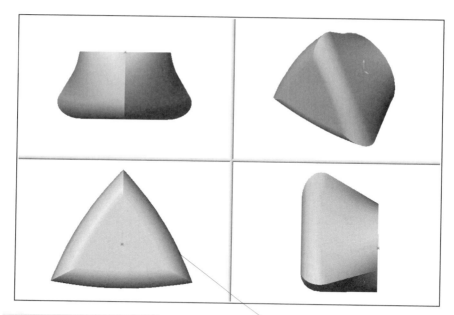

**STEP 12b -** Insert 10mm rounds on three edges.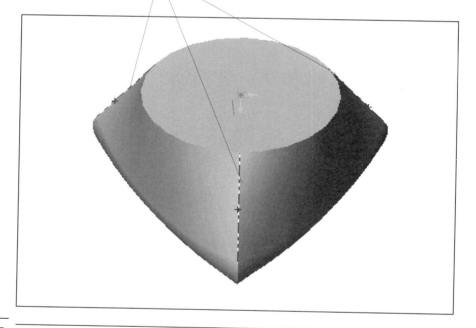

*Front face rounds*

**STEP 12c** - Insert a 30mm diameter hole 20mm deep.

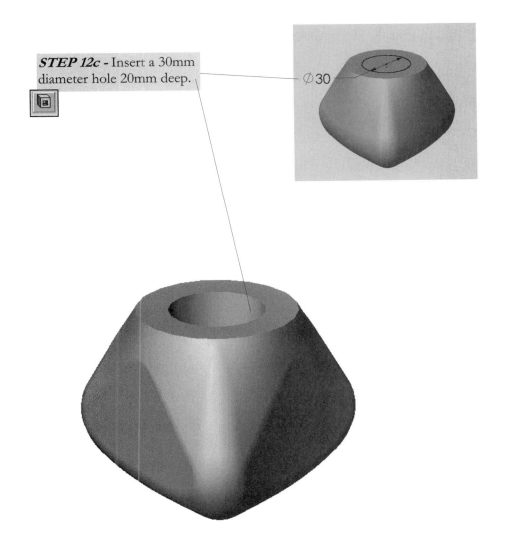

Ø30

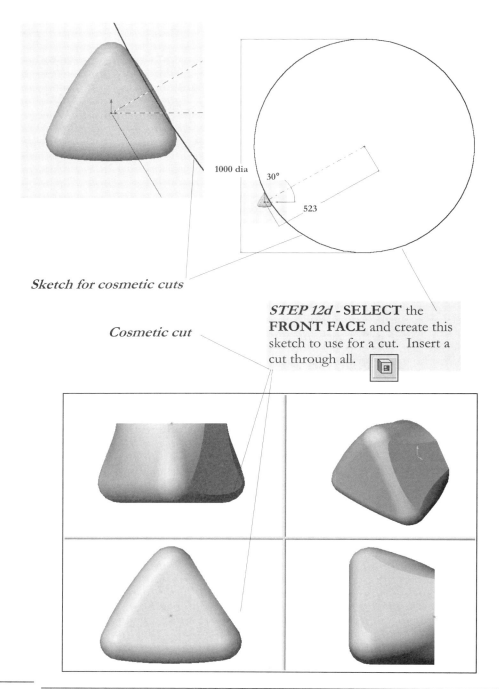

1000 dia

30°

523

*Sketch for cosmetic cuts*

*Cosmetic cut*

*STEP 12d -* **SELECT** the **FRONT FACE** and create this sketch to use for a cut. Insert a cut through all.

*STEP 12e* - **PATTERN** cut to the other sides of the knob. Remember to **Ctrl SELECT** the **CUT FEATURE** and an **AXIS** to pattern the cuts around.

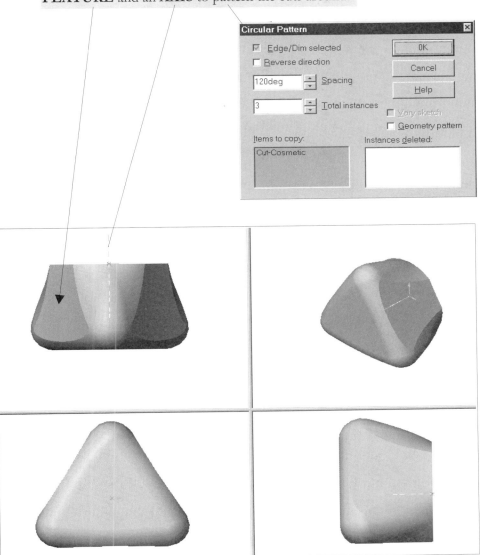

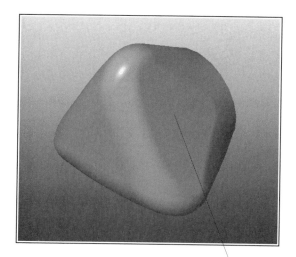

**STEP 13 -** Add 8mm rounds to the face cuts to give a nice, smooth appearance to the knob.

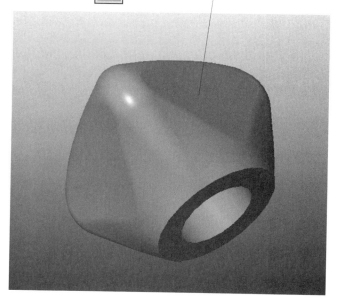

*Finished part*

**Lesson 4.4.2 - Shock Mount**

This lesson gives you practice with a simple loft, and introduces filleting by selecting faces.

**Try it:**                                                                           **objective**

Model the **SHOCK MOUNT** using the sprocket sketch from the **GROMMET** made in Lesson 4.2.2.

*STEP 1* - Open the **GROMMET** from lesson 4.2.2. From the FeatureManager, select the **SPROCKET SKETCH** and copy it to the clipboard by pressing **EDIT**, **COPY**. Close the **GROMMET** part.

*STEP 2* - In a new part, **INSERT** two planes **OFFSET** from the Front default plane, and **PASTE** the sketch on all three planes. Change the scale of the sketch on the middle plane by using the **MODIFY SKETCH** tool, then loft between the sketches. Experiment with the **PLANE OFFSET DISTANCES** and the **TOOLS, SKETCH TOOLS, MODIFY, SCALE FACTOR** of the sketch on the center plane for practice. See the next page for one variation to the part.

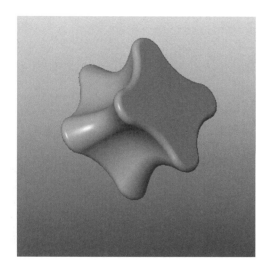

*Finished part*

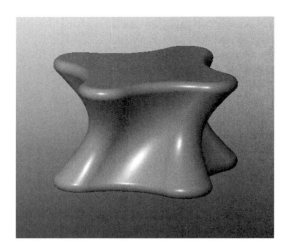

Note: This lesson
completes the chapter on
basic part modeling in
SolidWorks. Remember to
repeat any lesson that you
need more practice with.

*Chapter*

**5**

# Chapter 5 – PREPARING OUTPUT

After creating models in SolidWorks, you have various options for preparing output of the data. You can print images of parts. You can also link or embed SolidWorks part documents in Microsoft Word files or other programs that permit what Microsoft calls "object linking and embedding (OLE)." You can create IGES or stereolithography (STL) output of SolidWorks models to use in other CAD systems, or for manufacturing, analysis, or rapid prototyping. Finally, you can write SolidWorks part models in two forms that are readable by other solid-modeling applications: Parasolid by EDS Unigraphics and ACIS from Spatial Technology.

## Printing SolidWorks images

### Lesson 5.1.1 - Printing Parts, Part Details, and Sketches

You can send any image displayed on your screen to the printer.

**Try it:**                                                            **objective**

Open the part from Lesson 4.2.3 Head-Power Steering Box, and try the print options described on the next page.

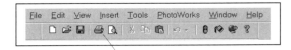

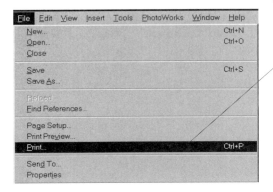

**STEP 1 -** Open and display the steering box head part (Lesson 4.2.3) and click **FILE**, **PRINT** or the **PRINT ICON**. The image displayed on your screen will be sent to the printer. The display shown is a full-section isometric in shaded view, but can be any view and display option you choose.

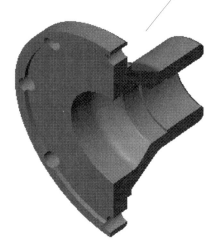

*Full-section isometric*

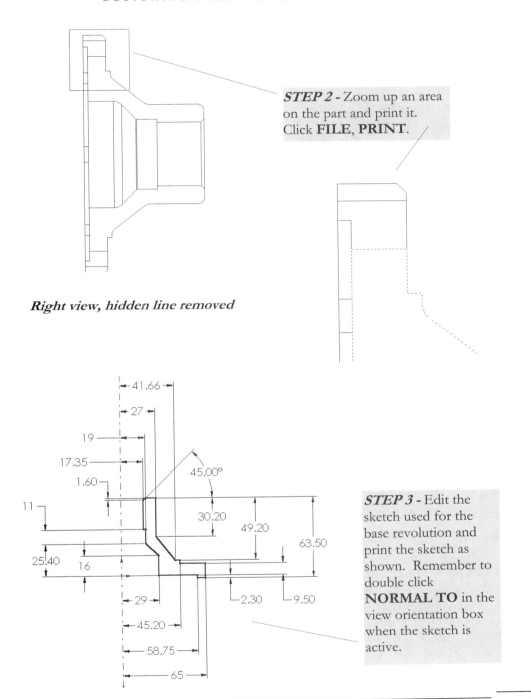

*Right view, hidden line removed*

**STEP 2** - Zoom up an area on the part and print it. Click **FILE**, **PRINT**.

**STEP 3** - Edit the sketch used for the base revolution and print the sketch as shown. Remember to double click **NORMAL TO** in the view orientation box when the sketch is active.

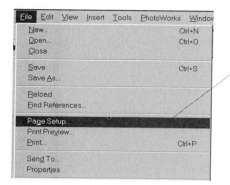

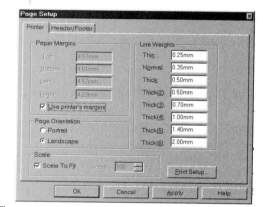

*STEP 4 -* Click **FILE, PAGE SETUP** to set margins and page orientation and other options shown in this dialog box.

*Click for preset options*

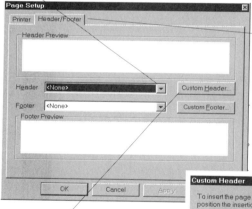

*STEP 5 -* Click **HEADER/FOOTER** tab to set the options shown in the **HEADER/FOOTER** dialog.

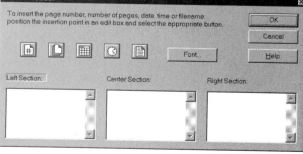

*STEP 6 -* Choose one of the preset header options or click **CUSTOM** to set up a header or footer with options that you select. See the next step for instructions on how to set up a custom header.

Figure 5.1 – Printer Page Setup Options

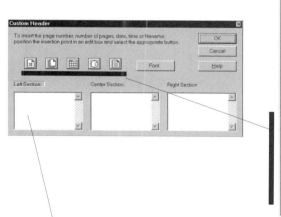

**Custom Header and Footer**

Creates a custom header or footer for every document page that you send to the printer.

**To create a page header or footer:**

1 Place the insertion point in an edit box: **Left Section**, **Center Section**, or **Right Section**.

2 Click the appropriate button to insert the information that you want to appear in that section.

3 If appropriate, enter spaces or text between the selections. For example, "**Page** &[pagenum] **of** &[pages]" would print as "Page 1 of 7" on the first page of a seven-sheet drawing.

4 Click the **Font** button to choose from a variety of font styles and sizes.

5 Click **OK** and view the result in the **Header Preview** and **Footer Preview** boxes.

6 Click **Apply** to accept the change. You can continue to make changes and then click **OK** to close the dialog.

or

Click **OK** to accept the change and close the dialog.

Page number

Total number of pages in the document

Date of the print

Time of the print

Name of the file

*STEP 7 -* To create a custom header, click in a section (left, center, or right) and click the icons of the options you want to display in that section. Click **OK** to preview the information you have chosen in the preview box. To accept, click **APPLY** then click **OK**.

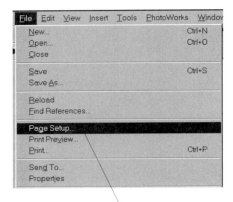

*STEP 8* - Click **FILE**, **PRINT PREVIEW** to preview what the printout will look like.

*STEP 9* - Click **PRINT** if your preview is acceptable or go back and make the necessary changes.

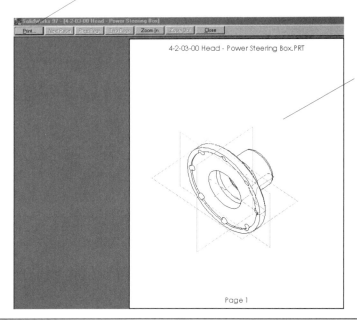

*Print preview display*

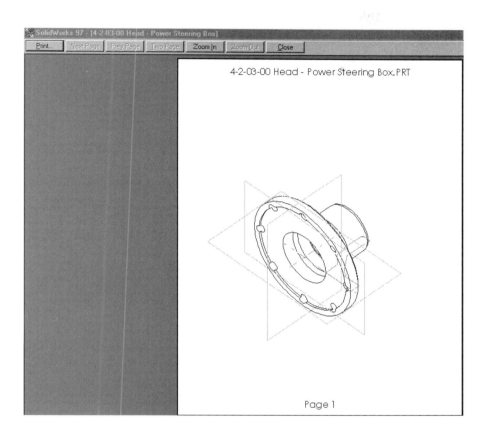

4-2-03-00 Head - Power Steering Box.PRT

Page 1

*Result of printout with a HEADER and FOOTER displayed*

## Cutting and pasting SolidWorks images

### Lesson 5.2.1 - Cutting and Pasting Images

You can copy a SolidWorks window to the clipboard and paste it into a paint program, Microsoft Word, or other Windows-compatible programs.

**Try it:**                                                                **objective**

Copy a SolidWorks Window of the **STEERING BOX HEAD** part and paste it into a Word document.

*STEP 1 -* While in the SolidWorks program, open the **STEERING BOX HEAD** part and go to a view of your choosing.  Press the **PRINT SCREEN** key on the keyboard to capture the active window into the **Windows clipboard**.

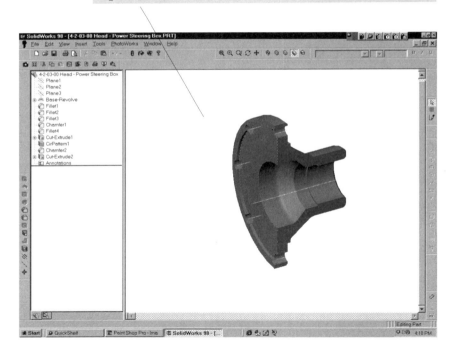

***STEP 2*** - Open a Word document, and click **EDIT**, **PASTE** or the **PASTE ICON** to copy the clipboard contents into the document. The picture can be resized or moved within the document. See Microsoft Word documentation for more details on manipulating pictures.

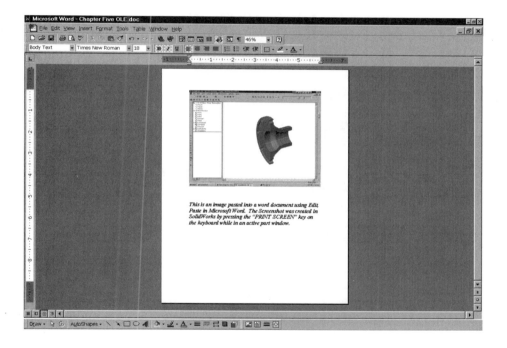

Figure 5.2 – Pasting a SolidWorks Image into Microsoft Word

***STEP 3*** - **PRINT** the Word document.

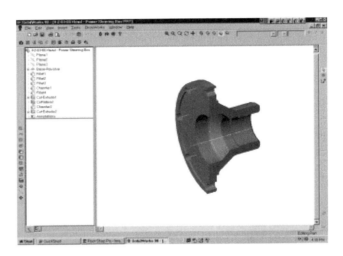

*This is an image pasted into a Word document using Edit, Paste in Microsoft Word. The Screenshot was created in SolidWorks by pressing the "PRINT SCREEN" key on the keyboard while in an active part window.*

*Result of printed Word document with a SolidWorks image pasted into it*

## Linking and embedding parts (OLE)
### Lesson 5.3.1 - Linking and Embedding SolidWorks Parts

You can link and embed SolidWorks documents into other OLE-compliant applications. Linking a SolidWorks document creates a "link" to the original document. Changes made to the original will be updated into the linked image. Embedded objects are not linked to the original. They are treated as separate documents, and changes made to them will be independent of the original. For more information on Linking and Embedding, refer to the SolidWorks User's Guide, and Microsoft documentation.

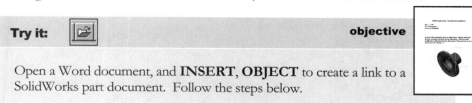

**Try it:**                                                          **objective**

Open a Word document, and **INSERT**, **OBJECT** to create a link to a SolidWorks part document. Follow the steps below.

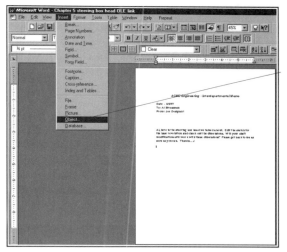

**STEP 1** - Open a Word document, and click **INSERT**, **OBJECT**.

**STEP 2** - Click the **CREATE FROM FILE** tab.

**Note:** You may create a new SolidWorks part document while within Word by clicking an **OBJECT TYPE** from the **CREATE NEW** options. Clicking the SolidWorks **PART DOCUMENT** option will load the SolidWorks program and SolidWorks tools will be accessible from within Word. For this lesson, you will create a link using the **CREATE FROM FILE** option.

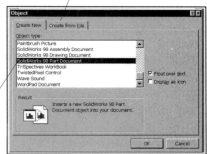

*STEP 3* - Click **LINK TO FILE** to create an image **linked** to the original SolidWorks part file. If the box is left unchecked, the SolidWorks part file will be **EMBEDDED** into the Word document.

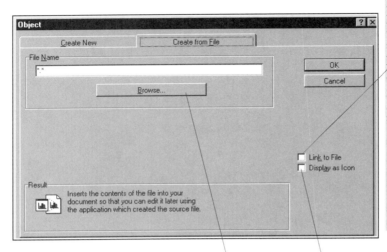

*If this option is checked, the linked image will be displayed as an icon in the word document. Do not check the icon box for this lesson.*

*STEP 4 -* Click **BROWSE**, and from your file folders, find the part from **Lesson 4.2.3 Head-Power Steering Box** to **LINK** the part into the Word document. Choose the part and click **OK** in both dialog boxes to create the link.

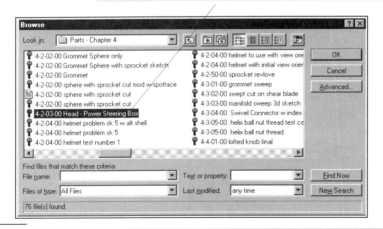

**Note: Close other Windows programs if you do not have enough memory to create the link.**

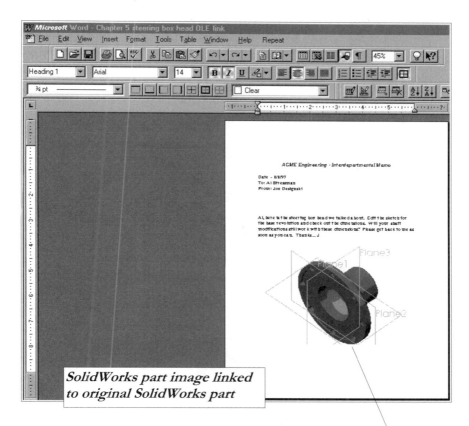

Figure 5.3 – Object Linking and Embedding (OLE) Exercise

**STEP 5 -** Double-click on the part image to activate the SolidWorks program from within Word. When SolidWorks is loaded, try to rotate, move, or zoom up on the part, and edit the sketch of the base revolution to observe the dimensions. Close SolidWorks without saving changes when you are through practicing.

*STEP 6 -* Print the Word document with
the linked SolidWorks image as shown.

ACME Engineering - Interdepartmental Memo

Date - 1/1/97
To: Al Stressman
From: Joe Designski

Al, here is the steering box head we talked about. Edit the sketch for
the base revolution and check out the dimensions. Will your shaft
modifications still work with these dimensions? Please get back to me as
soon as you can. Thanks...J

*Result of a SolidWorks part document
linked into a Word document*

# IGES
## What Is IGES?

The "Initial Graphics Exchange Specification" (IGES) was developed by the National Bureau of Standards to facilitate the exchange of CAD data between software systems. IGES is commonly called a "neutral file format." When one CAD system exports a file in IGES format, another program can import the file and perform work on it. The imported model is of limited use, however, because imported IGES files are treated as a single "entity" in the new system and do not have individual features. New features can be added to an imported model, but original "imported" features cannot be altered.

## When Is IGES Used?

Translating data with IGES files is required for:
1. Companies operating two different graphics systems that need to share data among systems.
2. Manufacturers that want to transmit design data to subcontractors who employ computer graphics for preparation of design details, tooling, analysis, or for numerically controlled machining.
3. Rapid prototyping service bureaus that prefer to have IGES files rather than STL files. (See the following section on STL files for an explanation.)

SolidWorks has the ability to import surfaces from IGES files and use them to model new parts or to modify existing parts. You can also export a solid model or selected surfaces of the model in the IGES format for use in other applications.

## Entity Types Supported

SolidWorks supports the following entity types for importing and exporting IGES files. See the SolidWorks Help screens for current data.

Figure 5.4 – IGES Entity Types

### Lesson 5.4.1 - Exporting IGES Solids

To export a solid model or selected faces of a model in IGES format that another system can use, you must first set IGES export options to match the target application of the IGES file.

**Try it:**    **reference model**

Open part **BRACKET MOUNT** from Lesson 4.1.1 and save the part as an IGES file in a new folder called "IGES Files."

*STEP 1* - Open the **BRACKET MOUNT**.

*STEP 2* - Click **TOOLS, OPTIONS, EXPORT**.

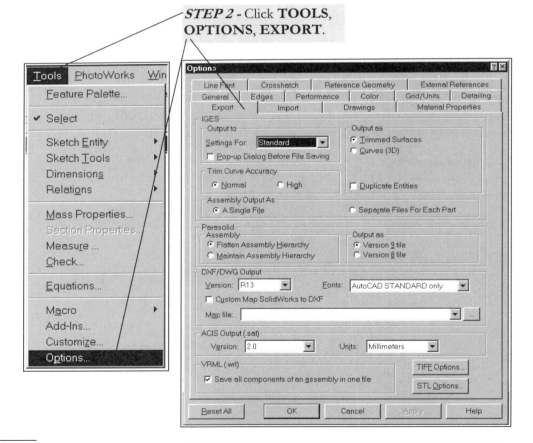

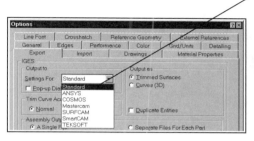

**STEP 3 -** Open the **OUTPUT TO, SETTINGS FOR** menu to see the options available. SolidWorks has different "flavors" of IGES for each of the applications listed in the pop-up dialog (see the **IGES EXPORT FORMAT TYPES** on the next page). For this exercise, choose **STANDARD**.

**STEP 4 -** Choose **TRIMMED SURFACES** option. See note.

*See Export Help screen on the next page for description of Trim Curve Accuracy*

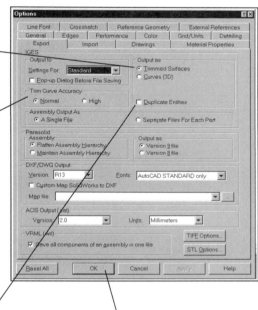

**Note: When exporting trimmed surfaces, the faces of the solid part are converted to trimmed surfaces IGES entity type 144 in the IGES file. The IGES entity types that compose the trimmed surfaces depend on the export format chosen from the SETTINGS FOR list.**

**STEP 5 -** Click the **DUPLICATE ENTITIES** box if you want to export composite curves (entity type 102) to any of the available export formats. See the note and table on the next page for a description of the entity types used to export 3-D curves.

**STEP 6 -** Click **OK**.

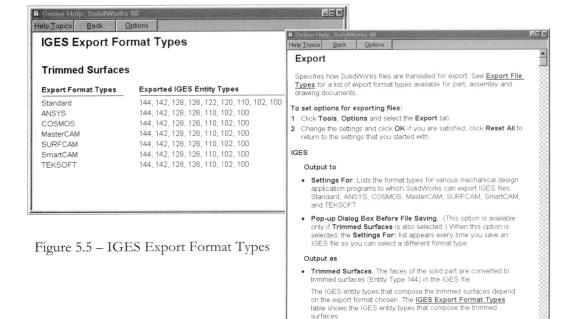

Figure 5.5 – IGES Export Format Types

Figure 5.6 – IGES Import Export Help Screen

**Note: Curves (3D) – When exporting curves, the solid body is converted to wireframe representation in the IGES file. Select either B-SPLINES or PARAMETRIC SPLINES, depending on the entity types required by the system where you will use the IGES file.**

**Note: For more clarification of IMPORT and EXPORT options, refer to the SolidWorks help screens and target system documentation for importing files.**

DESIGNING PARTS WITH SOLIDWORKS

**STEP 7 -** Click **FILE, SAVE AS**, and choose **IGES FILES** as the type of output. Save in the "IGES Files" folder.  Save as **4.1.1 BRACKET MOUNT IN STANDARD SOLID FORMAT TYPE 144**. (It is a good idea to identify in the filename what type of IGES file it is, such as trimmed surface, wireframe, Cosmos, etc.)  Since you selected no surfaces before saving, SolidWorks exports the entire solid.  IGES files are saved by SolidWorks with the extension **IGS**, a common convention used by a number of CAD programs.

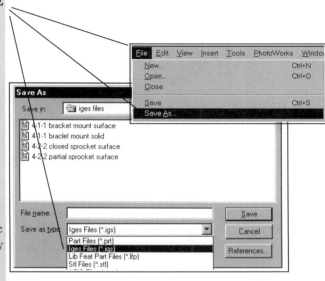

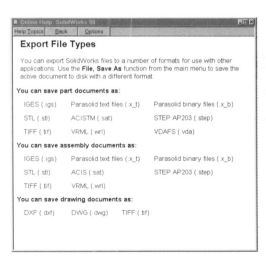

### Lesson 5.4.2 - Exporting Selected IGES Surfaces

You can select individual surfaces to export.

**Try it:** 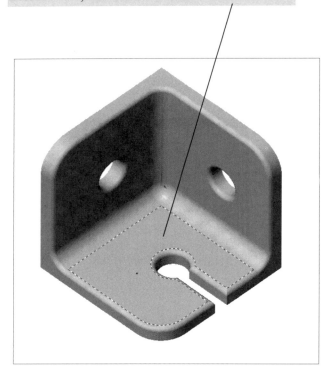  reference model

Export an IGES surface from the part shown.

*STEP 1* - Open the **BRACKET MOUNT** from Lesson 4.1.1, and select the surface shown.

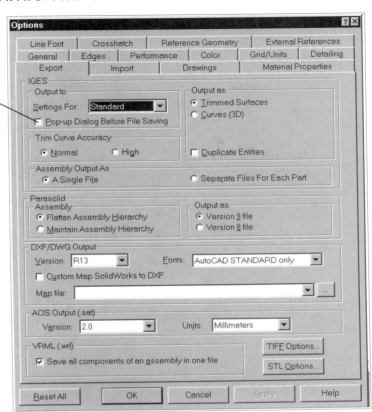

*When this box is checked you will have the option to choose a new format every time you save an IGES file, otherwise previous settings will be used when saving files. Leave this box unchecked for now.*

**STEP 2 -** Use the settings previously set in the **EXPORT** tab as shown above. These settings will remain the same as set for your previous save.

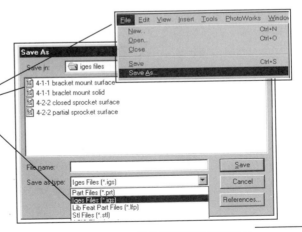

**STEP 3 -** Click **FILE, SAVE AS** and choose **IGES FILES** from **SAVE AS TYPE** options. Name the file **4.1.1 BRACKET MOUNT SURFACE**. At the dialog box, choose the option **SELECTED FACES** to export just the surface you selected.

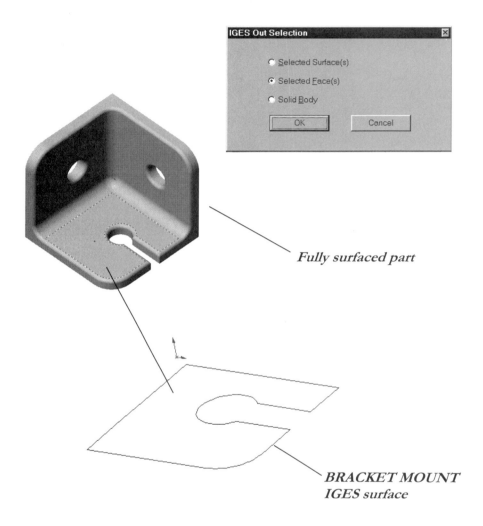

*Fully surfaced part*

*BRACKET MOUNT*
*IGES surface*

Note:  When exporting an IGES file from another system for use in SolidWorks, export the surfaces as trimmed surfaces (entity type 144) or as untrimmed surfaces (entity types 120, 122, or 126).  See Figure 5.4.

# Stereolithography output
## What Is STL Format?

Stereolithography (STL) file output is a triangulated surface representation of a CAD model. Originally developed by 3-D Systems Inc., the inventors of the stereolithography process, STL format has become the de facto standard of the rapid prototyping industry. Rapid prototyping systems convert CAD models in STL format to physical models using a variety of sophisticated techniques. Physical models aid designers because they provide the best tool for reviewing design concepts with other company personnel early in the design cycle. This review process maximizes the synergy of the concurrent engineering process. Because communications improve using physical models, design iterations become more focused and productive. Rapid prototypes help to reduce product development costs, improve product quality, and reduce the time needed to introduce new products to market. Rapid prototyping machines require STL files exported from SolidWorks. They then slice STL files into layers and build physical models one layer at a time using the slice data. An STL file consists of the X, Y, and Z coordinates of the three corners of each surface triangle as well as an indication of the surface normal for each triangle. The surface normal information designates what is inside and what is outside of the model. The "chordal deviation" determines the maximum distance that a point on a triangle may deviate from the true surface of the part.

SolidWorks allows users to output design data in STL format. Triangle size and deviation can be varied, depending upon the resolution set in SolidWorks when the STL file is generated. Generally, smaller triangles allow finer resolution of curved surfaces and improved part accuracy. Larger triangles allow faster part building, but you may lose entire features of your design if the triangles are too big.

## Using STL Files

STL files are used primarily for creating rapid prototyping parts and tools for parts such as molds. STL files can also be used for viewing, measuring, and manipulating parts, and for numerically controlled manufacturing and analysis.

Third-party software such as SolidView, from Solid Concepts Inc. (Valencia, California) and MAGICS VIEW from Materialize of Ann Arbor, Michigan, can be used to view, measure, and manipulate the solid part files on PCs. Users can cross-section parts or use parts to build assemblies for visualization purposes. This use can help engineering or manufacturing job shops, or rapid prototyping service bureaus bid on models made with SolidWorks and exported as STL files.

## IGES Versus STL File Output

As simple as the STL format is, there are still pitfalls to avoid. The resolution of an STL file affects the way a rapid prototyping part looks. STL files can't be adjusted to create a finer or coarser mesh after they have been generated, so it is important to get the conversion right the first time. For this reason, many service bureaus may prefer that you give them files in SolidWorks part format, (if the service bureau also has SolidWorks software), or as IGES files.

## Lesson 5.5.1 - Exporting Stereolithography (STL) Output

**Try it:** objective

Open the **SWIVEL CONNECTOR** from Lesson 4.1.3, and export an STL file of it.

***STEP 1*** - Open the **SWIVEL CONNECTOR**.

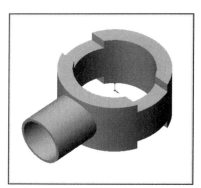

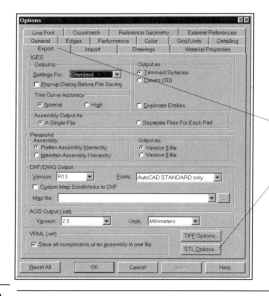

***STEP 2*** - In **TOOLS, OPTIONS, EXPORT,** click the **STL OPTIONS** button.

This display area shows approximately how the part tessellation will vary as a result of the settings.

*Usually you will want to output your file in binary because of the smaller file size and faster processing speed of the files. ASCII output files are generally used for debugging applications in development and for research.*

*Minimum-quality setting equals the highest values for deviation and angle tolerance.*

**STEP 3** - Click the **COARSE** quality, **PREVIEW**, and **SHOW STL** check-boxes. Click **OK** for both dialog boxes.

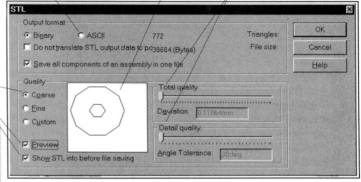

**STEP 4** - Set the **SAVE AS** option for **STL Files**. Then save the file. This preview will appear before saving so that you can reset the quality of the STL file if desired. Click **YES** to save the file. See the STL help screen on the next page. Access SolidWorks help for the most current information.

Figure 5.7 – STL Output Format Options

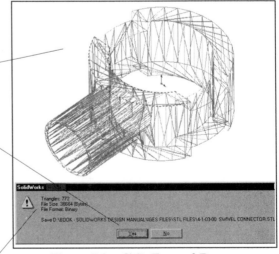

Figure 5.8 – STL Faceted Part

*Triangle count and file size data is a factor of the quality settings.*

*Note: To determine appropriate settings for your STL output, try coarser settings first. If your RP model quality is not acceptable, increase the quality settings to achieve the desired results. Remember that increasing the quality settings increases file size and time required generating rapid prototype models.*

*Maximum-quality setting equals the lowest values for deviation and angle tolerance.*

**STEP 5** - Click **CUSTOM**, then reset the quality settings to the values shown. Check the result preview before saving. See the STL help screen below for a description of output format and quality.

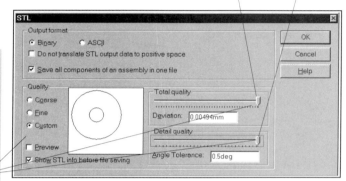

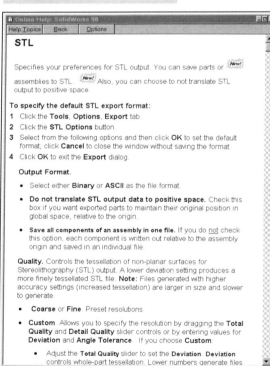

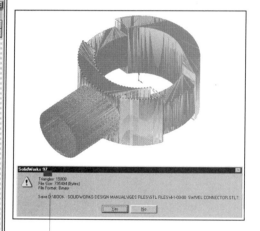

*Faceted part preview – highest quality settings*

*Notice the increase in the triangle count and the file size data due to the increased quality settings.*

## Miscellaneous output

### VRML Files

VRML files are similar to IGES files and allow SolidWorks parts to be viewed with Web Browser plug-ins such as Live 3-D. Click **FILE**, **SAVE AS** and click **VRML** as the type of file format to save in the pop-up dialog box. Click **SAVE** to finish.

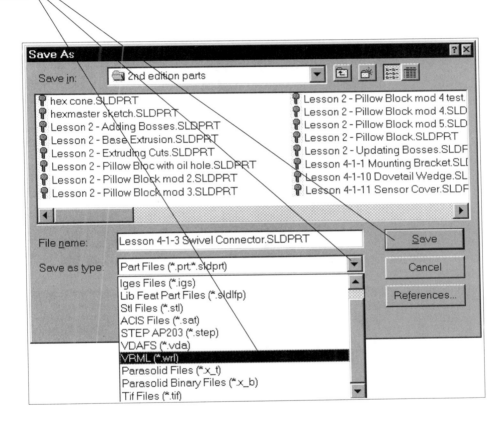

Other output options include Parasolid files for use with Unigraphics and other Parasolid-based applications and ACIS for creating .SAT files for use with ACIS-based applications. Click **FILE**, **SAVE AS** and choose from options listed.

*This lesson concludes DESIGNING PARTS WITH SolidWorks. Remember that to become proficient with any CAD program you need to practice. Retry lessons that you are not confident with. Also, occasionally review the index to test your memory of command applications you learned in this book. If you cannot remember the reference in the index, go to the pages that you need to review and retry the lesson if necessary.*

*When using SolidWorks for your production work, remember to model parts so that the part origin is located at your primary datum selection. Practice creating rough sketches of the features in your designs, then dragging sketch elements to resize and reshape your sketches as required. Finally, dimension each sketch starting with the largest dimensions first and working your way in. Add or remove constraints as necessary to get the shape you want, and to preserve design intent. To become really effective using constraints, experiment with them and observe how your model acts when you modify them. With a little practice, creating models that can be easily modified and still preserve design intent will become second nature.*

*The author and the publisher hope that you have enjoyed this book and benefited from the lessons in it. Your comments and suggestions are welcome. Please write to:*

*CAD/CAM Publishing*
*1010 Turquoise Street, Suite 320*
*San Diego, California 92109 USA*
*Web site: http//www.cadcamnet.com*

*Or:*

*Roy Wysack*
*e-mail:* rwysack@realteknet.com

The purpose of this appendix is to provide some guidelines for when operations do not work or when you get unexpected results. Items are listed in alphabetical order by a key word describing the function or problem. Refer to SolidWorks on line help for more detail about the items listed below.

## Any operation -

When the results of any operation are not acceptable, remember to click **UNDO** to back out of the command and return to the previous condition.

## Error messages –

### Dangling dimensions or relations
Dimensions or relations referencing entities that no longer exists.

### Dangling sketch geometry (geometry that cannot be solved)
This geometry's position cannot be determined using the existing dimensions or constraints. The geometry, relations, and dimensions that prevent the solution of the sketch are usually displayed.

### Feature that cannot be regenerated
In the FeatureManager Design Tree, a red exclamation mark flags items that cannot be regenerated because of errors. Right Mouse click on the item and choose "What's Wrong" from the pop-up menu for a description of the problem.

### Invalid geometry – no solution found
This geometry would be geometrically invalid if the sketch were solved.

### Invalid geometry – solution found
The sketch was solved but will result in invalid geometry, such as a zero length line, zero radius arc, or self-intersecting spline.

### Non-manifold solid (disjoint body)
A boss does not intersect the existing solid. Modify the sketch or the boss definition or direction.

*Over-defined sketch*
Caused by dimensions or relations that are conflicting or redundant and thus over-define one or more entities.

## Extrusion fails -
The most probable cause is that the direction is such that the extrusion does not intersect the part. Reverse extrusion direction. Also check for excessive draft angle.

## Feature modifications -
To modify features, right mouse click them for a context-sensitive pop-up menu which will allow you to edit the feature definition or to edit the feature sketch.

## Fillets won't work -
The usual cause is that the fillet value you entered is too big to fillet to existing geometry. Reduce the fillet size. Also, there may be a very small surface patch or cut feature that won't allow the fillet to be constructed. Try rolling back suspected features. Finally, try inserting intersecting fillets starting with the largest fillet first and following with smaller ones.

## Help!
Do not forget to access on-line help for assistance when you run into problems. Also access help for a description of sketch element color codes.

## Loft fails -

*Lofted surfaces twist incorrectly*
Need to define a guide curve. See on-line SolidWorks help for assistance.

*Total loft failure*
Geometry is probably too complex to loft.

## Patterning -

*Circular pattern won't work*
Be sure to select an axis around which to pattern the selected features.

## Reordering part features -

To change the order for part features or to add a new feature in the FeatureManager Design Tree, drag and drop the features in the FeatureManager or click a feature and click **EDIT, ROLLBACK** to roll back the part to the point selected. There you can insert a new feature and the other rollback features will follow the new feature after a rebuild.

## Revolved features fail -

When a sketch profile will not revolve, check that the sketch does not have a gap or that it is not self-intersecting. Also, be sure that there are no stray elements or centerlines in the sketch. Box select all to see if any stray elements show up. Finally, be sure that only one centerline is selected.

## Shell fails -

Shell thickness chosen creates geometry that cannot be calculated. Change thickness to see if this is the problem. To troubleshoot shelling problems, suppress some features in your part and recheck the shell function. If it works the problem is tied to the suppressed features. In complex parts like the helmet in Chapter 4, shells cannot be created if adjacent part features do not merge cleanly. Eliminate this problem by using the **CONVERT ENTITIES** tool to use existing edge geometry for adjacent features when possible. Otherwise, if geometry is too complex to shell, try using extruded or revolved cuts instead.

## Sketch problems -

### Cannot dimension to element endpoints
Remember to select the **HORIZONTAL** or **VERTICAL** dimension options from the right mouse pop-up menu while dimensioning.

### Cannot mirror
When a sketch profile will not mirror, be sure that only one centerline is selected.

### Cannot modify sketch position or origin
The sketch origin was probably automatically constrained to the part origin. Delete the constraining relations or recreate the sketch with the **AUTOMATIC RELATIONS** turned off in **TOOLS, OPTIONS, GENERAL** tab.

### Check Sketch
Allows you to check a sketch for errors that would prevent it from being used successfully in creating the type of feature you specify. To access this tool, click **TOOLS, SKETCH TOOLS, CHECK SKETCH FOR FEATURE**.

### *Modifications to sketch and sketch plane*

To edit a sketch, right mouse click a feature for a context-sensitive pop-up menu that will allow you to choose the **EDIT SKETCH** or the **EDIT SKETCH PLANE** options. The **EDIT SKETCH PLANE** option allows you to select another reference plane or planar face to move the sketch profile to and the **EDIT SKETCH** option allows you to change or repair a sketch profile.

### *Over-defined sketches*

This condition exists when there are conflicting constraints or redundant dimensions. Delete some dimensions or make them "driven" reference dimensions. Also delete the conflicting constraints.

### *Unexpected results when dragging sketch elements*

Look for relations or constraining dimensions that cause the unexpected results. You may have to add or delete these constraints depending on what you are trying to do.

## Sweep fails -

The sketch profile must not intersect itself during the sweep along the trajectory sketch. Also, the trajectory must intersect the sketch profile and be at right angles to it.

## Appendix B
## Additional help topics

The purpose of this appendix is to highlight SolidWorks 98 enhancements and to show the user where to find current information on additional items not covered elsewhere.

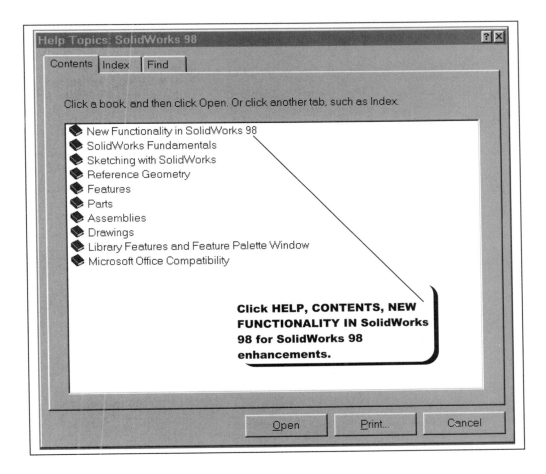

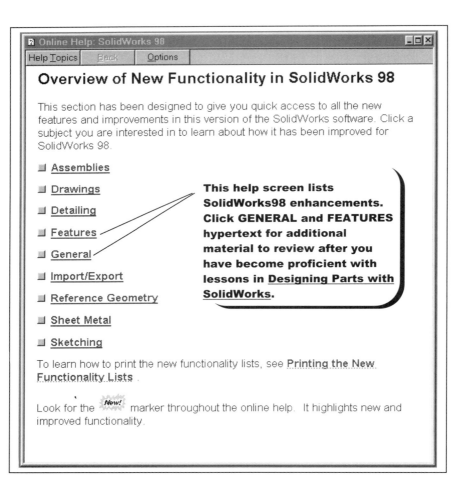

**Online Help: SolidWorks 98**

Help Topics | Back | Options

# Overview of New Functionality in SolidWorks 98

This section has been designed to give you quick access to all the new features and improvements in this version of the SolidWorks software. Click a subject you are interested in to learn about how it has been improved for SolidWorks 98.

- Assemblies
- Drawings
- Detailing
- Features
- General
- Import/Export
- Reference Geometry
- Sheet Metal
- Sketching

**This help screen lists SolidWorks98 enhancements. Click GENERAL and FEATURES hypertext for additional material to review after you have become proficient with lessons in Designing Parts with SolidWorks.**

To learn how to print the new functionality lists, see **Printing the New Functionality Lists** .

Look for the *New!* marker throughout the online help. It highlights new and improved functionality.

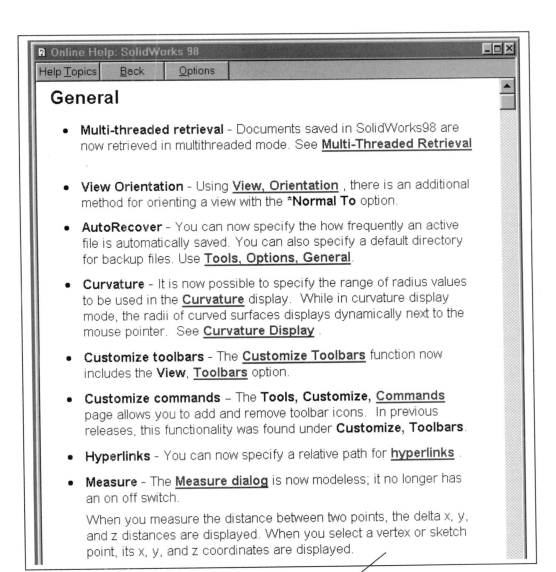

Help Topics | Back | Options

# General

- **Multi-threaded retrieval** - Documents saved in SolidWorks98 are now retrieved in multithreaded mode. See **Multi-Threaded Retrieval**

- **View Orientation** - Using **View, Orientation** , there is an additional method for orienting a view with the *\*Normal To* option.

- **AutoRecover** - You can now specify the how frequently an active file is automatically saved. You can also specify a default directory for backup files. Use **Tools, Options, General**.

- **Curvature** - It is now possible to specify the range of radius values to be used in the **Curvature** display. While in curvature display mode, the radii of curved surfaces displays dynamically next to the mouse pointer. See **Curvature Display** .

- **Customize toolbars** - The **Customize Toolbars** function now includes the **View, Toolbars** option.

- **Customize commands** – The **Tools, Customize, Commands** page allows you to add and remove toolbar icons. In previous releases, this functionality was found under **Customize, Toolbars**.

- **Hyperlinks** - You can now specify a relative path for **hyperlinks** .

- **Measure** - The **Measure dialog** is now modeless; it no longer has an on off switch.

  When you measure the distance between two points, the delta x, y, and z distances are displayed. When you select a vertex or sketch point, its x, y, and z coordinates are displayed.

**In the SolidWorks help screen, click links to other items you would like to review.**

# Features

- **Feature Palette™ window** – SolidWorks 98 provides a new **Feature Palette** window that lets you save commonly used features and components into specific folders, and then conveniently drag/drop them from the Feature Palette window onto the model. Users can also share the contents of the Feature Palette window with other members of the design group.

- **Chamfer** - The **chamfer feature** has new chamfer types: Distance-Distance, and Vertex-Chamfer. (The vertex may be concave or convex.)

- **Face Blend Fillet** - You can now select projected split line or an edge to set a boundary for a **face blend fillet** .

- **Dome** - You can use the closed split line to create a **Dome** on a planar surface, instead of using the outer boundary of that planar surface.

  Domes may now be created on any planar face, and are no longer limited to circular, elliptical, or four-sided faces.

- **Library Features** - The following items can now be used in **library features** : holes created with hole wizard, chamfers, sketches, reference planes, reference axes, and constraints across sketches.

  After inserting a library feature, you can now dissolve it into its individual features.

- **Hole Wizard** - The **hole wizard** functionality has been improved. You can now dimension the location of the hole while you are creating it.

- **Geometry Patterns** - When making linear or circular patterns, or mirroring features, you now have the option of creating a **Geometry Pattern** . Individual instances of the feature being copied are not solved; end conditions and calculations are ignored. Each instance is an exact copy of the faces and edges of the original feature. This speeds up the creation and rebuilding of the pattern.

- **Loft** - You can specify **end tangency** for lofts, including normal to the plane of the profile, tangent to a selected vector, and tangent to adjacent faces on existing geometry. You can use a **center line curve** to guide a loft.

- **Sweep** - You can specify end tangency for **sweeps with guide curves** , including tangent to the path or to a selected vector, and tangent to adjacent faces on existing geometry.

- **Move/Size features -** Feature handles are now available for changing feature size and location. A new **Move/Size Feature** icon that you can add to the Feature toolbar activates the feature drag mode.

- **Midpoint selection of model edges -** You can now use the **Select Midpoint** option from the right-mouse menu to select the midpoint of an edge. Previously, it was easy to accidentally select the midpoint when intending to select the model edge.

In the SolidWorks help screen, click links to other items you would like to review.

# INDEX